NEILL'S "BLUE CAPS"

NEILL'S "BLUE CAPS"

Vol. 2
1826–1914

by
COLONEL H. C. WYLLY, C.B.

The Naval & Military Press Ltd

in association with

The Imperial War Museum
Department of Printed Books

Published jointly by
The Naval & Military Press Ltd
Unit 10 Ridgewood Industrial Park,
Uckfield, East Sussex,
TN22 5QE England
Tel: +44 (0) 1825 749494
Fax: +44 (0) 1825 765701
www.naval-military-press.com

and

The Imperial War Museum, London
Department of Printed Books
www.iwm.org.uk

In reprinting in facsimile from the original, any imperfections are inevitably reproduced and the quality may fall short of modern type and cartographic standards.

[Photo: Kent & Lacey

THE LATE MAJOR C. H. DALE.
Military Knight of Windsor, late Madras Fusiliers.

Dedicated

IN
AFFECTIONATE
MEMORY OF
THE LATE
MAJOR C. H. DALE,
ROYAL MADRAS FUSILIERS,
MILITARY KNIGHT OF WINDSOR,
WHO SERVED IN THE INDIAN MUTINY,
1857–58 (RELIEF AND DEFENCE OF
LUCKNOW) AND IN THE RISING
IN THE N.W. TERRITORIES
OF CANADA,
1885.

Major Dale, before his death, had completed the manuscript of Vols. I. and II. of "Neill's 'Blue Caps,'" but the publication was deferred owing to the Great War. On his death his widow most generously gave all the documents and data to the Officer Commanding the "Blue Caps." All ranks, past and present, of the "Blue Caps" owe a very deep debt of gratitude to the late Major Dale for the records he compiled of the Battalion in which he was such a distinguished officer.

COLONELS OF THE REGIMENT.

FOREWORD

PUBLICATIONS such as these that record the glorious actions of our troops in the field are most valuable in directing the minds of our rising generation towards emulating the deeds of those who have left an example worthy to be followed. Our forces to be efficient must necessarily possess such regiments as these Fusiliers. The perusal of their records will undoubtedly induce many young men to enter military service, and for various good reasons. For instance, a laudable desire to deserve or win the Cross for valour or other honourable distinctions will not be forgotten. Many will have to be content with the satisfaction of having deserved the praise of their fellows, which is no small matter. In the armies of King David of old there are only thirty-seven names mentioned of men conspicuous for personal bravery; but doubtless there were many others who did not happen to come under the notice of their commander-in-chief, the brave but unscrupulous Joab.

Among Havelock's regiments the enemy had a particular hatred and fear of the "Blue Caps" which tells well in favour of the latter. And it is difficult to understand why such a corps should be disbanded now as if of no account. However, nothing in the world can belittle or stain its glorious name, for which God be thanked.

J. A. WOODS,
Lieut.-Colonel (retired),
late Madras Fusiliers.

47, EDITH ROAD,
KENSINGTON, W.14.

NOTE

I KNOW it will fire with enthusiasm all ranks of Neill's "Blue Caps" to hear that the "Foreword" to this volume has been written by an old, if not the oldest living, "Blue Cap."

Colonel Woods joined the Madras Fusiliers in 1855, and served with the greatest distinction all through the Mutiny under General Neill and other gallant "Blue Caps." He states that Sir Patrick Grant saw the Regiment, some 2,000 strong, off to Calcutta in 1857—the Adjutant-General of the Madras Army, his father, being present too.

Colonel Woods was brought to notice for great gallantry during the Relief of Lucknow, and it is known that had General Neill survived it was his intention to have recommended Colonel Woods for the Victoria Cross. Colonel Woods served 20 years in the old Corps, and set an example which has been handed down to the present day officers, enabling them to carry on to the last the high traditions of "Neill's 'Blue Caps.'"

C. N. PERREAU,
Lieut.-Colonel,
late Commanding Neill's " Blue Caps."

CONTENTS

CHAPTER.		PAGE
I.	1826–1856: THE SECOND BURMA WAR	1
II.	1857: THE INDIAN MUTINY—ACTIONS AT FUTTEHPORE, PANDOO NUDDI, AND CAWNPORE	36
III.	THE INDIAN MUTINY—THE FIRST RELIEF OF LUCKNOW	57
IV.	THE SECOND SIEGE OF LUCKNOW AND THE SECOND RELIEF—THE WITHDRAWAL OF THE GARRISON AND RELIEVING TROOPS	83
V.	1858: DEFENCE OF THE ALAM BAGH AND RECAPTURE OF LUCKNOW—THE END OF THE MUTINY AND RETURN TO MADRAS	107
VI.	1859–1870: THE TRANSFER FROM THE COMPANY TO THE CROWN—THE 102ND REGIMENT (ROYAL MADRAS FUSILIERS) PROCEED ON THEIR FIRST TOUR OF HOME SERVICE	132
VII.	1870–1899: HOME SERVICE—GIBRALTAR—BECOMES THE 1ST BATTALION ROYAL DUBLIN FUSILIERS—CEYLON—HOME SERVICE AGAIN—THE OUTBREAK OF THE WAR IN SOUTH AFRICA	150
VIII.	1900–1902: THE WAR IN SOUTH AFRICA	172
IX.	1903–1913: SERVICE IN MALTA—THE IONIAN ISLANDS—EGYPT—INDIA—BACK TO MADRAS	199
APPENDIX:	VICTORIA CROSSES CONFERRED DURING THE MUTINY	221

LIST OF ILLUSTRATIONS

COMMANDING OFFICERS, MADRAS EUROPEAN REGIMENT
Frontispiece
MAJOR C. H. DALE ... ... *Facing "Dedication"*
COLONELS OF THE REGIMENT ... ... *Facing "Foreword"*

	FACING PAGE
BURMESE BELL PRESENTED TO THE REGIMENT	30
LIEUT. HARCOURT IN OLD FUSILIERS UNIFORM, 1856	40
BRIGADIER-GENERAL J. G. SMITH NEILL, C.B. MAJOR-GENERAL SIR JAMES OUTRAM, G.C.B. ... ... MAJOR-GENERAL H. HAVELOCK, C.B. ...	68
MADRAS FUSILIERS STORMING CHAR-BAGH BATTERY, MAJOR STEPHENSON LEADING	78
THE ROAD UP WHICH NEILL'S "BLUE CAPS" ADVANCED TO RELIEF OF THE LUCKNOW RESIDENCY	80
AFTER THE CAPTURE OF LUCKNOW	83
OFFICERS PRESENT SEPTEMBER 25TH, 1857	92
STREET FIGHTING: MADRAS FUSILIERS LEADING TO THE RESIDENCY	96
LUCKNOW PICTURE AND DRUM	98
OFFICERS PRESENT SIR COLIN'S RELIEF, 1857	100
INTERIOR OF THE ALUMBAGH	102
JELLALABAD FORT	108
OFFICERS PRESENT DURING THE MUTINY, 1857–58 ...	114
NEILL CENTREPIECE	126
THE OLD SILVER ORIENT BOWL OR SOUP TUREEN ...	128
OFFICER AND CORPORAL, MADRAS FUSILIERS, 1857	130
COLOURS OF 102ND ROYAL MADRAS FUSILIERS	140
COLOUR BELTS	142

LIST OF ILLUSTRATIONS

	FACING PAGE
Officer's Buckle for Belt	144
Cap Badge and Buckle	146
"Plassey," the Pet Tiger of the 102nd Royal Madras Fusiliers	150
Boer Generals at Officers' Mess, Krugersdorp, May, 1902—Spion Kop—Allemans Nek—Hart's Hill	182
Royal Dublin Fusiliers: Memorial Arch, Dublin	200
Silver Loving Cup in commemoration of the South African War	202
"G" Company, 1st Royal Dublin Fusiliers, at Khartoum, 1908	210
The New Centrepiece	218
Placing a Wreath on General Neill's Statue, Madras, February 17th, 1913	220
Two Mutiny V.C.'s and other Medals in possession of Officers' Mess	222
Cases of Medals of Indian and South African Campaigns in possession of the Officers' Mess	222

LIST OF MAPS

	FACING PAGE
Route of 1st Madras Fusiliers during Mutiny, 1857–58	50
Road Sketches: Operations June 29th, 1900—Allemans Nek—Colenso	178

The coloured plates in this Naval and Military Press reprint are placed after this page.

INTERIOR OF THE ALUMBAGH

JELLALABAD FORT.

OFFICER AND CORPORAL, MADRAS FUSILIERS, 1857.

PART II

CHAPTER I

1826–1856.

THE SECOND BURMA WAR.

ON July 1st, 1826, the following officers were present and doing duty with the two Regiments of Madras European Infantry:—

1826 *1st Regiment European Infantry:* Lieutenant-Colonel H. M. Kelly; Captains B. Hooper, A. Calder and E. Franklyn; Lieutenants J. V. Brown (Quartermaster, Interpreter and Paymaster), G. K. Boyce, J. A. Howden, R. D. Weir, F. B. Doveton (Adjutant), W. J. Manning and N. Burrard; Ensigns F. H. Hopper, M. R. Taynton and S. Marshall, and Surgeon A. Campbell.

2nd Regiment European Infantry: Major J. F. Gibson; Captain St. J. B. French; Lieutenants J. B. Puget (Quartermaster, Interpreter and Paymaster), W. P. Gardiner, H. F. Barker, J. Kerr, T. C. Stinton, T. Duke, E. Simpson (Adjutant), W. Hill, J. C. Hawes, and W. Grant; Ensigns R. T. Welbank, C. Nutting, J. S. Mathews, H. Harriott and A. Barker, and Surgeon W. S. Anderson.

There were at least twice as many officers borne on the strength of the two regiments, but they were either attached to the staff, temporarily in civil employ, or at home on leave.

The ill-health from which the 1st Regiment had suffered in Burma continued for some time after its return to Madras, and there was considerable mortality among the non-commissioned **1827** officers and men; but with the beginning of 1827 matters began to improve, a large draft of recruits arrived from England, while in March Lieutenant-Colonel Waugh, a very smart and popular officer, was appointed to command, and when the 1st Regiment was inspected later in the year it was reported as being in excellent order.

1827 On June 12th, 1827, the thanks to the Army for its services in Burma from the Court of Directors were published in Orders:—

"Resolved unanimously, that the thanks of this Court be given to the Brigadier-Generals, Brigadiers, field and other officers of His Majesty's and the Company's forces, both European and Native, for their gallant and meritorious conduct in the field throughout the late operations against the State of Ava.

"Resolved unanimously, that this Court doth acknowledge and highly applaud the zeal, discipline, and bravery, together with the patient endurance of fatigue, privation and sickness, displayed by the non-commissioned officers and privates, both European and Native, employed against the Burmese, and that the thanks of the Court be signified to them by the officers of their respective corps."

About the same time in this year General McDowall presented Colours to the 2nd Regiment at Kamptee and highly complimented the Corps on its fine appearance and high state of efficiency.

1828 The 2nd Regiment remained in garrison at Kamptee throughout 1828 and 1829, while the 1st Regiment occupied quarters
1829 at Masulipatam.

In consequence of the annexation of the provinces of Assam, Arracan and Tenasserim on the conclusion of the Burma War, it had been necessary to make certain augmentations of the Company's forces and 12 native infantry regiments had been added to the Bengal Army and two to that of Madras. The Directors seem later to have been greatly concerned at the increased cost entailed by these augmentations, and only a year had elapsed when the Madras authorities were called on by the Supreme Government to report what could be done in the way of reduction. As a result, no doubt, of these representations, each of the two European Infantry Regiments in Madras was in May, 1829, reduced by two lieutenants and one ensign, while early in the following year—on **1830** February 1st, 1830, to be exact—the 1st and 2nd Regiments of European Infantry were formed into a single regiment, designated the "Madras European Regiment," consisting of two flank and six battalion companies, the 1st Regiment becoming the "Right Wing," and the 2nd Regiment the "Left Wing" of the new Regiment, the facings being again changed from French grey to white.

Notwithstanding this amalgamation, the promotion of officers continued to go separately in each Wing—a system which naturally produced in time considerable supercession. This was altered in 1838 when promotion again began to go regularly in the whole regiment, but many years elapsed before the matter was wholly put right again.

When on March 5th, 1830, the "Right Wing" arrived at Kamptee to relieve the "Left Wing," this latter left for Masulipatam via Hyderabad under Major Kyd, and had arrived on April 26th within 63 miles of the capital of the Deccan, when a despatch was handed to the Commanding Officer directing him to move on Hyderabad at once and as rapidly as possible in consequence of a mutiny which had there broken out among the native troops.

The thermometer at this time—3 in the afternoon—stood at 105°, but within two hours the Left Wing had started, marched all night, rested next day during the heat, and marching again at sundown on the 27th, arrived under the walls of Hyderabad at 7 a.m. on the 28th, not having left a single man behind; 63 miles in 38 hours at the height of an Indian summer!

Major Kyd and his men remained encamped outside Hyderabad for seven days, when the need for their presence was no longer felt and the Left Wing continued its march towards Masulipatam. It had not, however, proceeded very far on its way when it was overtaken by an outbreak of cholera, whereby upwards of 300 soldiers and followers died before they reached Bezwada, 40 miles from Masulipatam, where the disease ceased. The Regiment arrived at its destination in May.

1832 In 1832 some trouble which had been simmering during the last four years with a Malay chieftain came finally to a head.

In 1824 all the British possessions in Sumatra had been ceded to the Dutch in exchange for Malacca and its dependencies, and from this date therefore the Malay Peninsula came under British protection; but in 1828 the chief of Nanning, whose capital was distant some 22 miles from the town of Malacca, refused to acknowledge British sovereignty. The matter was referred to the Directors of the Honourable East India Company, and in 1831 orders reached Malacca to reduce the refractory chief to obedience by force of arms. An expeditionary force, far too weak in numbers for the work demanded of it, was sent out from the garrison of Malacca, and met with a serious reverse, having to abandon its two guns and having many men killed and wounded. Reinforcements were sent to Malacca in January, 1832, and these proved sufficient to bring the chief to terms after some very trying operations which were prolonged until March, 1834. But at one time it seemed likely that European troops might be needed, and in June, 1832, the Left Wing of the Regiment was ordered to Malacca from Masulipatam, embarking in two parties, the one under Captain Puget on June 27th in the *Alligator*, and the remaining companies in the *Imogen* under Captain French on July 11th. Captain Puget's party landed on July 13th, re-embarking again on August 5th and being back in Masulipatam on September 23rd. Captain French's detachment was not required to land, but returned almost at once in the *Imogen*, and was back in its peace-time garrison by August 21st.

On October 23rd the Left Wing marched to Secunderabad, which was reached after a very trying march on November 19th, many men and camp followers having died *en route* of cholera.

1833 The Wing remained at Secunderabad until May 10th, 1833, when it again marched under Captain Puget to join the Right Wing at Kamptee. Ten days after the start Captain Puget died, and on June 13th, after a particularly trying march during the hot season of the year, the Wing arrived at Kamptee, where for some months previously Lieutenant-Colonel Elderton had been in command of the Regiment.

The whole Regiment remained at Kamptee until the end of 1839 when "A" and "B" Companies under Major Howden, marched out on New Year's Eve, their destination being **1839** Kurnal, but the orders were later changed and they were ordered to Secunderabad, where they arrived on February **1840** 11th, 1840. On the same day "E," "G" and "H" Companies also left Kamptee under Captain Weir, joining Major Howden's detachment at Secunderabad on March 16th. The headquarters of the Regiment remained at Kamptee until March 7th, when it left for the same destination under Major Kerr, but prior to its departure new Colours were presented by Major-General John Woulfe, commanding the Nagpore Subsidiary Force, on February 28th.

The old Colours were returned to the Arsenal.

Before the Regiment moved to Secunderabad a very handsome marble tablet was placed in the Church at Kamptee, inscribed as follows :—

" Sacred

" To the Memory of the undermentioned officers of the 1st Madras European Regiment, who died at or near Kamptee during the time

" the troops served in

" The Nagpore Subsidiary Force.

" Captains

James Roy	died 5th September, 1825.
James Victor Brown	died 5th June, 1831.
Joseph Puget	died 20th May, 1833.
Charles Nutting	died 29th September, 1837.
Edward Simpson	died 30th July, 1839.

" Lieutenants

Stephen W. S. Shairp	died 23rd April, 1830.
Naylor Burrard	died 3rd February, 1834.
Charles Young	died 8th May, 1835.
Francis Hamilton	died 14th February, 1837.

"Ensigns

John Mathews	died 28th May, 1828.
James Clarke	died 21st September, 1833.
William Newby	died 16th February, 1836.
Surgeon Thomas Bond	died 28th July, 1829.
Assistant Surgeon John Davies	died 15th July, 1837.

"Also to

"Nineteen sergeants, two drummers, fourteen corporals and three hundred and ninety privates of the Regiment, whose remains are
"interred in the
"Churchyard adjoining.
"This Tablet
"Is erected by the Officers of the First Madras European
"Regiment on the
"occasion of the Corps quitting the
"Station in the year 1840 as a token of their esteem and regard
"for their deceased brother officers and soldiers."

In February of this year the establishment of the Regiment was fixed at 1 colonel, 2 lieutenant-colonels, 2 majors, 10 captains, 16 lieutenants, 8 ensigns, 1 surgeon, 2 assistant surgeons, 52 sergeants, 20 drummers, 50 corporals and 800 privates.

While Colonel James Bell held command of the Regiment he sent in a letter to the military authorities, setting forth the past distinguished services of the Madras European Regiment, and asking that these might be recognized in the usual way by the according of "Honours" to be borne on the Colours and appointments; the Commanding Officer's letter runs as follows :—

"To THE A.G. OF THE ARMY.

"FORT ST. GEORGE,
"SECUNDERABAD,
"*31st December*, 1840.

"SIR,

"*In doing myself the honour to request you will submit for the favourable consideration of the Commander-in-Chief the following representation, I trust that the motives which prompt the proceeding will be attributed solely to that which has originated it, the earnest desire to raise by every effort in my power the tone and 'esprit de corps' in the Regiment which it is my pride to command.*

2. "It were super-erogant to dilate on the manner in which the 1st Madras European Regiment has ever performed its duty in the field whenever it has been afforded an opportunity to serve against the enemy, and that opportunity has not been infrequent the annexed list will show. His Excellency is doubtless aware that the Corps has never once failed to uphold the British name as distinguished alike for enduring patience of fatigue in the Siege or Campaign or for hardy valour in the Battle, and I would not therefore trespass further on His Excellency's attention than to express my earnest hope that in the distribution of Honours which have lately been bestowed on some regiments of the Army, the oldest and not the least distinguished Corps in it may not be forgotten.

3. "Amongst the names of places enumerated where the Regiment has been engaged, it will be observed that it fought at Plassey, Java, Nagpore, Porto Novo, etc., names which Her Majesty's Regiments, as also some native corps, for the share they bore in the engagements are permitted to emblazon on their Colors, while the 1st Madras European Regiment can only boast of 'Mahidpore and Java.' I would leave it to His Excellency to select from the annexed list these places of which he may deem the Corps most worthy for the part it may have played therein.

4. "In conclusion I trust that some distinctive appellation may be given to the Regiment and venture to suggest that as the 2nd are distinguished as a Light Corps the 1st Regiment may be denominated the Fusiliers of the Madras Army, and trust His Excellency will be pleased to submit the same for the consideration of the Honourable Court of Directors. Such honor would, I feel convinced, be amply appreciated by all ranks and tend much to encourage and maintain that high soldierly feeling which it is so much my wish to promote in the Regiment." Then follows:—

"Statement of a portion of the Services of the 1st Madras European Regiment for the year 1758 to the year 1825.

Trichinopoly	*Defended and continued actions fought under its walls from 1750 to 1759 until its surrender in 1761.*
Arcot	*Defended under Clive.*
Plassey	*Present at the whole of the actions against the Nabob of Bengal which terminated in the glorious and eventful battle of Plassey; this badge is borne in the Color of other Corps engaged.*
Masulipatam	
Wandiwash	
Fort St. George	*Defence of against Lally in 1758–1759.*
Porto Novo	
Sholinghur	
During the Mysore wars against Hyder and Tippoo in every engagement and siege including the capture by storm of Bangalore, of Nundy-Droog, the General Action under the wall of Seringapatam, and several other affairs of consequence under Sir Eyre Coote, General Smith, and Lord Cornwallis.	The "Royal Tiger" on the Colors of all the corps in Her Majesty's Service employed with the Corps in these campaigns. Her Majesty's 36th have the Motto "Firm" on its Color for Nundy-Droog, where the 1st Madras European Regiment particularly distinguished itself.
Cuttack	
Pondicherry	*All its Captures.*
Amboyna	*Taken twice, once in 1795, the other twice in 1809.*
Java	*In the Colors of all corps there employed.*
During the Mahratta Wars and present at the siege and capture of Mallygaum, Asseerghur— etc.	
Kemedine	*2 Companies in 26th N.I. (sic.)."*

* It will be noticed that Colonel Bell lays no claim to "Condore."

This correspondence was "forwarded and recommended" by Brigadier J. Wahab, commanding the Hyderabad Subsidiary Force, "as one of the Colonels of the Regiment," and was then sent on by the A.G.—Lieutenant-Colonel R. Alexander—by order of the Officer Commanding the Army-in-Chief to the Secretary to Government for submission to the Right Hon. the Governor in Council, in a letter recapitulating the services of the Regiment, and His Excellency asked that the 1st Madras European Regiment might be accorded the motto *Primus inter Pares*, the badge of a "Royal Tiger," and be designated the 1st or Madras Fusilier Regiment, and be dressed and equipped accordingly.

In a Minute of Government the Governor generally agreed, but did not consider it expedient to permit the Regiment to adopt the suggested motto, but consented to allow the names of certain of these actions to be borne on the Colours and asked the Commander-in-Chief to cause a General Order embodying these several proposals to be framed. The Governor also promised to submit the suggestion as to the title of "Fusiliers" to the Court of Directors.

Then a Minute, No. 934, directed that a General Order corresponding with the draft submitted by the Commander-in-Chief be published.

As to the proposed title of "Fusiliers" the Court of Directors replied in a letter which might well have emanated from the War Office of to-day, saying:—"*The designation here proposed is inapplicable to present circumstances when the Fuzil has been discontinued even with the corps designated Fuziliers in Her Majesty's Army, and could only be properly given to the 1st Madras European Regiment if they had in former times, when distinguished in action, been armed with Fuzils. To the grant of any appropriate designation which may be recommended by you we shall most willingly accede.*"

Then later again—on September 29th, 1841—the Honourable Court of Directors wrote:—"*Your General Order of the 16th March, 1841, detailing the services of the Corps and ordering the names of the actions in which it has been distinguished to be emblazoned on its Colours has our entire approbation.*"

The answer to Colonel Bell's appeal was unusually generous and prompt, being contained in General Order No. 48 by the Right Honourable the Governor-in-Council, dated Fort St. George, **1841** 12th March, 1841; portions of this Order have already appeared in earlier chapters of this History, but it may now be quoted in full :—

"*The Right Hon'ble the Governor-in-Council having had under consideration the many honorable services of the 1st Madras European Regiment, whose career is to be traced through the most eventful periods of the military history of British India, has been pleased to order that, in commemoration of its victories under Lawrence, Clive, Sir Eyre Coote, Lord Cornwallis, and other distinguished Generals, it shall bear emblazoned upon its Colours the motto 'Spectamur Agendo,' and the names of the following battles and expeditions in which it has borne part :—*

"*Arcot, which it successfully defended under Lord Clive in 1751;*

"*Plassey, to which place it accompanied Lord Clive in 1756, and assisted in the victory gained on the 23rd June, 1757;*

"*Condore, where it greatly distinguished itself under Colonel Ford in December, 1758;*

"*Wandewash, for the victory on the 20th January, 1760;*

"*Sholinghur, where it fought with success on the 27th September, 1781;*

"*Nundy-Droog, which it assisted to capture in 1791, and for which His Lordship in Council is pleased to permit it also to bear a Royal Tiger on the Colours and appointments;*

"*Amboyna, Ternate, Banda, to which islands the Regiment proceeded with the expeditions in 1796 and 1809-10;*

"*Pondicherry, the Corps having been employed at the sieges and reduction in 1761, 1778 and 1793.*

"*In reviewing the services of this gallant Regiment, the Right Hon'ble the Governor-in-Council has had before him various records of its employment in the early wars of the Carnatic and in Southern India, of which the present brief notice gives but a general indication, and for which it is but necessary to refer to the military operations at different times near Trichinopoly, from the year 1746 to 1761, to its share in the resistance against the French under Lally, Conflans, Bussy, Law and other enterprising commanders; its various engagements in the Northern Circars and Cuttack, and its service in Ceylon in 1795–96.*

"*The 1st European Regiment was actively employed throughout the campaigns against Hyder Ally and Tippoo; during the latter it assisted in the storming of Bangalore, and in the engagement near the walls of Seringapatam under the command of Lord Cornwallis; and already does it bear on its Colours testimonials of the last Mahratta War, in which it was present at the sieges of Talneir, Malligaum, and Asseerghur, and of the bravery and devotedness which were so conspicuous in Burmah.*

"*The Right Hon'ble the Governor-in-Council feels that in conferring these distinctions upon the 1st Madras European Regiment, he does but accord a tribute of well-merited honour to the Army of Fort St. George; and His Lordship is assured that the decorated banners of its oldest Corps, while exhibiting a proud memorial of past achievements, will never cease to wave over soldiers whose good conduct in garrison and bravery in the field will well maintain what has been so nobly won by their predecessors in arms.*"

It will be noticed that in the opening paragraph of this General Order the Regiment is styled the 1*st* Madras European Regiment, the reason for this being that in October, 1839, a *second* European Regiment was ordered to be formed at Arnee as a Light Infantry Corps, and to be designated the "2nd Madras European Regiment," and in consequence of this augmentation of the Madras Army, the "Madras European Regiment" resumed the title of the "1*st* Madras European Regiment."

In December, 1841, new Colours were presented to the Corps by Major-General Riddell, the whole of the Hyderabad Subsidiary Corps being paraded on the occasion; Colonel James Bell was this day in command of the Regiment.

In February, 1842, there was some unrest among the native troops at Secunderabad owing to their batta having been stopped,

1842 the regiments specially affected being the 4th Light Cavalry, 7th, 10th, 32nd and 41st Native Infantry. For three or four days some of these corps were almost in a state of mutiny, but the conduct of the 1st Madras European Regiment, their promptness in getting under arms, and the temper and tact displayed by all ranks were specially commended by General Fraser, British Resident at Hyderabad, and by Major-General Riddell, commanding the Hyderabad Subsidiary Corps; and in commenting upon the reports forwarded by these two officers, the Governor-in-Council desired that it might be intimated to the Regiment that its "steady and soldierlike behaviour upon this painful occasion has received the most favourable notice of the Government."

During the two years and upwards that the Corps was stationed at Secunderabad it received many recruits and in 1842 was about 1,200 strong and in a high state of efficiency; the health of the Regiment had been good and it had lost no more than the average from sickness, but three young officers had died—Lieutenants McKenzie, Waller and Jourdan.

1843 The Regiment marched from Secunderabad on February 13th, 1843, under command of Lieutenant-Colonel R. J. Hussey Vivian,* for Arcot and Arnee, the Left Wing reaching Arcot on the 5th and the Headquarter Wing arriving at Arnee on April 9th; and while occupying these new stations the following was published:—

"*General Orders, Fort St. George, 11th April, 1843. No. 58 of 1843.*

"*The Honourable the Court of Directors having been pleased to authorise the designation of 'Fusiliers' to be conferred upon the 1st European Regiment as a mark of approval of its distinguished services, the Most Noble the Governor-in-Council directs that the uniform and equipment of the Corps shall be assimilated to those of Fusilier regiments in Her Majesty's service.*

---

* This officer commanded a Turkish contingent during the Crimean War.

"The Ensigns of the Fusilier regiment will be designated 2nd Lieutenants.

"His Excellency the Commander-in-Chief is requested to adopt the necessary measures for carrying this order into effect."

1845 The Regiment remained rather less than two years at Arcot and Arnee, for in January, 1845, the two Wings marched separately to Bangalore, the Headquarter Wing proceeding under Major Charles Butler on the 3rd and arriving on January 25th, while the remaining companies moved on February 13th and reached their new station on the 28th, marching in under the command of Major T. A. Duke; within a year, however, the Left Wing proceeded from Bangalore to Bellary, under Major P. Chambers.

1846 In this year—in September, 1846—the establishment of the Regiment was augmented by two captains—from 8 to 10.

1847 Early in 1847 the Headquarter Wing marched under Major Duke and joined the Left Wing at Bellary, and here the whole Regiment remained together until the autumn of 1852, Nos. 2, 3, 4 and 5 Companies being quartered in the fort and the remainder of the Regiment in the New Barracks. While stationed here drafts came out from home at the rate of from two to three each year, under the following officers:—

Lieutenant W. Brown on February 26th, 1847.
Captain Rees on October 4th, 1847.
Lieutenant Cattley on November 6th, 1847.
Lieutenant D. Brown on February 9th, 1848.
Lieutenant Cattley on June 19th, 1848.
Captain Babington on October 4th, 1848.
Lieutenant A. Ward on April 12th, 1850.
Captain W. R. Brown on May 3rd, 1851.
Lieutenants Hamilton and Harcourt on September 3rd, 1852.

1852 On July 16th, 1852, new Colours were presented to the Regiment by Mrs. Duke, the wife of the Commanding Officer, Lieutenant-Colonel T. A. Duke, the consecration service being conducted by the Rev. J. Morant, Chaplain of Bellary. This was the last event of any importance in which the Regiment was concerned while in this garrison, for in July orders were received to march to Madras to take part in the Second Burmese War. The 1st Madras Fusiliers left Bellary on August 2nd, reached Madras on September 1st, and on the 7th embarked in H.M.S. *Sphynx*, the transports *Moozuffer* and *Graham*, at a strength of 49 officers, 48 sergeants, 20 drummers and 892 other ranks. The following were the officers who embarked with the Regiment:—Lieutenant-Colonel T. A. Duke; Majors W. Hill and A. Barker; Captains Hawes (Brevet Major), J. Neill (Brevet Major), J. Stephenson (Brevet Major), Nicolay, Renaud, C. Tulloch, W. Brown, Rees, Geils, M. Galwey, F. Dickson and J. West; Lieutenants A. Ward, J. Harris, Carter, J. Fraser, D. Brown (Adjutant), J. Christie, T. Raikes, H. D. Taylor, J. B. Spurgin, C. Grant, T. Brown, C. Scott-Elliot, E. S. Daniell, J. Hamilton, P. A. Brown, E. Dangerfield, G. J. Hamilton, J. Woodcock, G. F. Gosling and G. R. Fisher; Second-Lieutenants R. Menzies, C. Bowen, W. Brice, S. H. Jones-Parry, E. B. Sladen, G. J. Harcourt, J. Wing, W. Groom, J. M. Williams and J. Seton; Surgeon A. Goodall; Assistant-Surgeons Carnegie, Cholmeley and F. Day.

The three vessels containing the Regiment entered the Rangoon River on September 13th, when the disembarkation was proceeded with, and by the 14th all were accommodated in barracks.

Of the officers about to take part in this Second Burma War, only Colonel Duke and Major Hill had served with the Regiment in the earlier campaign in this country.

The King of Ava, whose arrogance and presumption had been the causes of the first Burma War, resulting in serious loss of territory, had been deposed very soon after the conclusion of peace, being succeeded by his brother who assumed the title of King Tharrawaddy and at once made it known that he had no intention whatever of considering himself bound by the terms of the Treaty. He treated successive British Residents with conspicuous rudeness and even indignity, with the result that the Resident was at first withdrawn from Ava to Rangoon and finally removed from the country altogether. This King died in 1846, and his son and successor followed in his footsteps, while the different provincial governors, taking their tone from the Court, renewed the policy of exaction and extortion from British traders which had been largely responsible for the war of 1824–26.

The Indian Government for some time did nothing to enforce the terms of the Treaty; its hands at the time were very full, for the unfortunate Afghan War of 1842 had been followed by the Gwalior campaign, while this again had been succeeded, after a brief term of peace, by the two Sikh wars, and every soldier who could be raised had been needed either within India or on or beyond its north-west frontier of those days.

But by 1851 the Governor-General, Lord Dalhousie, had more time to look into affairs on the east of India and began seriously to consider the recital of the grievances of British merchants trading with Burma, and he then sent a squadron under Commodore Lambert to Rangoon with a peremptory order to the Burman Governor to mend his ways, and bearing a letter from the Governor-General to the Burmese King, which was to be sent on to that potentate should the Governor not at once comply with the new demands now put forward.

There is no occasion to describe in detail all that now took place—the studied and repeated insolence of the Burmese, the continued evasions of the agreed terms of the Treaty, the ceaseless extortions to which British residents and merchants were subjected; but at last matters went so far and assumed so threatening an aspect that Commodore Lambert embarked all British subjects in Rangoon in the ships of his squadron and dropped down the river, accompanied by all the British merchantmen and by a Burman Royal vessel which he had seized. A heavy fire was opened from the river banks, but this was returned and the Burmans driven from their entrenchments by the guns of the men-of-war.

The Second Burmese War may now be said to have begun.

The Indian Government had already made certain preparations and an expeditionary force, nearly 6,000 strong, and drawn partly from Bengal and partly from Madras, was detailed and placed under command of Major-General Godwin, C.B. This force left India in April, 1852, and during the six months that followed the operations met with general success; but the Burmese made no sign of submission, and Lord Dalhousie wrote to the Court of Directors stating that in his opinion it was absolutely necessary that the war should be continued until the British Government had obtained effectual pledges against any renewal of outrage. The Governor-General himself visited Rangoon in July and on his return to Calcutta in August wrote an appreciation of the situation as then existing, which was briefly, that the British were masters of the sea coast from east to west, that our ships controlled all the waters of the Irrawaddy from Prome to the sea, that there were hardly any Burmese troops in the Lower Province, and that no army had been collected in the Upper Province; and as a result of the Governor-General's visit and consultations with the Home Authorities, General Godwin was reinforced with two more brigades, one from Bengal and one from Madras. The army under his command was now organized in two divisions—a Bengal division of three brigades, under Brigadier-General Sir John Cheape, and a Madras division of equal strength, under command of Brigadier-General S. W. Steel.

The Madras Fusiliers were in the 2nd Brigade of General Steel's Division, with the 5th and 79th Madras Native Infantry, and the Brigade was commanded by Brigadier McNeill.

While the Regiment remained in Rangoon awaiting orders for the front, a court-martial was convened to try a Private Smith of the Corps for desertion; this man, who was in hospital at Madras when his regiment embarked, had escaped from hospital and reached the ship's side in a catamaran and so rejoined. The court had no option but to find Smith guilty of the charge, but sentenced him to the smallest punishment they could award; the proceedings were at once returned for revision, when the Court

ADVANCE ON PEGU

equally promptly, "respectfully adhered to their former sentence," and the proceedings were read out on parade with the addition of the words "Confirmed, but not approved." Private Smith distinguished himself in the campaign and became a non-commissioned officer.

Cholera, which had already attacked the Regiment while on the march to Madras, now again made its appearance, causing a good deal of depression which everything possible was done to remove; but it was not until October 18th that any move of the Regiment took place, when a detachment of Nos. 8 and 9 Companies under Brevet Major J. C. Hawes, with Captain Tulloch, Lieutenants Ward, Hamilton, Woodcock and Second-Lieutenant Harcourt, embarked for Bassein in relief of a detachment of the 51st Light Infantry.

Pegu had been captured from the Burmese in June and had then been handed over to our Allies, the Talaings, who had been confident of their ability to hold it, but it had been retaken by the Burmese within a week and its defences greatly strengthened; and General Godwin now dispatched a column to recapture Pegu before the main column moved forward from Rangoon. The column contained 300 of each of the Madras and Bengal Fusiliers, 400 sepoys, 70 sappers and two 24-pounder howitzers, and embarked on the evening on October 18th in four steamers, under command of Brigadier McNeill and accompanied by General Godwin. The Madras Fusiliers were composed of Nos. 1, 6 and 10 Companies, with Major Hill in command, and having with him the following officers of the Regiment:—Captains Nicolay, Stephenson and West; Lieutenants Spurgin, Scott-Elliot, Daniell, P. A. Brown, Dangerfield, and Gosling; Second-Lieutenants Menzies and Bowen, and Assistant-Surgeon Cholmeley.

On November 20th, after experiencing considerable and many difficulties, the steamers anchored 2 miles below Pegu, and early on the next day the troops were landed. There was a dense mist and it was not easy to find the way, but two men of the Regiment, Privates McClory and Kelly came across an old iron gun which the

Burmese had been unable to remove, and clung to this ancient weapon with laudable pertinacity.*

On the arrival of the main body in front of the Pagoda a halt was called, when the attacking column, under Major Hill, was formed up and harangued by General Godwin. "Now," said the General to the two regiments of Fusiliers, "*You* are Bengalis and *you* are Madrasis. Let us see who are the best men."† A deafening cheer and a forward rush was the response. The enemy fired a volley at the oncomers, but the bullets took but little effect, and after three hours' hard fighting the Burmese outworks were stormed through a gap on the south side. Later in the day the Madras Fusiliers, under Captain Stephenson, charged up the steps of the Pagoda and drove the defenders from the platform, Lieutenants Elliot and Daniell being, so it is said, the first to enter. In this action 12 men were dangerously wounded, 6 severely and 6 slightly.

General Godwin now returned to Rangoon with the bulk of his force including No. 6 Company of the Regiment with Captain West, Lieutenants Scott-Elliot and Gosling, leaving as garrison at Pegu the two remaining Companies of the Madras Fusiliers, 200 of the 5th Native Infantry, a few gunners with two 24-pounders and some small ordnance captured from the enemy, and 30 sappers, and the troops immediately began to clear the ground round the post and improve the defences—Major Hill was here in command with Lieutenant Dangerfield as staff officer.

The Pagoda here was built on a height on the upper of two terraces, connected with each other and with the level country by flights of steps. Both the Pagoda and the town at the south-west angle were enclosed by a wall, much broken and overgrown with jungle, while the Pagoda itself was overlooked and commanded on two sides by higher ground. Gunboats had been left on the river to keep open communications.

On the night of November 27th an attack was made simultaneously on the garrison, the gunboats and the river picquet,

* Jones-Parry, *An Old Soldier's Memories*, p. 54.
† Laurie, *Our Burmese Wars*, p. 214.

and the following account of what here happened is taken from Jones-Parry's " Memories."

" No sooner had the firing commenced than Brown got the powder barrels, sacks of provisions together, and with some timber dragged from the river made a sort of breastwork, which prevented the Burmese from closing in on them. From this breastwork, at intervals when the moon, emerging from a cloud, allowed them to see the enemy plainly, he made vigorous sorties. In this work, and in saving the stores which caught fire, Private Clancy, of No. 1 Company of the Fusiliers, greatly distinguished himself. . . .

" But repelling the attacks on the stores was not the only difficulty that Lieutenant Brown had to contend with. The Burmese, by means of trees, sunken canoes, etc., attempted to block the river, which at that time was shallow, and so prevent the boats from getting down-stream. Brown by his judicious arrangements kept down the enemy's fire until the sailors could remove the obstacles and get off safely.

" A curious feature connected with this gallant defence deserves to be noticed. The river picket was attacked from both sides of the river, the banks of which were very high above the water at this season of the year. One-half of our men had to front the river face, so as to keep down the fire of the enemy on the gunboats lying below. On their side the gunboats had to fire over both banks as occasion required, and when the Middies called out ' Starboard ready ! ' the whole picket had to lie down flat on their faces, whilst the gunboats fired over them. Lieutenant Mason, R.N., had his necktie shot off, and in the morning the awnings of the boats were found to be well riddled by bullets. Lieutenant Mason reported to the Admiralty that if it had not been for the assistance rendered by the picket, the gunboats would have run a great risk of being captured. The attacks continued all night and even after daybreak—in fact until the picket was strengthened from the Pagoda."

On December 3rd Second-Lieutenant Jones-Parry arrived at Pegu with arms and provisions. "On Sunday the 5th," he writes, "we had a busy day. We were employed cutting timber for a stockade to protect a large body of Peguers who had come in to seek protection the day before." These numbered some 2,000 men, women and children, and such of the men as had matchlocks were told off to help in the defence, while the walls were strengthened and the gaps filled up with sandbags, barrels and even with sacks of flour and rice. On this day too a party was sent out under Captain Nicolay, Second-Lieutenants Parry and Bowen, to rescue twenty sepoys of the 5th Native Infantry who were in danger of being cut off while coming up the river with supplies. On returning the combined party was followed up by large numbers of the enemy and got back with great difficulty. Second-Lieutenant Jones-Parry was very nearly cut off and was rescued by Private McClory of No. 10 Company.

From this date until December 14th the enemy closely invested the Pagoda with a force estimated at 6,000 men, made several vigorous attacks and kept up a very heavy fire on the upper terraces, Lieutenant P. A. Brown and three men of the Regiment being wounded. The men were greatly exhausted by the heavy duties and want of sleep and became very careless. "One man in particular," says Parry, "Private McKinley, was for ever exposing himself. He was repeatedly cautioned . . . one day just as he left the mess he was hit . . . and died from lockjaw."

The gun found earlier by Privates McClory and Kelly was now brought into use. It was, Parry tells us, "a bulldog looking thing with a touch hole as large as the handle of a church door. We had an excellent instructor in one Bombardier Sale, as grand an old soldier as ever wore a belt. . . . The men who volunteered to form a gun crew were from No. 10 Company and their names, as far as I can remember, were Liptrot, Vincent, G. Moore, Weir, Saunders, Dunsheath and Denis Kelly." The fault of this infantry gun crew was that they were too fond of "loosing off," thus causing a useless expenditure of ammunition, but it was difficult to check their ardour. On one occasion, however, Lieutenant Daniell was found seated on the gun, in front of an open embrasure, in order to prevent its being fired off unnecessarily!

DEFENCE OF PEGU

The post had been much harassed by fire from a large clump of bamboos in front of the north-west angle of the Pagoda, and gun fire upon it from the defenders seemed to have been of small effect. So one day Parry and Bowen collected all the dry wood and combustibles they could carry, and sallying forth, reached the clump, which luckily was unoccupied, and set it on fire, retiring hurriedly under a very hot fire from friend and foe. But relief was now close at hand and an account of how this was effected here follows, as drawn up shortly afterwards for Colonel Laurie, when writing his book, by the late General (then Captain) Neill of the Regiment.

"Two hundred and fifty Madras Fusiliers, under Captain Renaud, had been obliged to return to Rangoon in consequence of the disabled state of the river steamer *Nerbudda* in which they had embarked. These troops were transhipped to the *Mahanuddy*, a vessel whose boilers had seen rather too much service. It was not therefore until both these steamers had been repaired that the Headquarters in the *Nerbudda* and the Madras Fusiliers in the *Mahanuddy* were enabled to leave Rangoon. At noon on December 12th, 1852, the Headquarters leading in the *Nerbudda* and the Madras Fusiliers following in the *Mahanuddy* set out from Rangoon. At daylight next morning, which was very foggy, all the boats conveying the other troops, under convoy of Captain Tarleton, R.N., proceeded with the *Nerbudda* up the river; the other steamer was supposed to be following not far astern. They approached the village of Lower Seedee as the mist was rising, which was found, as expected, occupied by the enemy, and the river staked abreast of it. We were quite prepared for the foe; guns loaded, and a party of 25 men on each paddle-box—the starboard furnished by the Madras, the larboard by the Bengal Fusiliers. We had evidently taken the Burmese by surprise; some of them were seen about the village, also a large party with some horsemen moving about on the plain. The left bank, near where the steamer was anchored, was an open plain, higher up and out of shot stood the village. The troops were soon landed, and it was speedily determined to occupy the village as affording shelter, it having been taken for granted that the enemy had retreated. The Bengal Fusiliers were therefore moved up to some of the nearest houses, when about 20 shots were fired on them from the high grass and jungle adjoining One man was slightly wounded, but the Burmese escaped without being either seen or fired upon. The village was then occupied, the Madras Fusiliers being on picquet in advance.

"The *Mahanuddy* not having yet arrived with the rest of the Fusiliers, the other steamer was sent down to bring the men up. The day wore on, and there being no appearance of the steamer, arrangements were made to pass the night in the village and picquets were thrown out; but no attempt was made to drive the enemy further away, or out of the village of Upper Seedee, about a mile distant. This village had on several occasions, particularly on the last when the boats were obliged to retire, annoyed the Navy considerably. . . .

"About midnight a volley was fired into some of the houses, by which one Bengal Fusilier was killed and another was mortally wounded. A sailor was also mortally wounded. Irregular firing now commenced, and the sentries at other points of the line also giving the alarm, some firing, which was fortunately put a stop to in time, had nearly caused considerable confusion. . . . The steamer returned during the night with Captain Renaud's party, their detention having been caused by the *Mahanuddy* unfortunately grounding. The troops were landed early in the morning, and by 7 a.m. the whole force advanced in the following order :—Two ship's guns dragged by sailors of the Royal Navy under Captain Shadwell, R.N.; 250 Madras Fusiliers under Captain Renaud; 150 Bengal Fusiliers under Major Gerrard; and 300 Sikhs under Major Armstrong, formed the advance of 700 men, General Godwin commanding, with Brigadier Dickenson. Two hundred of the 10th Bengal Native Infantry under Captain Monro, 450 Bengal Fusiliers under Colonel Tudor (650 men) formed the reserve under Brigadier-General Steel, C.B.

"The force moved off, marching away from the river so as to avoid Seedee, and on nearing a small village came upon the high road leading to the south-west gateway of the mound or old wall round the ancient city of Pegu. In the outskirts of the village about 300 of the enemy were posted, and on the plain about 100 Cassay Horse.* On the approach of our advanced troops, the enemy cheered and came on towards us, their infantry flanked by their cavalry. Our skirmishers pushed on answering their cheers, firing commenced, and the Burmese retired, the infantry into the jungle in our front, the cavalry keeping to the plain on our flank. As the head of the column was entering the jungle near the south-west angle of the mound a short halt took place; the guides had evidently been leading the column in the wrong direction for that point, and counsel was now taken of an excellent guide in Captain Renaud's service, who having urgently represented that the defences at the west point were particularly strong (as was subsequently seen), and that the proper way, which he offered to show, was by the east side, he was at once directed to lead the column.

"The force continued its march, and after a very fatiguing morning's work, reached the gateway in the eastern *bund*. Here the head of the column first came in contact with the enemy. Captain Renaud's party quickly pushed over the *bund*, the Burmese came down through the jungle on the flanks of the column, and opened fire on the reserve. Their fire was speedily answered and they were compelled to retire. All then pushed forward and got within the *bund*. Firing had, up to the time of the column entering the *bund*, been heard near the Pagoda. Telescopes were now in requisition, but nothing could be seen of the garrison. A man was at last discovered on the Pagoda; he was made out to be a Burmese soldier, but was immediately afterwards declared to be a Madras lascar. General Godwin, who had been in a state of intense anxiety, was at once relieved.

"The force now pushed on to the east gateway of the Pagoda, and it was not until a very short distance from it that we observed the garrison, and then learned that the line of *bund* and old Pagodas from which it was commanded had been occupied by the Burmese

---

* Chiefly men from Manipur.

until within a few minutes of our entering the fortress, that we had taken them in reverse, and that, had we been aware of it, by detaching a party to our right on entering the first *bund*, we might have cut many, if not all, off.

"The troops were now dead-beat. . . . Few out of the whole force were equal to more exertion during the heat of that day It had been a long and fatiguing march, but not yet was there to be a rest of any duration. All the troops crowded into the Pagoda and completely covered its area. . . The men were lying about, taking their rest, when about 4 p.m. a fire was opened upon them from the old commanding ground which the enemy had again occupied. In a few minutes several men were hit. and it became necessary to dislodge and drive the Burmese out of the defences along the river bank and south and west faces of the *bund*. These services were performed in a very brilliant manner by the troops employed. . . ."

Lieutenant Jones-Parry's account supplements the foregoing. He writes:—"On the morning of the 14th December we were all anxiety; it was not, however, till about eleven that we heard firing on our east face. It grew nearer and nearer. . . . Presently we heard a cheer, then saw our men's red coats, and in a few seconds more Elliot of 'Ours' was in through the embrasure of our No. 10 Company battery. . . . General Godwin, on meeting Major Hill on the upper terrace, said 'I had given you up till ten minutes ago.' The fact was that the Burmese would not surrender their positions until driven out, and had General Godwin attempted the relief in any other direction than that indicated in Major Hill's letter, his loss would have been very great; as it was, it only amounted to three killed and nine wounded. In his despatch to the Governor-General he remarked: 'I know few moments that have been more gratifying to me than when I met that excellent and brave officer, Major Hill of the Madras Fusiliers, in the Pagoda.'"

The loss sustained by Major Hill's party was surprisingly small— 2 officers being wounded and 45 soldiers and followers killed and wounded, while of the Madras Fusiliers one man died of his wounds and Lieutenant P. A. Brown and 3 men were wounded.

In a General Order, issued at Pegu on December 17th, 1852, General Godwin wrote as follows:—

"Major-General Godwin is most proud to express his admiration of the noble defence of the Pegu Pagoda (against a host of enemies) made by Major Hill and the brave handful of officers and soldiers under his command for so many days and anxious nights, cut off as they were from the succour of their comrades by the works of the enemy on the river, as well as by the distant communication with Headquarters of the Army. It is a fine example to this Army of what bravery under the direction of cool courage can do, giving, as Major Hill has done, confidence to all, by which alone the Pegu garrison has gained so much honour."

Then in a Notification, dated Fort William, January 4th, 1853, it stated in Paragraph 3 thereof that:—

"The Governor-General in Council particularly desires to record his high approbation of the gallant conduct of Major Hill of the Madras Fusiliers, and of the officers and men under his command, in their defence of the position they held at Pegu."

On December 16th, two days after the relief, a force made up of 570 Bengal Fusiliers, 150 Madras Fusiliers (Nos. 3 and 5 Companies, with Captain Renaud and Assistant-Surgeon Day), and some 500 sepoys and sappers—total 1,230 men, was warned to move on the following morning to drive the enemy away from the neighbourhood. The expedition was not altogether a success and the following is Captain Neill's account of what occurred:—

"The force moved out of the Pagoda following Captain Latter's guides. We wound slowly through the jungle to the north of Pegu and emerged on the plain about 9.30 a.m. So little were the enemy expecting us that the garrison of Pegu saw from the Pagoda their elephants feeding in the jungle near us, and had we been aware of it we might have captured them all. On our column reaching the plain signal guns were fired from the enemy's lines evidently to collect their people. On reconnoitring their position it appeared to be three lines of entrenchments, the right on the river and extending across the Shwe Gheen road far into the plain. On the left of the road, which was the centre of their position, ran a jungly nullah, which we subsequently found had been so spiked and entrenched that had we advanced by that route our loss would have been very considerable. . . . After the force had turned the left of the first line of entrenchments it was halted, and dispositions made for attacking in two columns, one the left, under General Steel, the other under General Godwin. The left column was soon in its place impatiently waiting the signal to advance. It was not given. The enemy were seen moving in huge masses from their left. . . . An aide-de-camp was sent off to General Godwin to inform him of what was going on in front and returned with an order that the attack of the left column was not to take place, but it was to stand firm and cover his flank when he attacked. . . .

"When the advance by General Godwin at last took place the enemy were in full retreat. A few only remained on our front, and although the attacking party, European and Native, more particularly the Sikhs, were exceedingly forward and energetic, our men were never able to approach sufficiently near to do the execution they would have done, had they been permitted to attack at the proper time.

"The Burmese retreated by the Shwe Gheen road, and the column was halted in a tope of trees which had formed their headquarters. After more than an hour's halt, the men stood to their arms and formed upon a road leading nearly due west . . . the march in that direction was unfortunately persisted in, which ended in our reaching the village of Lephandoon before sunset. With the exception of a broken-down buffalo-cart and an old woman the post was abandoned. . . .

"For the night the force occupied the houses on the left bank of the river, and after sunrise on the 18th December moved off in a north-east direction. . . . Approaching the village of Mousakamu there was a thick belt of jungle, the force passed through it and found shelter in huts and sheds. The guides declared that the enemy had pushed on and were at least 20 miles off. . . However, the presence of the enemy within 2 miles of his headquarters became known by chance to General Godwin from two or three officers and men going out beyond the outposts to reconnoître. The guides asserted that it was all a mistake—there was no enemy near. However, an old ruined pagoda in a jungle, which had been used by the Burmese as a look-out, enabled others to see them as they had reported, and, a body of their infantry moving down into the belt of jungle in front of their centre, an officer with a small party went out again towards the bridge to reconnoitre, when the enemy attempted to cut off their retreat. . . .

" The bugles in camp now sounded, the men stood to their arms, and the force moved out to meet the foe, who, on seeing our troops advance, fell gradually back on his entrenchments, our skirmishers dislodging those who had entered the jungle on our left. After crossing the bridge two columns of attack were formed. . . . The skirmishers only of the left force were engaged, the right carried the village on the enemy's left ; night closed in and the force marched back to their former ground. . . . The following morning we left Mousakamu after sunrise and reached Pegu about 1 p.m. . ."

On December 20th General Godwin started for Rangoon, leaving Captain Renaud with 200 of the Regiment in Pegu as a reinforcement, also some guns but no gunners, while Captain Tarleton, R.N., and three gunboats also remained. Jones-Parry writes : " All was now activity in the work of erecting a stockade on the river bank. . . . The river was a mile and a half from the Pagoda, the immense *bund*, covered with jungle, intervened between **1853** us and it. . . . On the 4th January, 1853, a few shots were fired at the river picket and spies said the enemy were coming down on us in force. On the 5th I went up to the Pagoda to have a look round, and saw a number of the enemy busy stockading on the north and several shots were fired into the picket. Dangerfield later on discovered a body of Burmese making along the *bund* for our stockade and sent a rocket and a dose of canister into them.

" On the 5th January we were for river guard, which was relieved daily, in order to keep the road open. We took two days' supplies with us, in case of being hemmed in, but on account of the fog we did not start until 8 o'clock. Spurgin of 'Ours' commanded 50 of our men with a party of the 19th.* The Major told us that if any opposition should be made at the ghat, he would flank us right and left with a mortar and 24-pounder howitzer. I was sent out in front with skirmishers, but found the ghat clear so we arrived safely. . . . The work of stockading was instantly commenced and was no trifling job; our men were constantly being fired at while working so the main body had to act as a covering party. At 11 o'clock one of them was struck by a jingal ball right through the calf of the leg—a horrid wound, we gave him some brandy and water and put him in the ditch out of danger. Two other men were hit from the fire on the other side of the river—contusions only.

"Our position was now somewhat critical, for, owing to the enemy having taken up a position on the right bank, opposite our weakest face, we were in reality hemmed in on three sides, but still we managed to keep down their fire pretty well. Spurgin removed all our sentries from the east face, as the shot across the river caught them in the rear. The enemy next took possession of an old indigo factory, a brick building of considerable strength, situated exactly opposite to us across the river on our west face. We fired a 6-pounder into it with but little effect. . . . We lost pretty heavily that day in proportion to our numbers, but firing ceased at sunset. The night was one of intense watchfulness. Next day instead of being relieved as usual, we were kept down as a working party. . . ."

At mid-day the working party marched back to the Pagoda, leaving Captain Nicolay on duty, but on the morning of January 8th Nicolay was mortally wounded, dying next day; he was buried on the north front of the Pagoda.

On the night of the 10th the enemy made a final attack, and three days later a convoy arrived bringing supplies of food and ammunition.

By reason of the wise measures adopted by Major Hill the

* The 5th Madras Native Infantry had been relieved at the end of December by a party of the 19th Madras Native Infantry under a Captain Young.

losses during the investment were remarkably small, though they actually amounted to 10 per cent. of the force, while those of the river picquet were rather higher. Major Hill admitted that had the Burmese attacked really vigorously during the first few days the position might easily have been critical.

While Nos. 3, 4 and 5 Companies were engaged as above described at Pegu, Captain Geils, in command of Nos. 2 and 6—161 non-commissioned officers and men, had embarked for Martaban on January 3rd as part of a force ordered to proceed up the Sittang River to Tonghoo under Brigadier-General Steel. This force had several engagements with the enemy, notably on January 14th. In the despatch conveying the thanks of the Governor-General to General Steel and his command, Captain Geils and his detachment, which included Lieutenants Grant, P. A. Brown and Menzies, were mentioned.

During this time four separate parties were sent from Pegu to Myetkyo on the Sittang River with supplies, etc., for the force; the first was commanded by Captain Stephens with Lieutenant Elliot and Second-Lieutenant Sladen; the second by Captain W. R. Brown with Second-Lieutenant Wing; while Lieutenants Christie, Spurgin and Raikes and Second-Lieutenant Groom were employed with the other parties.

In March and April the force at Tonghoo was augmented by the arrival of Nos. 1 and 10 Companies with the Headquarters of the Regiment. There was now much sickness and many deaths among both officers and men, Lieutenants Bowen, Brice and Wing and Surgeon Anderson all dying of dysentery.

A detachment of 2 captains, 2 subalterns and 216 other ranks had been left behind at Pegu, and on April 14th No. 5 Company, which formed part of this detachment, set out from Pegu under Lieutenant Raikes and Second-Lieutenant Groom, accompanied by two guns and some Bengal artillerymen, and proceeded by forced marches to Sittang to assist in the capture of Belling, which had been taken by the Burmese. In the operations 2 men of the Regiment were wounded. No. 5 Company remained at Sittang, being reinforced by a small party from Pegu.

The remaining events of the Second Burma War, so far as they concerned the Madras Fusiliers, were briefly as follows:—In November, 1853, No. 8 Company moved to Pegu from Bassein, and in December the force at Pegu, under Captain A. Ward—with whom were Captain D. Brown, Lieutenants Dangerfield, T. Brown, Woodcock and Harcourt and Assistant-Surgeon Joseph—set out for Shwe Gheen to relieve a detachment of the Bengal Fusiliers. On the way Ward attacked and drove a dacoit chief from his stronghold at Waingyee.

1854 In January, 1854, an insurrection occurred in the Bassein District and No. 9 Company, under Lieutenants Gosling and Græme, was employed in quelling it.

In the same month Nos. 1 and 7 Companies left Tonghoo as escort to the Boundary Commission; these companies were commanded by Captain Geils and Lieutenant Grant, and were accompanied by a detachment of Madras sepoys, some sappers and a few Irregular Horse. The party was attacked on four separate occasions and both officers of the Madras Fusiliers were wounded. "On the receipt of the news of Grant's wounds," writes Jones-Parry, "Lieutenant P. A. Brown and Dr. Boutflower were sent out on an elephant with only three men as a guard. They travelled 17 miles through dense jungle and reached the force only to learn that it had been again attacked and that Geils was severely wounded . . . a matchlock ball had hit him in the shoulder, and the bullet, imbedded beneath the clavicle, could not be extracted." He lingered for some weeks and died on March 4th.

On February 5th, 1854, Lieutenant-Colonel Apthorpe assumed command of the Regiment at Tonghoo.

On the occupation of Prome and Pegu the Governor-General in Council had issued a proclamation declaring the annexation of the latter, and now that military operations were at last at an end the Burman King, while refusing to sign any treaty, promised to make no effort to resist the British occupation of Pegu, and petitioned that the Irrawaddy blockade should be withdrawn and trade between the two nations re-established. Lord Dalhousie recognized that

BURMESE BELL.
Presented to the Regiment.

no useful purpose could result from insistance on a treaty which would, with such a king, hardly be worth the paper upon which it was written, and accordingly issued his own Proclamation of Peace and fixed upon a frontier line between British and Burmese territory. The King of Burma abided by this Proclamation.

1855 At the end of 1854 all the detachments were called in and the Regiment was quartered at Tonghoo until December 27th, 1855, when the Headquarters and Left Wing set out for
1856 Martaban, whence on February 2nd, 1856, they sailed for Madras, marching on the 11th into Fort St. George, where on April 5th the Right Wing joined.

During the operations the services of the following officers of the Madras Fusiliers received honorable mention :—Major William Hill, Brevet Major J. G. S. Neill, employed as Adjutant-General to the Forces, Captains S. G. C. Renaud, A. A. Geils and D. Brown, Lieutenants C. Scott-Elliot, P. A. Brown and E. Dangerfield; Major Hill and Brevet Major Neill were promoted Brevet Lieutenant-Colonels, and Captain Renaud was given a brevet majority.

The following were the casualties incurred by the Regiment during the campaign :—Brevet Major Hawes, Captains W. Brown, Nicolay, Geils and Tulloch were killed or died of wounds, Lieutenant Bowen, Second-Lieutenants Wing and Brice and Surgeon Anderson died of disease, and Lieutenants Grant and P. A. Brown were wounded, while 118 non-commissioned officers, drummers and rank and file of the Madras Fusiliers fell during the war. The Regiment brought back to Madras two brass guns which it had captured, and a large bell presented to it by the General.

Under G.O.C.C. No. 26 of January 5th, 1855, the name " Pegu " was permitted to be borne on the Colours and appointments of the Regiment; while on April 24th, 1856, medals, with clasp " Pegu," for the Second Burma War were presented to all ranks of the Madras Fusiliers at a special full dress parade of the garrison of Fort St. George by Lord Harris, the Governor of Madras. The event was celebrated by the officers of the Regiment by a ball given on May 2nd.

INDIA REGISTER.
(1835).
EUROPEAN REGIMENT.
(Right Wing.)
"Mahidpoor"—"Ava."

Station—Nagpore.

Rank.	Names.	Rank in the Regiment.	Army. (L.G.)	Remarks.
Colonel	Robert Mackay	21 Sept. 1804	19 July 1821	On furlough.
Lt.-Col.	C. Aug. Elderton	18 June 1831		
Major	Alexander Calder	27 Mar. 1832		
Captains	Edw. Francklyn	12 Jan. 1826*		
	James A. Howden	7 Nov. 1828		Do.
	Charles Butler	3 Mar. 1830		
	Philip Chambers	6 June 1831		
	Robt. D. Weir	27 Mar. 1832		Do.
	F. B. Doveton	4 June 1825		Sub. assist. com. gen.
Lieuts.	Wm. J. Manning	23 Aug.		On furlough.
	Thos. W. Jones	14 Oct. 1827		
	T. Hillman Hull	31 Dec.		
	Jas. Geo. Neill	7 Nov. 1828		
	Thos. F. Nicolay	6 June 1831		
	S. G. C. Renaud	27 Mar. 1832		
	Thos. Mears	3 Feb. 1834		
Ensigns	J. N. Warington	26 June 1831	6 June 1831	
	Wm. F. Newby	19 Apr. 1832	27 Mar. 1832	

Facings—White.   *Lace*—Gold.

| Surgeon | W. A. Hughes | | 10 Oct. 833 | |

* Dep. ass. qu. mas. gen., Mysore div.

INDIA REGISTER.
(1835.)
EUROPEAN REGIMENT.
(Left Wing.)
"Mahidpoor"—"Ava."

Station—Nagpore.

Rank.	Names.	Rank in the Regiment.	Army.	Remarks.
Colonel	Wm. C. Fraser	5 June 1829		L.C.C. 7 Oct. 1819.*

* On furlough.

Rank.	Names.	Rank in the Regiment.	Army.	Remarks.
Lt.-Col.	Thos. McLean	3 Mar. 1830		Sec. Mil. Board.
Major	Benj. S. Ward	21 Feb. 1834		
Captains	William Stuart	12 Sept. 1825		Hyderabad.
	St. John B. French	25 Feb. 1826		Sub. assist. com. gen.
	Hen. F. Barker	9 Nov. 1831		
	James Kerr	20 May 1833		On furlough.
	Thomas Duke	21 Feb. 1834		
Lieuts.	Edward Simpson	21 Sept. 1823		
	William Hill	27 Mar. 1825		Do.
	J. Chas. Hawes	12 Sept.		
	Chas. Nutting	23 Aug. 1826		
	Francis Hamilton	12 Dec. 1828		Do.
	Thos. Jas. Ryves	16 Oct. 1829	11 July 1827	
	Arundel Barker	20 May 1833		
	Chas. R. Young	21 Feb. 1834		
Ensigns	J. L. Stephenson	11 May 1830	29 Apr. 1830	
	Henry Houghton	25 do. 1831	29 do. 1831	

Facings—White.   Lace—Gold.

Adjutant to the Regiment	J. G. Neill	7 Mar. 1834	
Qr.-mas. and paym. do.	John Chas. Hawes	19 Apr. 1831	
Surgeon			
Assist. do.	John Davies	4 Mar. 1833	

INDIA REGISTER.
(1839.)
EUROPEAN REGIMENT.
(Right Wing.)
" Mahidpoor "—" Ava."
Station—Kamptee. Arrived March, 1838.

Rank.	Names.	Rank in the Regiment.	Army. (M.G.)	Remarks.
Colonel	F. W. Wilson	23 Dec. 1832	28 June 1838	Com. Ceded Dis.
Lt.-Col.	James Dalgairns	15 May 1834		
Major	James A. Howden	4 Jan. 1839		
Captains	Charles Butler	3 Mar. 1830		
	Philip Chambers	6 June 1831		
	Robt. D. Weir	27 Mar. 1832		
	F. B. Doveton	24 Oct. 1837	27 Apr. 1837	On furlough.
	Wm. J. Manning	4 Jan. 1839	do.	
Lieuts.	T. Hillman Hull	31 Dec. 1827		
	Jas. Geo. Neill	7 Nov. 1828		
	Thos. F. Nicolay	6 June 1831		
	S. G. C. Renaud	27 Mar. 1832		Do.
	J. N. Warington	2 Feb. 1835		
	John M. Rees	24 Oct. 1837		
	And. Alex. Geils	30 Dec.		Do.
	W. R. Brown	4 Jan. 1839		
	J. Fotheringham	29 do.		

D
[*Vol. II.*

Rank.	Names.	Rank in the Regiment.	Army. (M.G.)	Remarks.
Ensigns	Nich. Newberry	30 Jan. 1839		
	Cha. W. Tulloch	do.		
	G. W. Mackenzie	do.		
	C. J. Allardyce	1 Mar.		

Facings—White.

INDIA REGISTER.
(1839.)
EUROPEAN REGIMENT.
(LEFT WING.)
"Mahidpoor"—"Ava."
Station—Kamptee. Arrived June, 1833.

Rank.	Names.	Rank in the Regiment.	Army.	Remarks.
Lt.-Col.	Thomas King	8 Sept. 1826	C. 18 June 1831	Com. Neilgherries.
Major	James Kerr	6 Sept. 1836		
Captains	Thomas Duke	9 Feb. 1834		Com. Res. Esc. Nagpore.
	Edward Simpson	19 June 1835		
	William Hill	22 Sept.		
	J. Chas. Hawes	25 Jan. 1836		
	Thos. Jas. Ryves	29 Sept. 1837		
Lieuts.	Arundel Barker	20 May 1833		
	J. L. Stephenson	8 do. 1835		
	Henry Houghton	19 June		
	H. R. H. Steer	22 Sept.		
	Andrew Walker	25 Jan. 1836		
	Michael Galwey	6 Sept.		
	J. M. Walhouse	14 July 1837		

Facings—White.

Adjutant to the Regt.	... ...	J. L. Stephenson	7 Oct. 1836
Qr.-mr. and inter.	... ...	T. F. Nicolay	27 Mar. 1838
Surgeon	... ...	Samuel Stokes	22 Sept. 1836
Assist. do.	... ...	W. L. O. Moore, M.D.	28 Feb. 1838

INDIA REGISTER.
(1853.)
FIRST EUROPEAN REGIMENT—FUSILIERS.
(RIGHT WING.)

Colonels	... ...	F. W. Wilson, C.B.	On furlough.
		J. Laurie	Do.
Lieut.-Colonels	... ...	T. B. Forster	Mil. and Gen.
		T. A. Duke	
Major	... ...	—	

INDIA REGISTERS 35

Captains	Jas. Geo. Neill	
	Thos. F. Nicolay	Brig.-Maj., Bangalore.
	S. G. C. Renaud.	
	And. Alex. Geils.	
	W. R. Brown	
	Cha. W. Tulloch	
	F. F. C. Dickson	
	Wm. Henry West	
	Alfred J. de H. Harris	On furlough.
Lieutenants	Arnold Ward	
	John Christie.	
	David Brown	
	Thomas Raikes	
	G. M. Carter	
	E. L. Grant	
	H. D. Taylor	
	J. G. C. Fraser	On furlough.
	J. B. Spurgin	
	Chas. S. Elliot	
	Wm. Down	
	T. Brown	
	E. S. Daniell	
	P. A. Brown	
	E. Dangerfield	
	G. I. Hamilton	
	J. Woodcock	
	G. F. Gosling	
	J. Corstophine	
	Robt. Menzies	
2nd-Lieutenants	G. R. Fisher	
	S. H. J. Parry	
	E. B. Sladen	
	W. Bryce	
	J. H. Bowen	
	G. J. Harcourt	
	J. F. Wing	
	W. T. Groom	
	J. M. Williams	

(LEFT WING.)

Major	William Hill
Captains	J. Chas. Hawes
	Arundel Barker
	J. L. Stephenson
	Michael Galwey
Adjutant to the Regt. ...	D. Brown
Qr.-Master and Interpreter...	H. D. Taylor
Surgeon	A. Goodall
Assistant do.	H. Cholmeley
Do. ,.. ...	H. Carnegie

CHAPTER II

1857.

THE INDIAN MUTINY—ACTIONS AT FUTTEHPORE, PANDOO NUDDI, AND CAWNPORE.

1857 On February 6th, 1857, a draft of 247 recruits joined the service companies of the Madras Fusiliers at a very opportune time—opportune for the reason that although the Regiment had only very recently returned from an arduous campaign, the authorities were already contemplating sending it forth again to war.

Since November of the previous year the Indian Government had been at war with Persia. A force, commanded by Major-General Sir James Outram, and composed of two divisions under Major-General Stalker and Brigadier-General Havelock, had fought several actions and traversed a large extent of country, but in the early part of 1857 it appears to have been considered that reinforcements were needed to bring the war satisfactorily to a close, and the Madras Fusiliers were ordered to proceed to Persia, embarking on March 17th under command of Colonel Stevenson, at a strength of 26 officers and 868 non-commissioned officers and men, in the steamers *Oriental* and *Tasmania*. On the departure of the Regiment the following General Order was published by the Governor of Madras:—

"*The 1st Madras Fusiliers being under orders for embarkation this evening are struck off the strength of the garrison from this date.*

"*The Right Honourable the Governor cannot allow the Fusiliers to leave Fort St. George without recording his satisfaction with their conduct during the period they have been quartered within the garrison of Madras.*

"While expressing his sincere wishes for their welfare to Colonel Stevenson, the Officers and Men of the Regiment, Lord Harris feels it scarcely necessary to add his conviction that the distinguished character which their Corps has ever maintained on active service will be upheld by them on the present occasion to the fullest extent."

The two ships touched at Point de Galle and Tellicherry, and the voyage then became a tedious one, the *Tasmania*, which conveyed the two companies commanded by Major Renaud and Captain Grant, breaking down and having to be towed by the *Oriental*. At the mouth of the Persian Gulf the ships were overhauled by a steamer which had been sent after them from Bombay, and which brought the news that peace had been concluded with Persia on March 4th and that the Regiment was to return as speedily as possible to Madras.

The return voyage was uneventful except that a man fell overboard but was fortunately rescued, and on April 20th the Fusiliers disembarked at Madras and again garrisoned Fort St. George, where on the 29th Brevet Lieutenant-Colonel James Neill assumed command *vice* Colonel Stevenson, whose health had broken down and who was ordered home to England. Colonel Neill had then nearly 30 years' service, and at the close of the Second Burma War he had gone home on furlough, after enjoying which he had proceeded to the seat of war in Eastern Europe where he was attached to the Turkish Contingent under Sir Robert Hussey Vivian. He was "a soldier of extraordinary energy, valour, daring and activity . . . who had as adjutant done much to maintain the discipline and proud traditions of the Corps."*

The causes of the Great Mutiny which this year broke out in India and imperilled British rule have been written in histories which abound, and there is no particular object in recapitulating all that caused the catastrophe; it is for the purposes of this history enough to say that while the Fusiliers had been voyaging from Madras to the mouth of the Persian Gulf and back again very serious disturbances, amounting to the mutiny of two regiments of Bengal

* Forrest, *Selections from State Papers*, Vol. II, p. 116.

Native Infantry, had occurred at Barrackpore, a few miles distant from Calcutta; but the officers and men of the Madras Fusiliers and the Europeans living in the south of India generally, do not appear at the time of the return of the Regiment to Fort St. George, and even for some time after, to have had the faintest conception of the real seriousness, still less of the grave danger, of the situation. Even the contents of the following telegrams, and the effect that their receipt had upon the movements of the Regiment, do not appear to have led any of its subordinate members to realize all that was before them in the dark days that were coming. As an officer who was then a subaltern in the Fusiliers writes :—" They," he and his brother officers, " imagined that they were going to relieve the Calcutta garrison in consequence of the disturbances that had taken place at Barrackpore in March, and by a show of force to calm the disturbed sepoys in Bengal, and they thought it would be a pleasant change to go to the Governor-General's ball instead of attending the same old function in Madras."

The following telegrams show how events were moving :—

" *From :* THE MILITARY SECRETARY TO THE GOVERNMENT OF INDIA, CALCUTTA.

" *To :* THE MILITARY SECRETARY TO GOVERNMENT, MADRAS.

" 14*th May,* 1857.

" *It is understood that the 43rd Foot and the 1st European Regiment are at or near Madras, you are requested that both the Regiments may be held in readiness so that either may be brought to Calcutta without delay if required.*"

" *From :* THE GOVERNOR-GENERAL OF INDIA,
" CALCUTTA.

" *To :* THE GOVERNOR OF MADRAS.

" 15*th May,* 1857

" *Urgent. If you have the means of sending one European Regiment to Calcutta immediately and can spare it, let it be despatched at once. Perhaps the ' Zenobia' can bring it, she may then be required here.*"

ORDERED TO BENGAL

The next day Colonel Neill received the following communication :—

"*To :* THE OFFICER COMMANDING,
  "1ST MADRAS FUSILIERS.
    "*16th May*, 1857.
"SIR,
  "*I have the honour by order of the Commander-in-Chief to request you will be good enough to hold the Regiment under your command in readiness to embark fully equipped for service as soon as transport can be provided.*
  "*I have the honour to be,*
    "*Sir,*
      "*Your obedient Servant,*
(Sd.) "W. A. WOODS, *Lieutenant-Colonel*
  "*A.G. of the Army.*"

A further telegram was despatched from Madras to Calcutta on the 17th stating :—" *Zenobia* to leave this evening with part of Fusiliers. Remainder on the *York*, sailing vessel, to-morrow. Fusiliers take only pouch ammunition 60 rounds, further supply to be provided at Calcutta. They have 250 Enfield Rifles." But another telegram dispatched on the 18th shows that further alterations in the programme already announced had become necessary ; it runs: "I have the honour to report for the information of Government and by order of H.E. the Commander-in-Chief that the Headquarters and Right Wing 1st Madras Fusiliers embarked this morning on the Honorable Company's steamer *Zenobia* for Calcutta, and that the Left Wing will embark to-morrow morning for the same place on the *John Wells*. A detachment of 50 men will be sent up by P. and O. steamer, there being no room for them in the other vessels."

Neill with Nos. 1, 7, 8, 9 and 10 Companies embarked in the *Zenobia* at 9 a.m. on May 18th—a Monday, the remaining five companies following next day in the *John Wells* under Captain Galwey, the ten companies numbering just 917 non-commissioned officers and men. It will have been seen from the last but one of the telegrams above quoted that little more than a fourth of the Regiment was armed with the Enfield rifle, which had, moreover, only recently been issued so that the men armed with it had had but small experience of it; but while the number of rounds issued to the Regiment amounted only to 60 per rifle, the Madras authorities refused not only to send with it a larger quantity, but even declined to arm the whole Regiment with the new weapon from the stocks in the arsenal. A further proof of the failure of the Madras Government of this date to realize the gravity of the crisis, appears from the fact that Neill was obliged to leave behind on embarkation for Calcutta *seven* of his most experienced officers for the reason that they happened to have been appointed members of a court-martial!

The following are the names of the officers who embarked with the Regiment at Madras on May 18th and 19th, 1857:— Lieutenant-Colonel J. G. S. Neill, Captains Fraser, Spurgin, Renaud (Brevet Major), Grant and Galwey, Lieutenants Harcourt, Groom, Arnold, Seton, Richardson, Hargood, Beaumont, Bailey, Woods, Barclay, Dale and Cleland, with Assistant-Surgeon Robertson.

The *Zenobia* arrived at the entrance to the Hooghly on the 23rd and on Sunday evening May 24th steamed past Garden Reach. It was the Queen's Birthday and the band of the Fusiliers was playing; there seemed more excitement on shore than was likely to be caused merely by the arrival of a new regiment, people coming down to the water's edge, cheering and waving their handkerchiefs. But it was not until the ship anchored and some of the local staff came on board, that the officers and men of the Regiment heard of all that had occurred up-country within the last fortnight—the mutiny at Meerut, the seizure of Delhi by the mutineers, and all the resultant horrors. Neill made immediate preparations for pushing on to Benares and the authorities in Calcutta were not backward in rendering all possible assistance.

"I landed," wrote Neill, "and saw the Military Secretary and the Deputy Quartermaster-General and made all arrangements to start off the men I had brought up by the steamer to Benares.

LIEUT. HARCOURT IN OLD FUSILIERS UNIFORM, 1856.

However, next day there was a change. Only 130 men went up country by steamer and the rest I am starting off by the train." That same evening the men handed in "Brown Bess," and the whole Regiment was re-armed with the Enfield Rifle, of which there were some thousands in the Calcutta arsenal, and the work of fitting accoutrements and issuing ammunition went on till long after dark.

Colonel Neill had been anxious that, of the five companies with him, four should go up the Ganges in flats towed by river steamers and that the other should proceed by road by horse-dâk; but this proposal was negatived and No. 10 Company was put on board a river steamer with the band, staff sergeants and the bulk of the ammunition, while the other four Headquarter Companies were to entrain for Raniganj, which was then railhead, some hundred miles distant. All these arrangements were carried into effect on Monday, May 25th, on the morning of which day Colonel Neill and the four companies going with him were ferried across the river to Howrah railway station there to board the train for Raniganj.

At the hour when the train was timed to move some of the regimental baggage was still being transhipped, but the stationmaster gave the order for the train to start. Neill explained that the Regiment was not yet ready and asked for a few minutes' grace. The official did not know the sort of man with whom he had to deal, and curtly told Colonel Neill that the train would certainly start at scheduled time and that those unable then to proceed could follow next day. The Colonel promptly put the stationmaster in charge of a guard, placed another guard over the driver and firemen, entrained all his men, then released all the railway officials, the train finally starting no more than ten minutes behind time.

As it was imperative to reach Allahabad with the least possible delay, for here was a fort covering the road to Oudh and the Punjab without any British garrison, while the sepoy regiment there stationed was known to be very unsettled, Neill on arrival at Raniganj impounded all the horse-dâk gharries and sent on every soldier for whom carriage could be provided. But, as was only to be expected, the horse transport did not suffice for all the men of the four companies with Neill, so some were sent on in bullock-drawn carts, and Neill himself started off on May 30th, accompanied by 25 men only, and on June 3rd reached Benares, a hot-bed of fanaticism, where the troops were on the verge of mutiny. The garrison consisted of two regiments of native infantry, one of native cavalry, a weak detachment of the 10th Foot and a battery of artillery commanded by Captain Olpherts, with whom Neill had served in the Crimea.

At the suggestion of Brigadier Ponsonby, commanding at Benares, all the English women in the place had taken refuge in the Mint, whither Neill at once despatched a guard of 2 officers and 22 men of his regiment. On the 4th—by which date 200 more men of the Madras Fusiliers had fortunately reached Benares—there was a Council called, composed of the leading civil and military officials, at which the question of disarming the 37th Native Infantry was debated, and it was decided that this should be carried out next day. On leaving the Council, however, the Brigadier met Neill who urged that no time should be lost and that the disarmament should be carried out without delay, and to this Ponsonby hesitatingly agreed. A parade of all the troops in garrison was ordered for 5 p.m. and the troops turned out; on one side was the battery with a few men of the 10th Foot and the 200 Fusiliers armed with Enfields; in front of these was the 37th Native Infantry flanked by the 13th Irregular Cavalry and a regiment of Sikhs. On being ordered to pile arms, the men of the 37th unwisely replied with a volley, upon which Olpherts opened with grape, the Madras Fusiliers with their Enfield rifles, and the men of the 10th Foot with "Brown Bess." In a few moments all was over and Benares was saved; the mutineers broke and fled in wild confusion, throwing down their muskets and tearing off their accoutrements.

Neill was unable to leave Benares just yet, but he was very anxious as to the safety of the fort at Allahabad, so on June 6th he sent forward Lieutenant Arnold with 50 men of the Regiment, followed next day by another party of 57 under Lieutenant

ARRIVAL AT ALLAHABAD

Beaumont. The latter was attacked *en route* and he and his men lost all their baggage. Arnold arrived within a very few miles of Allahabad on the day following the mutiny of the 6th Native Infantry; he and his men were wearied by their forced march in an Indian summer, the bridge of boats was in the hands of the mutineers, and it was not until late at night that the Fusiliers were able to cross the river and help to secure the fort at that time held by a detachment of Sikhs under Captain Brasyer.

Neill himself left Benares on the evening of June 9th with 40 of his men under command of Captain Spurgin, and covered the 70 miles to Allahabad in two night marches; on the 11th he entered the fort. " Thank God, Sir," said the sentry who admitted him, " you'll save us yet."*

His march had been an arduous and a hazardous one, testing to the full the pluck and endurance of Neill and his followers. The men were crowded into the few conveyances procurable and the party was several times in very real danger while all ranks suffered greatly from the heat; the relays of horses gave out and Neill impressed a number of villagers to draw the carriages, while at one halting place an armed and angry mob blocked the road and matters looked ugly, till Spurgin, fixing bayonets, cleared away all opposition. Then when they reached the banks of the Ganges, the bridge of boats was held by the rebels and Neill's party had to cross a mile lower down, many of the men nearly prostrate from sunstroke and their Colonel in a fainting condition.

Lieutenant Woods of the Regiment who reached Allahabad later writes :—" Cholera was raging when I arrived and a large barrack room used as a hospital was full of our sufferers. Life seemed worth less than a day's purchase owing to various visible and invisible agents of death. Sunstroke, fever, cholera, bullets might be expected at any moment. I visited the hospital in the fort, and in the midst of the horrors of the frightful blue plague, saw Neill among the doctors and orderlies administering medicines and

* Holmes-Rice, *A History of the Indian Mutiny*, p. 217.

wine to those still able to receive help. Eighty men died in three days."

"The first of the great objects for which Neill had left Calcutta had been gained. Within a few days he had paralysed the insurgent population of a crowded city and a wide district, and had rebuilt the shattered fabric of British authority. He had done this while labouring under a physical weakness that would have prostrated many energetic men. But nothing could overcome the resolute heart of Neill. When he arrived in Allahabad, after a week of ceaseless activity and anxiety at Benares, he had felt almost dying from complete exhaustion; but 'yet,' he wrote to his wife, 'I kept up heart.' Unable to move, barely able to sustain consciousness by taking repeated draughts of champagne and water, he had had himself carried into the batteries, and there, lying on his back, had directed every operation. And now he felt that his work was only begun. For he knew that Lucknow was even then threatened by a mutinous soldiery, and that Cawnpore was hard pressed by the army of the Nana Sahib."*

On June 12th Neill attacked the rebels holding the bridge of boats, drove them off and secured the bridge; this was then at once repaired and was ready on the 13th for the crossing by it of 100 more Fusiliers under Major Stephenson, with whom were Lieutenants Bailey and Groom, who had left Benares at the same time as Colonel Neill. On this day the suburbs of Kydganj and Jhusi were attacked and cleared of the enemy, in which operations 2 men of the Regiment were killed, Lieutenant Bailey and 4 men wounded; and on June 14th, 16th and 18th further parties of the Madras Fusiliers joined their Colonel at Allahabad.

Colonel Neill now wrote to Calcutta :—†" As soon as a sufficient number of Europeans arrive I shall push on as large a body of Fusiliers to Cawnpore as I can, but almost fear it will be impossible until a shower or two of rain falls. The heat here is fearful; all are suffering from its effects. No European soldier could survive

* Holmes-Rice, p. 219.
† Neill to the Military Secretary, Government of India, dated June 17th, 1857.

beyond a day or two a forced march, badly provided with carriage (and consequently tents and provisions) on the Cawnpore road, which has been for some time in the hands of the insurgents. When cooler weather sets in, after a little rain, I will make the attempt, and I doubt not, if it is to be done, with success. I will also endeavour to send up men by steamer when the river rises. However, of this feel assured, I will push on troops to Cawnpore with the utmost dispatch."

On June 22nd the *Mirzapore* brought 240 of the Madras Fusiliers and on the next day Neill wrote to Calcutta : " Am lightly equipping 400 Europeans and the two 9-pounders with veteran European soldiers, 300 Sikhs, with all the cavalry here, taking 20 days' rations, to move by march on Cawnpore. It will be four days at least before I can start ; carriage and provisions difficult to get."

More delays, however, ensued, and it was not until the 30th that the first party was able to make a start on the march to Cawnpore. It was placed under the command of Major Renaud of the Madras Fusiliers, who had with him no more than 200 of the 84th Foot, 200 of the Madras Fusiliers, two guns manned by invalid gunners from Fort Chunar, and 120 Irregular Cavalry, whose fidelity then was at least doubtful. Before the little force marched off it was inspected by Brigadier-General Havelock, who had been appointed to command the troops detailed for the relief of Lucknow, and who had arrived early that morning at Allahabad.

Neill was naturally disappointed, not so much perhaps at finding himself in a measure superseded, but because Havelock's appointment made it necessary for Neill to remain for some little time longer at Allahabad ; but he had at least the satisfaction of knowing that he had won golden opinions for all the work he had done to make things easier for his successor, and he must have been very gratified about this time to receive a letter from General Sir Patrick Grant, the Commander-in-Chief, in which he wrote: " The ' Sweet Lambs ' are doing their work most nobly, every enterprize is carried out with a vigour and decision that cannot fail to command success, and it is indeed a fortunate circumstance that such a regiment should be available at a time like the present."

Havelock soon found himself infected by Neill's enthusiasm, and he intimated his intention of pushing on in support of Renaud on July 3rd, but this was found to be impossible. No cavalry was available and Maude's battery, which had come up with Havelock, needed both horses and equipment. For European cavalry there were, however, available many British officers of revolted regiments, civilians, planters and business men without employment, and from these, with some men of the 84th and Madras Fusiliers, a squadron of volunteer cavalry was improvised.

On July 3rd Captain Spurgin's Company of the Regiment, with Lieutenant Arnold, with two guns and supplies for the Cawnpore garrison, was embarked on a river steamer and was sent up-stream to act on Renaud's flank. On the 6th this little party landed on the left bank of the Ganges and engaged the enemy, who was repulsed with the loss of a gun, captured by Privates McCarthy, McGee and Preston. On hearing of Spurgin's success the Commander-in-Chief telegraphed to Colonel Neill: "Well done, Spurgin! He deserves great credit both for his firm observance of your orders, and his successful fight."

But on the same day that Spurgin left, the terrible news of the massacre at Cawnpore reached Allahabad: "I was on main guard yesterday," writes Groom, "and at 2 o'clock p.m. had to open the gate for an officer who had come in with despatches from Renaud, 40 miles ahead. He says they have received intelligence in camp of the fall of Cawnpore and the massacre of the whole of the Europeans there."[*] For some time all appear to have hoped against hope that the news might be false, but it was not long before it was corroborated, and then, the need for haste being now no longer so urgent, Renaud was ordered to halt where he was until the force with Havelock should come up with him.

With those who died in the entrenchment at Cawnpore, or who were murdered in the boats at the ghat on the river, were

* *With Havelock from Allahabad to Lucknow*, p. 15.

15 non-commissioned officers and men of the Madras Fusiliers—Sergeant McGrath, a corporal and 13 privates, who had been sent on in all haste by horse-dâk from Benares to Cawnpore under a young officer, Lieutenant Glanville of the Bengal Fusiliers. "I heard," wrote Woods of the Regiment, "from the accounts of the only two officers who survived the Cawnpore tragedy, that McGrath and our men were killed one by one before the surrender took place. Always in the worst places in that dangerous spot, drawing water for the others from that unhappy well, constantly exposed—behaving in fact just like all Madras Fusiliers did in that Sepoy War."

It was not until July 7th that Havelock felt himself able to move forward towards Lucknow, and on the evening of that day the march commenced in torrents of rain; the little force, including Renaud's advanced party near Lohanga, totalled barely 2,000 men, made up as under:—

Royal Artillery	76	Volunteer Cavalry	20
64th Foot	435	Bengal Artillery	22
78th Highlanders	284	Sikhs	448
84th Foot	190	Irregular Cavalry	95
Madras Fusiliers	376	Golandaze	18

The Madras Fusiliers were the only regiment completely armed with the Enfield rifle,* which was not generally issued until September, and when the march began, No. 10 Company, Captain Grant's, one of the first in the Regiment to be specially trained in the use of the new weapon, covered the advance. The dress worn on service by the Regiment consisted of trousers, a white smock frock and forage cap covered with blue cloth having a curtain and peak. Practically the whole of the Madras Fusiliers was now with Havelock or with Renaud and remained with the former throughout his campaign; the only men remaining behind in Allahabad was a detachment of some 150 men—mostly recruits—under Major Harris.

* The flank companies of the 64th and 78th also had them.

After Havelock's column had left Allahabad intimation reached Neill, who was still there, that he had been appointed a Brigadier-General on the Staff of the Army, and Major Renaud, as senior officer, assumed command of the Regiment. Before handing over the command of the Regiment and following the column, which he joined at Cawnpore on July 20th, Neill brought the services of the following officers of the Madras Fusiliers to notice :—Major Stephenson, Captains Fraser and Spurgin, Lieutenants Arnold, Richardson, Beaumont and Bailey.

Restricting the length of his marches to a limit of 8 to 10 miles each day, Havelock reached Koh on the 9th, whence he wrote that he expected to be joined by Renaud's party on the 12th, and hoped soon to announce the capture of Cawnpore; but on the evening of the 11th information came in from Renaud that the Cawnpore mutineers, strongly reinforced and estimated at 4,000 men, were marching down to attack him. Renaud could not be left to meet such a force unaided, so Havelock pushed on, and, making a forced march of 17 miles during the night, he overtook Renaud at Syanee, some 60 miles on the road to Cawnpore, at 2 a.m. on the morning of July 12th. Lieutenant Cleland of the " Blue Caps," who was with Renaud, thus describes the meeting : " At midnight our small force was drawn up on the side of the road and at 2 o'clock in the morning of the 12th July the General joined us with his force. We presented arms and gave him a cheer which would have sent the whole army of the Pandies to the devil."

The united force now marched some 15 miles further and reaching Batinda, 4 miles from Futtehpore, halted to encamp on a fine open plain. " Arms were piled in line, ground was taken up for each corps, and the weary, way-worn men, overcome by the oppressive heat and brilliant sunshine, lay down in groups, a little in the rear, anxiously expecting the arrival of the tents and baggage which was close behind."*

Lieutenant Cleland of the Regiment tells us of the opening of the action of Futtehpore :—" A reconnoitring party had been sent

* North, *Journal of an English Officer in India*, p. 40.

ACTION AT FUTTEHPORE

out . . . and we were resting under a tree. We had lain there a few minutes when I descried the reconnoitring party coming back. Having mentioned this to the Major, he pulled out his field glass, looked for a little, and remarked that there appeared to be men further off. The truth of this remark was soon proved by a puff of white smoke, and a round shot flying over the head of the reconnoitring party came lobbing down the road. All was now excitement. We rushed to our lines; the men left their tents and got under arms, the bugles sounded, and in less than five minutes we were ready to receive them."

A volunteer present with the force, speaking of the British soldiers, says, "Out they came, eager for the fray, like so many bulldogs and as jolly as possible, although just off a long march."

"The rebels, thinking they had only Major Renaud's force in front, insolently pushed forward two guns and a force of cavalry and infantry, cannonaded our front, and threatened our flanks. Havelock, earnestly wishing to give his harassed soldiers rest, made no counter-disposition beyond posting 300 Enfield riflemen (64th) in an advanced copse. 'But the enemy maintained his attack with the audacity which his first supposition had inspired and my inertness fostered. It would have injured the *morale* of my troops to permit them to be thus bearded, so I determined at once to bring on an action.' His dispositions were quickly made. The guns, eight in number, were formed in the centre under Captain Maude, protected and aided by 100 Enfield riflemen of the 64th; the infantry were formed in quarter-distance column at deploying distance behind, while the Volunteer Horse and Irregular Cavalry guarded the flanks. And now the word to advance being given, the artillery pushed on in line with the Enfield rifles and soon came into action with the enemy's guns. Maude's fire electrified them. . . . And the rifle fire reaching them at an unexpected distance increased their dismay. They fled from their guns and retreated to a second battery placed on the road in the rear. Here they again made a stand. Maude pushed his guns on through flanking swamps in which the wheels sank deep, till after much pulling by tired bullocks and gunners they surmounted the difficulties of the ground, and arrived within point blank range. Then the guns on both sides again exchanged salutations. In the rear of the enemy's principal battery was a large body of infantry, and moving to and fro among them, giving orders, could be seen the leader on a richly caparisoned elephant. Maude dismounted, laid the gun at line of metal, and the first shot, striking the poor beast in the rear came out at the chest, and the Nana general's fighting was suddenly all done. The rebels, on seeing their leader fall, abandoned their guns and retreated. 'In succession they were driven by skirmishers and column from the garden enclosures, from a strong barricade on the road, from the town wall, into the rough, out of and beyond the town.' "*

Had the Irregular Cavalry only performed their duty properly in the pursuit, the enemy's loss must have been very heavy, but the sowars refused to follow their leader, and the infantry and guns had again with great labour to be pushed to the front, when, in the words of Havelock's despatch: "Their fire soon put the enemy to final and irretrievable flight, and my force took up its present position in triumph, and parked 12 captured guns."

The British troops did not have a single man killed or wounded; of the Fusiliers Groom gratefully wrote: "We did not lose a man! Three have died of fatigue, which was to be expected as we were all in the sun until 3 o'clock," while the men had been under arms since 12 o'clock the previous night, marching and fighting, without tasting food.

In his report on the action Major Stephenson wrote: "The conduct of the Fusiliers was all that could be wished," while Brigadier-General Havelock published the following complimentary order to his troops on July 13th:—

"*General Havelock thanks his soldiers for their arduous exertions of yesterday, which proved, in four hours, the strange result of a rebel army driven from a strong position, eleven guns captured, and the whole force scattered to the winds without the loss of a British soldier.*

* Forrest, *The Indian Mutiny*, Vol. I, pp. 376, 377.

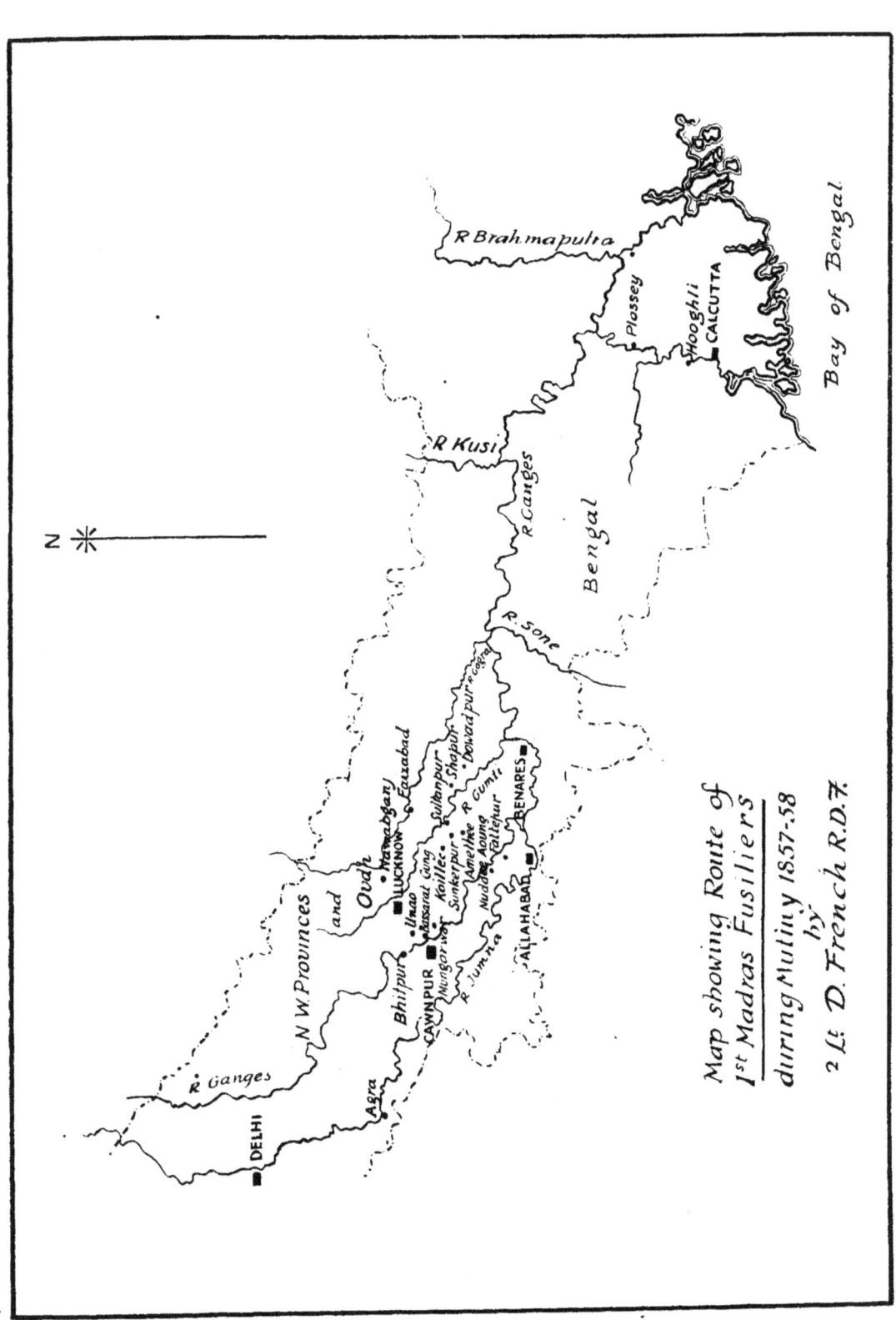

To what is this astonishing effect to be attributed? The fire of the British artillery, exceeding in rapidity and precision all the Brigadier-General has ever witnessed in his not short career, to the power of the Enfield rifle in British hands, to British pluck—that good quality which has survived the revolution of the hour, and gained intensity from the crisis—and to the blessing of Almighty God in a most righteous cause."

On the 15th the column started at daybreak, knowing that the village of Aong was strongly occupied by the enemy, that he was entrenched across the road, and that he had two big guns in position. This day two actions were fought and the operations are thus briefly described by Lieutenant Cleland: " On the morning of the 14th " (15th?) " we came up with the enemy at Aong, posted in a number of small enclosures, from which, after some sharp musketry firing, we drove them, followed them up and at 1 p.m. halted in a *tope*, and rested for two hours. We again advanced and at about 4 p.m. came upon the enemy in a strong position in the rear of the bridge at Pandoo Nuddi. We formed up in a *tope* of trees, but soon found the vagabonds had got the range of it, as a shot came crashing through the trees into the very midst of us. We rapidly advanced; the Madras Fusiliers extended in skirmishing order and proved the efficiency of the Enfield rifle. The astonishment of the rebels was great when bullets flew about them from distances which they imagined quite out of range. So great was it that the Nana, who commanded, issued an order cautioning his men to beware of the soldiers with the blue *topees* and dirty shirts as they killed before they fired."*

Lieutenant Groom adds some details of these two engagements: " We have had two fights this morning, but have of course held our own. The enemy's practice with a 24-pounder siege gun which was planted on a bridge over a wide nullah was mighty creditable but very disagreeable. . . . As usual we were in front and to-day

* Groom, p. 50, corroborates this: " Did I tell you," he wrote, " what that miscreant Nana Sahib said to his army after the Battle of Unao? ' Kill all the men in dirty shirts and blue caps; they kill all my men before they fire ' I am glad we made such an impression on him."

got rather peppered. Poor Renaud was very badly wounded leading the men into action; I fear he will lose his leg. Fraser a contused wound in the elbow; my pay sergeant is also badly wounded but none of *us* killed. . . . We have taken four guns."

In his telegram to the Commander-in-Chief sent off this day Havelock said: "At noon we attacked their entrenchment at the bridge over the stream. The resistance was short but spirited, and the two guns taken"—later he gave the number captured as four—"were of large calibre. Major Renaud is severely wounded. The Madras Fusiliers particularly distinguished themselves." In the more detailed despatch the Brigadier-General wrote: "The whole of the Madras Fusiliers were extended as Enfield riflemen, as being the most practised riflemen in the force. They lined the banks of the stream and kept up a biting fire. . . . These two affairs" (Aong and Pandoo Nuddi) "cost me 25 killed and wounded. . . . Amongst the latter I regret to have to particularise Major Renaud, 1st Madras Fusiliers, to whose gallantry and intelligence I have been under great obligations. His left thigh was broken by a musket ball in the skirmish at Aong, but I hope from the fortitude with which he endures all suffering a favourable result."

These two actions of July 15th cost the "Blue Caps" 1 private killed, 2 officers—Major Renaud and Captain Fraser—and 10 other ranks wounded; but Major Renaud did not long survive his injuries, for he died on July 18th—" The zealous, daring Renaud, Madras Fusiliers, whose courage and fortitude were proverbial! He sank rapidly after the amputation of his left leg above the knee. I had gone to see him, found him in cheerful spirits, hoped for his ultimate recovery, and now he is not."*

In the dead of night on July 15th tents were struck, and the little force moved on towards Cawnpore, halting during the heat of the day on the 16th near a large grove of trees close to the village of Maharajpore. The baggage arriving, food was cooked and eaten, and at 1.30 p.m. the column was again on the march. " In the full mid-day heat of the worst season of the year did the troops

* North, p. 81.

start, each man fully armed and accoutred, with his 60 rounds of ball ammunition on him. The sun struck down with frightful force. At every step a man reeled out of the ranks and threw himself fainting by the side of the road; the calls for water were incessant all along the line. On they trudged till they reached the junction of the two roads, and found the enemy posted about a mile beyond the fork. His entrenchments cut and rendered impassable both roads, and his guns, seven in number, two light and five of siege calibre, were disposed along his position which consisted of a series of villages; behind these his infantry, consisting of mutineers and his own armed followers, was disposed for defence."*

Cleland describes how " we made a *détour* to the right in doing which we suffered severely from the enemy's batteries, which were, however, soon charged and the enemy driven off only to retire to another position in the rear. It was here that a party of the Regiment, numbering about 40, became detached and were suddenly charged by the enemy's cavalry. They quickly formed square, the fourth side being filled up by a *tattoo* ridden by the adjutant, Lieutenant Seton, who commanded, and a little subaltern—Bertie. As they approached the square delivered its fire, several troopers were seen to reel in their saddles, and the remainder, swerving to the right, galloped off without attempting a second charge."

The enemy fell back about a mile, then rallied and occupied a village in a grove of trees against which the British columns again advanced—the 64th and 78th directly upon the village, the Madras Fusiliers moving against the grove; abreast the two regiments on the left raced at the village and drove the enemy out of it, while the " Blue Caps " cleared the plantation on the right. But the day's work was not nearly done; the British reformed and resumed their march, when, presently, they saw a 24-pounder planted on the road, and in rear and far to either side stretched the army of the Nana, who had come down from Cawnpore to make a final bid for victory.

* Forrest, Vol. I, pp. 384, 385.

"He had an army consisting of 10,000 highly trained men; and opposed to him were 900 English soldiers, worn with marching and fighting during the whole of a burning Indian day. The artillery cattle, wearied by the length of the march, had not brought up the guns; the Sikhs were in rear."

The word was passed to lie down and the fire of the enemy's guns threatened to become almost annihilating, when Havelock, "with clear and firm tone," gave the order: "The Line will advance."

"The whole," wrote an officer of the Regiment, "gave a cheer—such a cheer! It must have made the villains tremble from head to foot—and advanced in line against their battery (always the one gun) under a very heavy cross-fire, which they kept up very well, but did not do us much damage as they fired too high. They evacuated their battery and fled in every direction. We fired into them until they were out of range, and then we rushed up the hill and found to our joy Cawnpore about half-a-mile in front."*

It was now beginning to grow dark, so the force bivouacked that night 2 miles outside the Cawnpore cantonments. "At daybreak," wrote Lieutenant Cleland, "several of our men were found lying dead where they had lain down to sleep the night before; their death was supposed to have been occasioned by the heat and the fatigue of the previous day . . . at about 9 o'clock the whole force moved forward and encamped in Cawnpore."

In the action of the 16th the losses of the column amounted to 6 killed, 86 wounded and 10 missing, and of these the casualties in the Fusiliers were 1 private killed, 2 sergeants, 1 corporal and 12 privates wounded, 1 sergeant and 7 privates missing. In his despatch General Havelock specially mentioned Major Stephenson of the Regiment, and in an Order of July 20th, he wrote as follows:—

"*Soldiers, your General is satisfied and more than satisfied with you. He has never seen steadier soldiers or more devoted troops, but your labour is only beginning. . . . We must make great sacrifices if we would obtain great results. Three cities have to be saved—two strong places to be de-blockaded. Your General is confident that he*

---

* Maude, *Memories of the Mutiny*, Vol. II, Appendix J.

can effect all these things and restore this part of India to tranquillity, if you only second him with your efforts, if your discipline is equal to your valour."

"In nine days Havelock and his veterans had marched 126 miles under an Indian sun in the hottest season of the year, each man carrying a heavy weight of ammunition, and had won four pitched battles and sundry combats against highly disciplined troops far exceeding them in number. During the four days' fighting they had killed or wounded many hundreds of their enemies and had captured 23 pieces of artillery. Their advance had been one of suffering, of privation, and of fatigue; but the burning desire to save the captive women and children nourished the energy of the British soldier. Battle after battle was won by desperate fighting, the cholera and the sunstroke slew many survivors of the combat, but on they went with unflinching resolution till the outskirts of Cawnpore were reached. Then on the morning after their crowning victory, as they were about to fall in, news reached the men which quenched the hope that had burned clear in them through all the weary marching and hard fighting, and when they entered the city the evil tidings were confirmed, and they saw a scene which drove them mad with horror and excitement. But the firm hand of their commander held them in check."*

---

* Forrest, Vol. I, p. 393.

NEILL'S "BLUE CAPS"

INDIA REGISTER.
(1857.)
FIRST EUROPEAN REGIMENT—FUSILIERS.
(RIGHT WING.)

Colonels	Sir S. W. Steel, K.C.B.	On furlough.
	J. Laurie	Do.
Lieut.-Colonels	M. Carthew	
	D. H. Stevenson	
Major	Jas. Geo. Neill	
Captains	S. G. C. Renaud	Dep. Ju. Adv. Gen., Mysore div.
	F. F. C. Dickson	
	Alfred J. de H. Harris	
	David Brown	Civil employ.
	Thomas Raikes	
Captains	G. M. Carter	
	E. L. Grant	
	H. D. Taylor	On furlough.
	J. G. C. Fraser	
	J. B. Spurgin	
	Chas. S. Elliot	
	Wm. Down	Do.
Lieutenants	T. Brown	Do.
	E. S. Daniell	Do.
	P. A. Brown	Sap. and Miners.
	E. Dangerfield	Civil employ.
	G. I. Hamilton	
	J. Woodcock	Hyderabad Cont.
	G. F. Gosling	
	Robt. Menzies	On furlough.
	S. H. J. Parry	Do.
	E. B. Sladen	
	G. J. Harcourt	Seikh inf.
	W. T. Groom	
	J. M. Williams	Dep. Pub. Works.
	N. H. Arnold	
	C. E. Lennox	Hyderabad Cont.
	J. L. Seton	
	L. A. M. Graeme	
	J. A. Richardson	
	W. Hargood	
	H. F. Hornsby	
	W. H. Beaumont	
	W. S. Bailey	
2nd-Lieutenants	J. A. Woods	
	J. J. Barclay	
	V. C. Bertie	

(LEFT WING.)

Major	Arundel Barker.	
Captains	J. L. Stephenson	
	Michael Galwey	
Adjutant	—	
Qr. Mas. and Interp.	—	
Surgeon	J. Arthur, M.D.	

CHAPTER III

THE INDIAN MUTINY—THE FIRST RELIEF OF LUCKNOW

1857 WHILE the events resulting in the re-capture of Cawnpore were taking place, General Neill was still at Allahabad, where he had been left with some 200 men to secure the town and see to the prompt forwarding of reinforcements and stores to the front. Neill had arranged for a river steamer, the *Brahmaputra*, to move on Havelock's right flank during his advance, the vital parts of the vessel being built round with wooden logs and the steersman being protected from fire as well as possible. The garrison of this vessel consisted of 100 Fusiliers under Captain Spurgin, while its armament was composed of two 9-pounders and a 5½-inch mortar.

On July 10th Neill received news from Lucknow which caused him to describe the position there as " very critical," and he asked that artillerymen should be hurried on from Benares ; at this date he was " getting in no end of supplies and carriage." Two days later Lord Canning, the Governor-General, telegraphed from Calcutta that a steamer and pinnaces carrying guns would start for Allahabad in three days, and that Neill would " receive all help in artillerymen that can be spared. It will not be much." Then on the 11th came an urgent request for help from another station in imminent danger of attack by overwhelming forces, and Neill could do no more than reply encouragingly and tell them to hold out since he could " give no assistance at present."

Meanwhile the news from Lucknow became graver and graver. On July 13th a letter arrived announcing the death on the 4th of Sir Henry Lawrence, that the garrison had been closely besieged since the end of June and were having 10 or 11 men killed daily. They had food for a month but looked " for relief anxiously."

On Havelock's arrival at Cawnpore he ordered Brigadier-General Neill up with a party escorting ammunition, and on the 15th Neill sent on 227 men of the 84th Foot in bullock carts with orders to march 25 miles a day until they reached Cawnpore, and he followed himself next day, arriving at Havelock's headquarters on the 20th to find the column just crossing the river *en route* for Lucknow, and General Neill was himself again left behind with two companies of the " Blue Caps " to hold a small entrenchment which had been thrown up on the bank of the river.

The day before Neill reached Cawnpore Major Stephenson had been sent to destroy the Nana Sahib's house at Bithur; he took with him his Fusiliers, the Sikhs, two guns and some cavalry. "We started at 10 a.m.," wrote Groom, " and got there about four. We found that he had fled and all his following dispersed. We found 20 guns, the whole of which we brought in yesterday, having bivouacked in the Nana's compound. He had a magnificently furnished English house. . . ."

On the same day that Neill joined Havelock's force the little river steamer *Brahmaputra* came in with Spurgin's party, having experienced a most eventful voyage.

Lieutenant Groom's narrative gives some account of the happenings at this time and of the delays that hampered Havelock's advance. Writing on July 22nd from Cawnpore, he says :—" Here we are still and the rain falling in torrents. Nearly the whole of this force are now on the other side of the river without tents. They say that the Sikhs are to cross this morning and we cross this evening. No tents or baggage are to be taken to Lucknow, so you may fancy what a comfortable time we shall have of it. Raikes and a hundred men remain here with some other troops in an entrenched camp under General Neill. We have heard no firing for some time now, I think they must really be getting short of ammunition. The camp shave is ' they are all quite comfortable at Lucknow and can hold out till August.' Still no news from the

ADVANCE TO UNAO

north. The rebels are in full possession for the present. However, we have made all clear from Cawnpore to Calcutta which is a good slice of road.

"I do not think I told you that the General, after the Battle of Cawnpore, gave ourselves and the 78th a Victoria Cross for the man most worthy of it. When all behaved so well, it was very difficult to find any one man who had distinguished himself above his comrades. But I believe that Colour-Sergeant James Kelly, acting Sergeant-Major of our detachment, is to have the decoration. I am sure that the whole Regiment will be proud of having such an honorable decoration in its ranks, and I believe that a better soldier than Kelly cannot be found anywhere to carry it. He has been very badly wounded in the hand and arm, but is getting well rapidly." Then writing on the 23rd Groom says:—"Here still. All well. All have now crossed or are crossing the river except ourselves and the Sikhs. I suppose we shall be off in an hour or two."

Having assured himself of the safety of Cawnpore, Havelock advanced on July 29th as far as Unao, some four miles out, where the enemy was holding a strong position, and of the action which ensued an account is given in a report by Major Stephenson of the Madras Fusiliers, now in command:—

"The column proceeded to Woonai" (Unao) "where some 6,000 or more of the enemy had taken post with 15 guns. The battle lasted for a couple of hours, the force capturing all his guns. The Fusiliers were in front with skirmishers and supports, took possession of the *tope*, and drove large bodies of the sepoys before them; the guns then advanced and their fire drove the enemy from his guns. The line advanced, Fusiliers on the right, skirmishers and supports in front. These all the morning had been under the command of Captains Grant and Fraser, whom, with Lieutenants Groom and Arnold, I beg particularly to bring to the notice of H.E. for their dashing and forward conduct. During the action Lieutenant Richardson was killed and Lieutenant Seton, acting A.D.C. to Brigadier-General Havelock, severely wounded. The force bivouacked on a plain, the enemy remaining in sight for some time but subsequently decamped. At 2 p.m. the column proceeded to Basaratgunge" (Bashiratganj), "the enemy being again in position. The Fusiliers were sent on with 4 guns, and after a brisk cannonade, which was returned from the village, the skirmishers advanced and captured the place. The number of guns captured this day was 19.

"Lieutenants Dangerfield and Hargood were the first in the place and their conduct was a fine example to our own brave fellows who followed them."

Of the action at Unao, young Hargood wrote:—"Poor Richardson was shot through the brain and died instantaneously. I was talking to him about four minutes before he was shot, and poor Seton was shot through the cheek, he has a fractured jaw, but it is hoped he will get over it. . . . The General asked Major Stephenson, who now commands the Regiment, to recommend an officer for the Victoria Cross. The Major said that he should recommend Lieutenants Dangerfield and Hargood, as they were the first into the battery. The General said that he could only send in one name for the Cross, and Dangerfield being the senior and being a few seconds before me, his name was sent in."

Writing from Bashiratganj on the 30th Groom states:— "Yesterday we were literally fighting from morning till night. We got under arms at 4 o'clock in the morning and marched at 5, before 6 we were under fire and by 9.30 we drove the enemy off the field, having captured 15 guns. . . . We marched at 2 o'clock and found our friends in a very strong village with 5 guns with which they fought right well. We lost a great many in wounded here, and it was past 7 o'clock when we got through the village and bivouacked on the Lucknow side of it. . . . The General says he intends making a *splendid* report of the Regiment for the way in which we skirmished in the morning and evening. . . . We have lost 200 men since we have been in Bengal, and we can only muster about 200 men in the field at headquarters; the rest are all sick and scattered."

Hargood gives fuller details of the Regiment's casualties,

saying :—" On the 29th July out of 230 men of our Regiment who went into action, we had 5 killed and 17 wounded, and within the last three months out of 800 men we have buried from sickness, killed in action, and died of their wounds 150."

As General Havelock " rode back over the causeway, thronged with weary soldiers leaning on their arms, a cry was raised, ' Clear the way for the General.' ' You have done that *well* already, men,' was the prompt reply. For a moment there was silence; then their feeling found expression, and ' God bless the General ! ' burst forth from them as he galloped away."*

That evening in an order of the day Havelock wrote :—
"*Soldiers, your General thanks you for your exertions to-day. You have stormed two fortified villages and captured 19 guns. . . Major Stephenson, in command of the Regiment which the rebel chiefs know and fear as ' the Blue Caps,' showed throughout the day how the calmest forethought can be united with the utmost courage. Lieutenant Dangerfield has merited the Cross reserved for the brave. He was the first to mount the barricade at this place.*"

The opposition which Havelock's column had met with, showed that the chance of reaching Lucknow was but small. " What soldiers could do Havelock's men had achieved. But they could not fight against the pestilence of the tropics. For some days cholera and dysentery had done their deadly work among them. A sixth of his force had perished, half on the battlefield, half by disease. . . . Having given due weight to all the circumstances, Havelock made up his mind to retire to Mangulwar till the sick and wounded had returned to Cawnpore, and till reinforcements could reach him."†

On July 31st Havelock telegraphed to the Commander-in-Chief : " My force is reduced by sickness and repeated combats to 1,364 rank and file, with 10 ill-equipped guns. I could not, therefore, move on against Lucknow with any prospect of success, especially as I had no means of crossing the Sye or the canal. I have therefore shortened my communications with Cawnpore by falling back two short marches, hitherto unmolested by an enemy. If I am speedily

* Forrest, Vol. I, p. 487.   † *Ibid.*, p. 489.

reinforced by 1,000 more British soldiers and Major Olpherts' battery complete, I might resume my march towards Lucknow, or keep fast my foot in Oudh, after securing the easier passage of the Ganges at Cawnpore by boats and two steamers; or I might recross and hold the head of the Grand Trunk Road at Cawnpore."

This order for retirement and the consequent indefinite postponement of the relief of Lucknow was most unwelcome to all ranks of the force; the very idea of a retrograde movement filled them with consternation; and murmurs were heard on all sides, while Neill addressed a letter to his leader criticizing in unmeasured terms the decision at which he had arrived. Havelock sent a very severe reply, threatening Neill with arrest and concluding with the words: " You now stand warned. Attempt no further dictation."

On August 3rd Havelock was reinforced by a company of the 84th and Olpherts' half-battery, and then, hearing that Bashiratganj had been reoccupied by the enemy, he determined to evict them and advanced again on the 5th.

Lieutenant Groom describes as follows the events of the day in a letter dated August 6th :—" The day before yesterday we had to march to meet the enemy at Bashiratganj from which place we had driven him on the 29th. We slept on our arms at a place about 4 miles from the enemy's position, and yesterday morning went at him and gave him the best licking he has had yet, but we could not take his guns; they were all horsed. The enemy was so numerous that we were twice completely surrounded and our rearguard threatened, so we had again to beat a retreat to our old position. The General yesterday divided his force into three divisions, and we found ourselves taken from the Highlanders and brigaded with the 64th. We were the rear division, but at last we got an order to move to the right flank, and cover 3 guns that had been sent round to harass the enemy as they crossed the bridge on the other side of the town. We lined the edge of the water and kept up a jolly fire for a long time, wondering when the bridge was to be taken. At last we heard a cheer, and the 84th dashed over it with 4 guns, but they did not seem to get any further, and the bridge being now crowded with guns and limbers, etc., the enemy opened from the front. Then was the cry ' Where are the Fusiliers ?' and away we went some distance back to get on to the road, and threaded our way through the mass which choked the bridge, and supported by the Highlanders, cleared the village in a crack. As we were forming on the other side ready to make a rush, Havelock said ' Hurrah ! Blue Bonnets, that's right, show 'em the way !'—and we *did* show them the way in style !

"But the day's work was awful, three hours' fighting and 20 miles' march. We got back about 8.30 p.m. . . . We went into action yesterday morning in one of the heaviest downpours of rain I ever remember, and then were baked on an open plain for the rest of the day. Poor old Fusiliers ! . . . I wish some of the good folks at home could see how cheerfully and nobly the old ' Lambs ' bear up against all kinds of fatigue and privations."

Major Stephenson's report is more official in tone :—" On the 5th August the force advanced from Mangulwar again to Bashiratganj where the enemy was in greater force than before. In the attack on their position the 1st Madras Fusiliers took their place in line between H.Ms. 78th and half a battery of guns, and thus advanced on the right flank of the village which consisted of a long *pucka*-built street with fortified turrets at the entrance. In this order the advance was made against the enemy's battery and skirmishers. H.Ms. 84th, having pushed through the village, drove the enemy across a causeway over some deep water about 600 yards in length and unfordable. The Fusiliers advanced with the 84th at the double, lined the edge of the water and kept up a brisk fire on the enemy beyond the causeway, thus covering the advance of the 84th. After, the Fusiliers pushed across the causeway and moved forward in skirmishing order in front of the whole force and co-operated with the leading guns. The enemy was driven from every point of his position losing a number of men, but owing to his batteries being horsed, he managed to carry off his guns. The conduct of the Fusiliers elicited the high approval of the Brigadier-General ; their conduct was all that could be wished. After bivouacking on the plain beyond which we had driven the enemy, we burnt his camp and in the evening returned to Unao."

In proof of the interest with which the Madras authorities were following the operations in which the Regiment was engaged, a letter may be quoted which was addressed at this time by the Adjutant-General of the Army to the Secretary to Government, Military Department :—

"*I have the honor, by order of the Provincial Commander-in-Chief, to forward for submission to the Right Honourable the Governor-in-Council the annexed copy of a letter dated 8th August, 1857, from the D.A.G., Bengal Army, transmitting telegrams received by H.E. Lieut.-General Sir P. Grant, K.C.B., from Brig.-General Havelock, C.B., Commanding the Moveable Column from Allahabad, expressive of the distinguished conduct of the 1st Madras Fusiliers serving with that force, and I am directed to express the pride and satisfaction which Major-General Beresford experiences, and in which all must participate, in the just tribute therein paid to our fellow soldiers.*"

On the 8th a steamer, containing 2 guns and 50 Fusiliers under Lieutenant Dale, was sent up the river to disperse a party of mutineers of the 42nd Bengal Infantry which had halted a few miles above Bithur on the bank of the river, and which was forming something of a rallying point for all evilly-disposed natives in the neighbourhood. Considerable damage was inflicted upon these mutineers.

Writing on August 9th young Groom announces :—" We have, I deeply regret to say, just lost our Sergeant-Major from cholera, a man whose loss to the Regiment is irreparable. He leaves a wife and three children at Palaveram. . . . The whole Regiment attended his funeral this afternoon."

On August 11th Havelock's spies brought him intelligence that the rebels were once more collecting in force at Bashiratganj and again he put his small force in motion, marching in the afternoon to Unao, bivouacking there, and " in the morning " (of the 12th) " we advanced, the small, gaunt, careworn remains of our force, the men almost dropping out in tens from cholera, but with courage as high and as undaunted as of old."

"We found," wrote Major Stephenson, "that the enemy had erected some batteries on a plain near the village. Our force debouched to the right of the road, the left being impracticable. The Fusiliers were now to right of line in direct echelon of battalions, H.Ms. 78th about 500 yards in rear, a battery of artillery with the Fusiliers. In this order we advanced under a heavy cannonade from 3 guns. The Fusiliers turned the battery, the 78th advanced and took it, the Fusiliers at the same moment rushed forward and engaged a large body of the enemy occupying a *tope* in our front. These were driven away with some loss, the guns were left in our hands, and the enemy completely routed. Captain Grant of the Regiment was wounded and a fragment of a shell struck Lieutenant and Adjutant Gosling in the chest abrading the skin. Captain Fraser led the skirmishers with great judgment and bravery, and he was ably seconded by Lieutenant Arnold, an officer of great merit and gallantry, and who has been conspicuous for his dashing conduct throughout this arduous campaign."

Of this day's fighting Havelock placed on record :—"*The exertions of the troops in the combat of yesterday deserved the highest praise the Brigadier-General can bestow. In this fight the conduct of the artillery was admirable The Fusiliers and Highlanders were as usual distinguished.*"

Havelock now telegraphed to Calcutta :—"If I am speedily reinforced by 1,000 European infantry and Olpherts' battery is completed might resume march towards Lucknow." He knew that many of the mutineers had marched direct on Delhi to support the shadow of the "Great Mogul," and that others had moved in the direction of Cawnpore to rally round the Nana Sahib, and among these were the men of the Gwalior Contingent—a well-organized and well-drilled force of all arms—and the garrison of Nasirabad. This force was encamped within some 30 miles of Cawnpore, and that no attack was delivered by those composing it until November, when General Windham was entrenched in the city with 3,000 men while Sir Colin Campbell with 5,000 more was within striking distance, instead of falling upon Neill's weak force during Havelock's absence, was one of those fortunate happenings which enabled the British to hold India.

Havelock, however, was aware that this force was in the neighbourhood and also of the arrival at Bithur of the Nasirabad mutineers, consisting of two battalions of sepoys and a couple of batteries. Even with further reinforcements it would have been impossible to advance on Lucknow until Bithur was cleared, and he therefore decided, on the morning of August 16th, to try conclusions with the enemy at that place.

"On Sunday morning the 16th August, the miserable remnant of Havelock's force, some 750 Europeans and 250 Sikhs, advanced towards Bithur. The march was long and tedious and the slanting rays of the morning sun struck down many a wearied soldier. After a tramp of eight hours the column reached a wide plain covered with thick sugar-cane and tall castor-oil trees rising high above the head. It was flanked by villages, and had two streams flowing through it not fordable by troops of any arm, and only to be crossed by two narrow bridges, the further of which was protected by an entrenchment armed with artillery. After passing the second bridge the road took a turn which protected the defenders from direct fire, and behind lay the town of Bithur with brick houses rising one above another, surrounded by walls and buried in trees. 'One of the strongest positions I have ever seen,' wrote Havelock; and the streams prevented him from attempting his favourite turning movement."*

This day the "Blue Caps" mustered no more than 249 rifles, and they made up five companies only—No. 1 under Lieutenant Arnold, No. 2 under Lieutenant Dale, while Nos. 3, 4 and 5 were respectively commanded by Captains Galwey and Raikes and Lieutenant Beaumont. The Colours were carried by Lieutenants Chisholm and Cleland, and this was the last occasion until after the relief of Lucknow, on which the Colours were taken into action, for when the advance on Lucknow commenced and it was realized that there must be much street fighting, General Neill gave orders

* Forrest, Vol. I, p. 503.

that the Colours of all regiments in his brigade should be left in the entrenched camp at Cawnpore.

The account of this action may be given in extracts from the letters of an officer of the 60th Rifles* who was at this time attached for duty to the 78th Highlanders. "The Madras Fusiliers," he wrote, "followed by the artillery under Captain Crump, took up position on the plain, and the 78th Highlanders completed the right centre, on one side of the road. Our left wing, 64th, 84th, and Sikh Regiment of Ferozepore, with Olpherts' battery, prolonged the line to the left on the other side of the road. Soon our right was found to be enfiladed by matchlock-men posted in a village masked by trees, but this was speedily met by throwing back the right companies of the Madras Fusiliers who had the honour of carrying the village. On our leaving the road the enemy's guns opened on us with much precision, directing their fire upon our right centre, consisting of the 78th. . . . We were then assailed by a well-directed rifle fire, which was briskly answered from our right by the Madras Fusiliers, who poured a withering volley upon the enemy from a long range, and followed up their volley by an admirable advance in line. . . ."

"A considerable number of the mutineers had posted themselves in a square redoubt earthwork, from which their riflemen fired upon our right wing and with much effect. The position was concealed till the Highlanders . . . advanced within a hundred yards and pushed them out of it. Our right battalion, the Madras Fusiliers, led the charge giving simultaneously a long and thrilling cheer. . . . We here advanced upon the heels of the mutineers to the bridge adjacent to the road before described. . . . A large enclosure surrounding the Residency afforded a welcome halting place to the overtasked troops who lay down to rest under the shade of umbrageous trees. Short, however, was the rest for they were quickly warned to go on as it was necessary to clear the town. It being exceedingly intricate, there was much trouble in dislodging

* North, *Journal of an English Officer*, p. 129 *et seq.*

the enemy from it, nor was it effected without severe fighting in the barricaded houses.

"A Highlander and one of the Madras Fusiliers, possessed of but one rifle between them, in the heat of excitement rushed into one of these houses where they discovered seven sepoys. Not one of the seven escaped; they all were victims to the avenging spirit of these two Europeans, who proudly related the adventure."

The casualties in Havelock's force amounted to 49 killed and wounded, while 12 men died of sunstroke; young Groom writes:—"Fusiliers had 7 killed and 5 wounded, 78th 13 wounded and 1 officer. It was a sharp affair."

On the return march rain fell so heavily that at times the whole force was compelled to halt and turn about. Major, then Second-Lieutenant, Dale records:—"We reached Cawnpore wet to the skin. I carried the Colours on the return march with Chisholm, Cleland being in command of my Company, and pretty heavy they were, soaked with rain. When we reached camp Galwey told off the pickets and guards. . . . Chisholm was detailed for outlying picket and said to me, 'I am wet through, I know I shall get cholera before I am relieved.' I said, 'I'll send you dry clothes as soon as I reach camp and you'll be as snug as possible in a bungalow.' (The pickets were always kept under cover as much as possible and there were a number of bungalows which were occupied.) Next day after tiffin as I was in the hospital talking to my Captain—Grant—who had been wounded at Bashiratgunj, in came an orderly with the order book detailing me to relieve Chisholm who had been taken with cholera. He died, poor chap, on the 19th August and I got my lieutenancy."

In his report on the action Major Stephenson stated that Captain Galwey, Lieutenant Arnold and Second-Lieutenant Dale "deserve the highest commendation for their daring and bravery. The conduct of the men has been most praiseworthy, and their bravery and devotion have called forth high encomiums from the Brigadier-General."

After the action as Havelock rode down the line, the men,

MAJOR. GEN. SIR JAMES OUTRAM G.C.B.
Commissioner for Oude.

BRIGADIER GEN J.G. SMITH NEILL C.B.
Commanding 1st Brigade

MAJOR. GEN H. HAVELOCK. C.B.
Commanding Oude Field Force

weary with marching and fighting and stricken with disease, sprang up and cheered him. "Don't cheer me, my men," he exclaimed, "you did it all yourselves"; and in a General Order dated August 17th Havelock wrote:—"*The Brigadier-General congratulates the troops on the result of their exertions in the combat of yesterday. The enemy were driven, with the loss of their guns and 250 killed and wounded, from one of the strongest positions in India, which they obstinately defended. They were the flower of the mutinous soldiery of the Presidency, flushed with the defection of Saugor and Fyzabad, but they stood one short hour only against a handful of the soldiery of the State, whose ranks have been thinned by sickness and the sword. . . . Soldiers, your labours, your privations, your sufferings and your valour will not be forgotten by a grateful country. You will be acknowledged to have been the stay and prop of British India in the time of her severest trial.*"

On the return of the column to Cawnpore Havelock found awaiting him the *Gazette* containing the announcement that Major-General Sir James Outram was to command the Dinapore and Cawnpore Divisions which were to be amalgamated. Outram did not reach Cawnpore until September 15th and on the very next day he published what is surely the noblest General Order that has ever been penned by any soldier. In it he recalled that the relief of Lucknow had in the first instance been entrusted to Havelock, and that he considered it was due to that officer, and to the exertions already made to effect that object, that the honour of the achievement should be his and his only. "The Major-General, therefore," so runs the order, " in gratitude for and admiration of the brilliant deeds of arms achieved by General Havelock and his gallant troops, will cheerfully waive his rank on the occasion, and will accompany the force to Lucknow in his civil capacity—as Chief Commissioner of Oudh—tendering his military services to General Havelock as a volunteer."

About this time General Neill received a letter from Sir Patrick Grant containing the following message:—"Give your Lambs my assurance that one of my first steps on returning to Madras shall be to see myself that their wives and families are thoroughly well-cared for in every respect ; they shall want for no reasonable comfort or accommodation that I can procure for them. Tell your gallant Regiment so from me with my earnest wishes for their every success."

While the Fusiliers were on active service in northern India their families in Madras were supplied with free rations at Government expense, and in Madras also a fund, known as " the Madras Fusiliers' Fund " was inaugurated to assist the widows and orphans of the Regiment.

After the affair at Bithur the force settled down to await the arrival of reinforcements, and the ordinary routine of cantonment life was as far as possible resumed. There were morning parades, orderly room when prisoners were seen and told off, and amongst many curious crimes committed and punishments awarded, the following taken from a defaulter sheet of the period is surely very hard to beat :—

" Pte —— Hanging a native without permission—two days' C.B. ! "

But sickness was very prevalent and the death roll terribly high. On August 19th Lieutenant Groom wrote :—" We have a fearful number in hospital, and 70 men, who are too much exhausted to do anything, live in the theatre with a surgeon to look after them. They are called 'invalids,' but the whole force might be classed in the same category. Such a lot of woe-begone, ragged, bearded ruffians you never saw ! " On the 20th he wrote that " I hear we have 370 men in the field hospital this morning so I fancy that the men are improving a little in health " ; while four days later he writes in a still more jubilant strain, saying, " Our men are rapidly getting better and are daily improving on good rations and rest." But that the sickness in the force had been very serious is apparent from a letter of about this period from Lieutenant Cleland to his mother, in which he says :—" Cholera has broken out in the entrenched camp and committed frightful havoc. How officers escaped who were called upon to make men's wills in the worst and last stage of the disease seems miraculous."

During this time of enforced inaction news was received from Allahabad that a party of Fusiliers with a few Sikhs had been sent up the Ganges in the steamer *Jumna* towards Cawnpore in order to sever the enemy's communications between Oudh and the Doab. This party burned seven boats, destroyed 43 more and had a skirmish with the rebels at a village 16 miles above Allahabad, one of the Madras Fusiliers being wounded.

Sports were encouraged for the men at Cawnpore, a race meeting was actually held, and with so much that was ordinary going on it was difficult at times to realize that this little force of barely 1,200 men was in the heart of a rebel country with some 32,000 enemies and 40 guns posted only a very few marches distant.

No wonder that reinforcements were eagerly awaited. On August 27th Groom wrote :—" Two hundred of the 78th and 50 of our men are really coming up from Allahabad, and I believe Harris, Graeme, Hornsby, Woods, 'the Shepherd' (Lieutenant Barclay) and Duncan will come up with them. We also expect Down and Parry very shortly and we shall then have almost as many officers as men. Grant's wound is getting on well, and I hope he will be able to return to duty in a day or two. Seton goes to Allahabad with the rest of the sick and wounded to-night. Fraser only had a contused wound and never suffered an hour from it—much the same with Gosling's scratch. Our men, I think, still pick up in health. . . ."

On August 29th General Havelock received the welcome news that some 1,200 men were on their way to Cawnpore, and that he was to be further reinforced by details of the 64th, 78th and 84th and Madras Fusiliers from Calcutta, and he determined as soon as the first contingent should have arrived to re-cross the Ganges and move again on Lucknow. But he was once more doomed to disappointment. Small parties did indeed come in on August 30th, but others followed very very slowly, while the heavy and continuous rains, which delayed the recovery of the sick, made any advance of the force impossible before the middle of September at earliest.

By September 15th Outram had arrived in person and the Cawnpore troops had been considerably reinforced. Lieutenant Barclay with 56 Madras Fusiliers, 80 of the 78th, and 50 men of the 84th came in on the 1st; the 5th Fusiliers and 90th Light Infantry arrived on the 15th and 16th bringing details of some of the battalions already in camp, and the little force was now reorganized in three brigades, two of infantry and one of cavalry, the Madras Fusiliers being in the 1st Infantry Brigade, commanded by Brigadier-General Neill, with the 5th Fusiliers, and a detachment of the 64th and the 84th Regiment.

The following was the strength of the different arms with the force :—

Artillery	282
Volunteer Cavalry	109
British Infantry	2388
Brasyer's Sikhs	341
12th Irregular Cavalry	59

On the night of September 18th the bridge was laid over the Ganges and on the two following days the troops crossed over to the Oudh bank; then at daybreak on the 21st, in a deluge of rain, Havelock's column again began its advance for the relief of Lucknow. "We all take our bands complete to make as much noise as possible at Lucknow," wrote Groom joyously. "We—Fusiliers—are taking up lots of comforts for the ladies and children in our Mess; even sugar-plums for the children have not been rejected"; but for the troops everything had been cut down to the smallest scale and only three days' rations and one blanket per man were carried.

On crossing the Ganges, the Fusiliers and the Sikhs had been pushed on ahead over some sandhills to within about two miles of the enemy's position, and from here with glasses the rebels could be seen throwing up earthworks and otherwise improving their position at Mangulwar, where Havelock had already twice before engaged them in the previous July and August. The enemy's right rested on a village and walled enclosure, while his centre and left were covered by a line of breastworks behind which were 6 guns, and these last opened on the British artillery as it came in sight on the road. Maude, Olpherts and Eyre with their guns replied and shelled the enemy's position till Havelock considered that sufficient impression had been made, when he made a wide turning movement to the left with his main body, delivering a frontal attack with the 1st Brigade under Neill, whereby the enemy's line was quickly in ruins. The enemy fled, vigorously pursued by the Volunteer Cavalry with which Outram was serving. Here Sergeant Mahoney of the Madras Fusiliers, who was acting as Sergeant-Major to the British Cavalry, captured the Regimental Colour of the 1st Bengal Infantry, severing at the wrist the hand of the native officer who was carrying it.

No. 10 Company of the Madras Fusiliers was then extended in skirmishing order until the force was ready to move, and Havelock now coming up, said to the men of No. 10—" Fusiliers, you are always in front whether you are wanted or not "—a remark which was received with a hearty cheer.

The rebels were given no time to rally, the cavalry harried their rear, the infantry pushed on as fast as possible in support, and Havelock did not halt his men until the column entered Bashiratganj, the scene of three stubborn fights in the earlier advances.

The next day's march was unopposed and the 14 miles to Bani Bridge were accomplished in torrents of rain; the bridge was found to be intact and the formidable entrenchments were unoccupied, and here a Royal Salute was fired from the guns of the column to let the Lucknow garrison know that help was at hand.

On the 23rd the troops moved off again at dawn, still drenched to the skin for it had rained steadily nearly all night. There were now but 16 miles separating the relieving force from Lucknow, and it was certain that there would be many encounters with the mutineers before a meeting with the besieged could be effected. The Alam Bagh, a small palace or hunting lodge of the Kings of Oudh, lay between the column and the Lucknow Residency, and it was expected that this building, within a walled enclosure, would be stubbornly held. After marching some ten miles the enemy was seen drawn up in force in front of the wooded ground near that spot, and Outram and Havelock rode forward to reconnoitre. They found that the rebels appeared to be about 12,000 strong with numerous guns.

A change was now made in the order of advance, and the 1st Brigade changed front on the road by the stiff but time-honoured manœuvre of wheeling back sections, thus bringing the rear regiment, the 84th, to the front. Maude's guns opened a very accurate fire on the enemy who quickly replied, one of their shells bursting close to some of the Fusiliers but without doing any harm, and the force then wheeled off, the 1st Brigade to the left, with the Madras Fusiliers on the left and most exposed flank.

No. 10 Company covered the movement, directed by Captain Grant, still partially disabled from his wound, and General Outram rode beside this company.

On reaching the outskirts of the city Outram expressed his intention of taking the Yellow House, which stood in front on the road, directing Grant to move to the right for this purpose, and was only restrained by the sounding of the regimental call and the "Retire." On hearing this Sir James Outram cocked his head on one side and said with a smile to Lieutenant Dale, beside whom he rode, " Well, my boy, I think we had better retire." The call had been sounded by the order of Major Stephenson who feared that No. 10 Company was too much isolated.

Meanwhile Major Olpherts had been in action with the enemy on the left of the road, Maude's battery covering the advance of the 2nd Brigade. When the 1st Brigade had advanced some little way, Olpherts came up at a gallop, and as he passed the Regiment to come into action about a quarter of a mile to its front, he was greeted with rousing cheers, for the Fusiliers took more than an ordinary interest in this dashing battery since several of their comrades were acting as gunners with it.

The 78th and 90th went straight for that part of the Alam Bagh enclosure immediately in their front, while the 5th and Madras

NEARING LUCKNOW

Fusiliers advanced on their side of the road, so that as dusk fell Havelock was in complete possession of the Alam Bagh, capturing five of the enemy's guns. As the firing ceased a despatch was handed to the General and the news it contained quickly passed round and was signalized by a salute of 21 guns—it told the force that Delhi had fallen.

"Next day some annoyance was felt from a distant cannonade, but no serious attempt was made to reply to it; and, while the troops recruited their energies, the Generals consulted as to what plan of attack they should pursue on the morrow. Havelock had all along intended to seize the Dilkusha, cross the Goomtee, and, gaining the Fyzabad road at the Kokrail Bridge, occupy a building called the Badshah Bagh, re-cross the Goomtee at the iron bridge, and thence advance to the Residency. By the adoption of this route the relieving force would have been saved from the perils of street-fighting. The rains, however, had rendered the country impassable for artillery; and no alternative remained but to cross the canal at the Charbagh Bridge, and pursue the road along its left bank to the Residency.

"Meanwhile a great change had come over the feelings of the besieged garrison. For some days after the last departure of Ongud* there had been nothing to vary the monotony of their life. The death-roll grew longer. More natives deserted. But at 11 o'clock on the night of the 22nd a man came into the entrenchment, breathless with excitement, having just been fired upon by the enemies' sentries. It was Ongud. He announced that Outram and Havelock had crossed the Ganges and might be expected within a few days. The news spread like wild-fire. Next day firing was distinctly heard close to the city. The spirits of all rose to the highest point, and the native portion of the garrison were now at last convinced that relief was really at hand."†

Fortunately the morning of September 25th broke dry though cloudy. The rain of the past week had sent many good men to hospital, and all the sick and wounded and footsore men, as well

* The spy sent out from the Residency. † Rice-Holmes, pp. 298, 299.

as the picquets and baggage guards, were sent into the Alam Bagh enclosure. A force of 250 men was told off to hold this place under Major McIntyre, 78th Highlanders.

The distance from the Alam Bagh to the Residency was no more than 2 miles in a direct line, but the troops covered at least twice that distance before reaching it. The thickly-wooded gardens about the city, surrounded by high mud walls, afforded excellent cover for the enemy, while further on long narrow lanes between houses and mud huts crossed the route in all directions and equally gave protection to the rebels.

The following are the names of the officers of the Madras Fusiliers who were this day present:—Major Stephenson in command, Captains Galwey, Raikes, Grant and Fraser, Lieutenants Groom, Beaumont, Barclay, Arnold, Bailey, Dale and Cleland, with Surgeon Arthur and Assistant-Surgeon Robertson; while Brigadier-General Neill commanded the 1st Brigade, Captain Spurgin was Brigade Major, Lieutenant Hargood was officiating as A.D.C. to General Havelock, and Lieutenant Woods was temporarily attached to the 64th Foot. Lieutenant Bertie had been left at Cawnpore in charge of sick.

The Brigade of which the Madras Fusiliers formed a part led the advance, the 5th Fusiliers in front, with Maude's battery in rear of their two front companies, and Outram riding beside Maude. The Yellow House soon came in sight and here the enemy had placed 6 guns, two on either side of the road and two in front of the house itself, while the rebel infantry was well disposed in the fields bordering the road.

The troops, especially the gunners of the battery, suffered many casualties at this point from the rebel fire, particularly from that of 2 guns, which were loaded in the lane behind the Yellow House and then run out on the main road and fired. "At last," writes one who was present,* "Havelock sent the welcome order to advance," and the 5th Fusiliers, dashing forward, carried the Yellow House by storm. On went the column till it was checked

---

* Maude, *Memories of the Mutiny* Vol. II, pp. 292 et seq.

half-a-mile beyond the Yellow House by a sharp bend in the road. Two hundred yards in front flowed the canal; straight before them was the Charbagh Bridge. To the right and left of it were lofty houses, loopholed and held by musketeers. Lieutenant Arnold with the skirmishers of the Madras Fusiliers was sent forward to hold the canal bank on the left of the road and check the fire that streamed from the houses. Outram with the 5th went to the right to clear the walled gardens from which the bridge derives its name, and to proceed on till he gained the high banks of the canal, whence he could bring a flanking fire to bear on the bridge. General Neill continued on the main road with Maude's guns and the Madras Fusiliers. On turning a corner of the wall on the left this force came full on the bridge.

The men lay down on the side of the road fairly under cover, with their rear company (Grant's) in line with Maude's 3 guns. These were no match for the enemy's and were disabled one after another, the last being worked by Maude, his subaltern, Maitland, and a few Fusiliers.

Outram was away some time with the 5th Foot, the fire grew heavier from the loopholed houses, and men chafed at the delay. At last young Havelock, A.D.C. to his father, the General, rode up to Neill suggesting his Brigade should advance and take the bridge. " Not without orders," was Neill's reply, for he knew that Outram had gone to seek another bridge, though he was unaware that it had been destroyed. Had the Charbagh Bridge also been destroyed the difficulty of reaching the Residency would have been very greatly enhanced.

Havelock galloped off and obtained the necessary order, and Neill then at once turned to his " Blue Caps," saying, " Fusiliers, there is the bridge, take it ! "

(Young Havelock had gone in front apparently proposing to lead the Fusiliers, as at the action of Cawnpore he had led the 64th when his father, the General, had recommended him for the Victoria Cross. But here Major Stephenson recalled him and quietly told him that the Madras Fusiliers were led by their own officers and not by aides-de-camp!)

On hearing Neill's words the Fusiliers, with some men of the 84th, sprang up with a cheer, when the last round fired from one of the enemy guns knocked over Lieutenant Arnold and the leading section. Willis, 84th, states:—" I well remember during this charge the leading officer of the Madras Fusiliers (Lieutenant Groom*) had his foot shot off at the ankle, at my side"; while another writer† tells us that " Arnold fell hit through both thighs. . . . Havelock and Corporal Jacques " (Madras Fusiliers) " alone remained. They were the target for many muskets. 'We'll soon have the beggars out of that, Sir,' said the Corporal. . . loading and firing as fast as he could. . . . Before the rebels had time to re-load, they " (84th and " Blue Caps ") " leapt forward with a terrible shout, dashed across the bridge, cleared the breastwork, stormed the battery, and bayonetted the gunners. The Charbagh Bridge was won."

Sir James Outram fully recognized the importance of this feat. He wrote:—"*Under the tremendous fire of guns and musketry which the enemy directed across the Charbagh Bridge, Lieutenant Havelock, with the Madras Fusiliers, stormed the bridge, took the guns, and cleared the street sufficiently to allow of the troops in rear closing up. I cannot conceive a more daring act than this forcing of the bridge, and the officers who led the Fusiliers on that occasion in my opinion most richly deserve promotion.*"

The force now moved down the canal until it came to a trench dug across the road; this was quickly filled up sufficiently by the regimental pioneers to allow the guns to cross, and the men then advanced within sight of the Begum Kothi, from the windows of which some native women seemed to be looking out. The men were warned not to fire, but presently the women disappeared, and a rapid discharge of musketry came from these same windows against the advancing columns. From that point to the Kaisar

* He died of his wounds in Lucknow. Willis evidently meant Arnold.
† Forrest, Vol. II, p. 42.

MADRAS FUSILIERS STORMING CHAR-BAGH BATTERY,
MAJOR STEPHENSON LEADING.

Bagh a continuous fire of grape and musketry, with an occasional round shot, poured from every building within range. The 2nd Brigade for a time missed their way and had much stiffer fighting than the 1st as they had the big guns with them and very narrow lanes to negotiate.

Nearing the Kaisar Bagh, the fire met with by Neill's men grew even more murderous, and some of the " Blue Caps "— Lieutenant Dale among them—got penned in a verandah opposite the gateway and suffered several casualties. Here there was temporarily some confusion, gunners and infantrymen became intermingled, and soldiers were separated from their companies and companies from corps, and there was a brief halt to reorganize before going on.

General Neill now pushed forward across a large square with a big gateway on the left, and got into what seemed something of a blind alley, and Major Stephenson here ordered Captain Grant to hold this gateway with his company, directing Lieutenant Dale at the same time to bring on the rest of the men. Neill's cheery words :—" Go on, my lads, follow your officers," were the last these two companies heard him speak.

When the gateway was reached Outram rode into the square with some of the 78th, calling out—" Now then, 78th, the Residency." Someone, however, suggested that two companies were hardly enough for the work still ahead of them, so Outram told a bugler to sound the regimental call, and now, Captain Grant, seeing that the 78th were ready, shouted " Come on, No. 10, for the Residency ! " and away they went up the street. At the first turning Sir James overtook the company and pointed out the right route to follow, this slight check enabling the 78th to get up and rush on with the Fusiliers. As the soldiers pressed on musketry poured from all the houses and even women hurled missiles from the roofs, while trenches were cut across the road and guns fired grape into the ranks. Wounded men had to lie with the dead where they fell awaiting their chance of being picked up later.

In the last street leading to the Residency, Lieutenant Swanston of the 78th, while carrying one of the Colours, was shot and Lieutenant Dale and Corporal Youral of the Fusiliers both stooped at the same moment to pick it up, but the Corporal was the nearer of the two and carried it on.

"General Neill sat his horse near the archway giving orders with consummate coolness, meant to prevent too hasty a rush through the archway. One of the guns had not been got out of the lane. He sent an officer back to see what was the reason of the delay. As he turned his head to watch for its appearance a mutineer took a steady aim at him through a loophole in the archway, fired, and the bullet struck Neill on the head behind and a little above the left ear. Then, like an ash that on the crest of a far-seen hill is smitten with the axe of bronze, even so he fell, and his body was brought to the ground as his frightened horse galloped towards the lane."*

Of the death of Neill, Captain Spurgin of the Madras Fusiliers, his brigade major, wrote :—†" My poor good friend General Neill was killed by almost the last shot that was fired on the 25th. I was close to him. A wretched man shot him from the top of a house. He never spoke again and could not have suffered a moment's pain. There was a gun between us at the time, but I got round and saved his body by carrying it into the entrenched camp on a gun-carriage. . . . What am I to write or say to poor Mrs. Neill ? and he asked me before we went into action, in case he fell, to do so."

Of the very many tributes paid to the immortal memory of General Neill, two only will here be given, the one from a private soldier of the 78th Highlanders, the other by the highest in India, Lord Canning, the Governor-General. The private soldier wrote in a letter home :—" And here, when success had crowned our efforts, shocking to relate, our brave General Neill fell. He was an honour to the country and the idol of the British Army." While

* Forrest, Vol. II, pp. 50, 51.
† *Galignani's Messenger*, January 16th, 1858.

THE ROAD UP WHICH NEILL'S "BLUE CAPS" ADVANCED TO THE RELIEF OF THE LUCKNOW RESIDENCY.

when the despatches of Outram and Havelock were published, Lord Canning wrote of the deceased soldier in language of admiring regret :—" The Governor-General-in-Council," so runs his minute, " cannot refrain from expressing the deep regret with which he hears of the death of Brigadier Neill, of the 1st Madras European Fusiliers, of which it is feared that no doubt exists. Brigadier-General Neill, during his short but active career in Bengal, had won the respect and confidence of the Government of India ; he had made himself conspicuous as an intelligent, prompt, and self-reliant soldier, ready of resource and stout of heart ; and the Governor-General-in-Council offers to the Government and to the Army of Madras his sincere condolence upon the loss of one who was an honour to the service of their Presidency."*

While Neill lay dead his beloved " Blue Caps " stormed on— all that were left of them—to the Residency, which Captain Grant and some of the Fusiliers were among the first to enter ; once inside the scene was intensely pathetic, " the joy of the garrison," wrote young Hargood, " can be better imagined than described " ; women and children came down to meet their rescuers ; and by now it was almost dark and the troops were quite worn out.

The first relief of Lucknow was accomplished, that is to say, nearly one-third of the little army had forced its way through the city and had managed to get into the Residency, while another third came in next day.

Of the final rush and of the meeting of rescuers and rescued an historian has written :—" Like a life-boat ploughing its way through a tempestuous sea to the rescue of some sinking ship, the column rushed on, now plunging through deep trenches which had been cut across the road to bar their progress, now staggering, as they rose, beneath the storm of bullets which hailed down upon them

---

* Later a *Gazette* announced that H.M. The Queen had " been pleased to ordain and declare that Isabella Neill, the widow of the late Colonel James George Neill, of the Madras Fusiliers, shall have, hold and enjoy the same style, title, place and precedence, to which she would have been entitled had her husband, who fell in the gallant discharge of his duty, survived and been invested with the insignia of a Knight Commander of the Bath."

from the loopholes of the houses and the missiles which were flung from the roofs. But they were now within a few yards of their goal; they could see the tattered flag of England waving on the roof of the Presidency; and, though men fell fast at every step, the survivors never paused till Outram and Havelock led them through the gate into the entrenchment.

"Then the exultation, the sympathy, the loyalty of their hearts found expression in a burst of deafening cheers; the garrison caught up the cry; and from every pit, and trench, and battery, from behind the roofless and shattered houses the notes of triumph and welcome echoed and re-echoed. Women crowded up to shake hands with the men who had fought twelve battles to save them; and the Highlanders, with tears streaming down their cheeks, caught up in their arms the wondering children, and passed them from one to another. Anxious questions were tenderly answered; kinsmen long separated met once more; old comrades fought their battles over again; and the garrison, as they told their own tale, and learned with pride the admiration which their struggle had aroused, heard in their turn, with reverent sympathy, how and at what a cost they had been relieved."*

* Rice-Holmes, p. 301

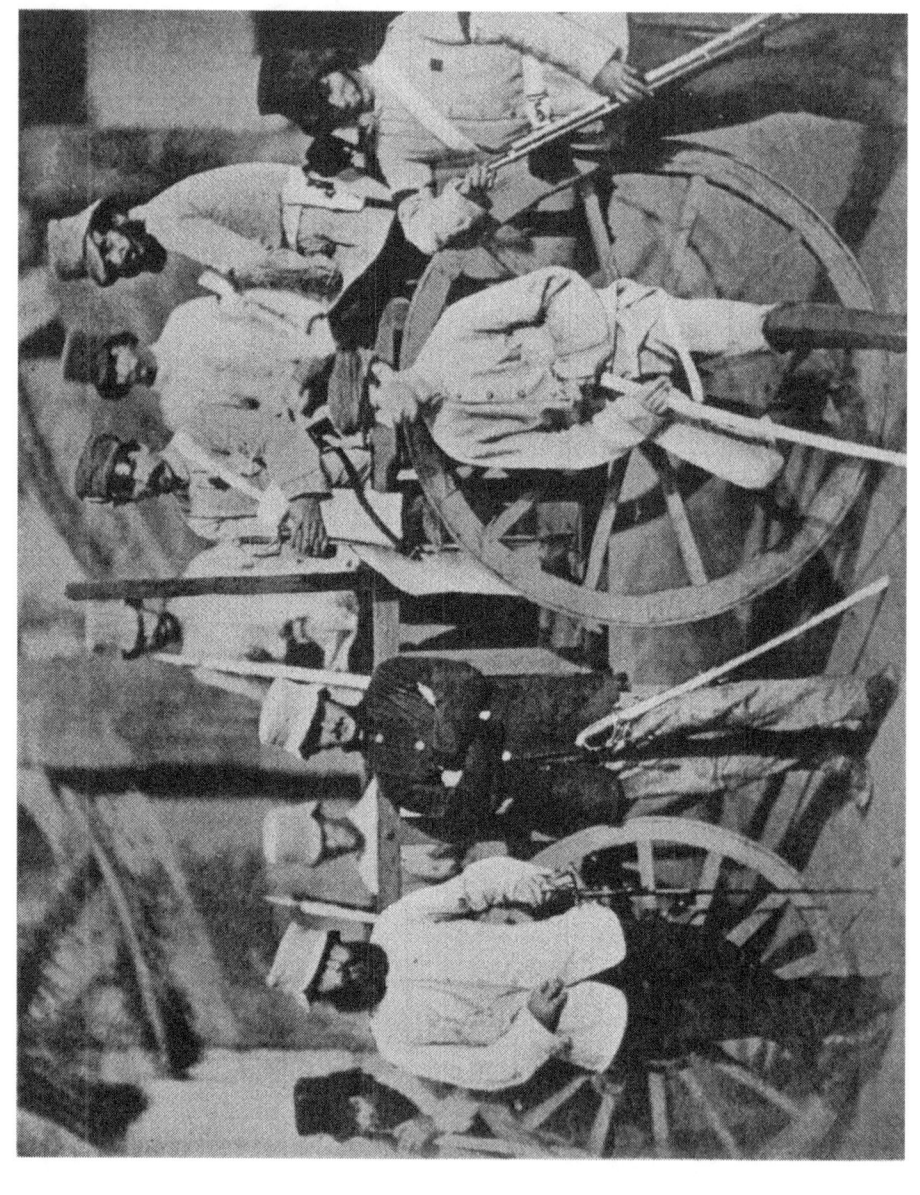

AFTER THE CAPTURE OF LUCKNOW.

Pte. Duffy, V.C.   Pte. Smith.   Sergt. Williams.   Pay-Sergt. Pierce.   Color-Sergt. Cunningham.
Capt. C. Scott Elliott.   2nd-Lieut. R. C. Parry.   Lieut. S. H. Jones Parry.   Lieut. C. H. Dale.   Lce.-Corpl. Coghlan.

CHAPTER IV

THE SECOND SIEGE OF LUCKNOW AND THE SECOND RELIEF—THE WITHDRAWAL OF THE GARRISON AND RELIEVING TROOPS.

ON September 26th, the morning after the relief column had marched in, General Sir James Outram assumed command, and the combined forces were now reorganized. Brigadier-General Havelock took over command of the 1st Brigade, while Colonel Inglis of the 32nd, who, on the death of Sir Henry Lawrence, had taken command of the Lucknow garrison, was given charge of the 2nd Brigade.

Havelock's Brigade comprised the 5th Fusiliers, the 64th—a very weak regiment, the 84th, the 90th and Brasyer's Sikhs, while Inglis's Brigade contained the 32nd, now greatly reduced in numbers, the 78th Highlanders and the Madras Fusiliers.

To the 1st Brigade was assigned the occupation of the palaces and gardens lying to the east of the Residency; and it was further decided, now that the garrison had been so considerably reinforced, to enlarge the scope of the defences by occupying some of the houses on the banks of the river, and also to try and open out a road towards Cawnpore in order to enable the horses of the cavalry to obtain a sufficient supply of fodder.

The very first thing to be done, however, was to get in the wounded, the guns and the rearguard, which had all been left behind the previous evening while the relieving force was making its way into the Residency. Colonel Napier, who had been appointed Military Secretary to Outram and had now taken over the duties of C.R.E., went out in command of a search party early on the 26th, while Olpherts went with him to superintend the bringing in of the guns. Some of the wounded met with a fearful fate; the rescue party missed its way, got into the enclosure where

Neill had received his death wound, was exposed to a very deadly fire from the neighbouring houses, and the dhooly-bearers abandoned their charges and fled. The deed of heroism which saved Lieutenant Arnold from a cruel death is thus narrated by Sir George Forrest*:—
"From their position at this time the mutineers could fire freely on our dhoolies in the square. In one of the dhoolies lay Lieutenant Arnold of the Madras Fusiliers. Private Ryan" (of the Regiment) "was sorely distressed at the cruel fate that awaited one of his officers, and he called for a volunteer to assist him in removing him. McManus" (5th Fusiliers) "had been wounded but he instantly came forward. . . . The two rushed across the gateway through the deadly fire into the square. They tried to lift the dhooly but found it beyond their strength. They then took Arnold out of the litter and carried him to the house. The ground was torn by musket balls about them, but they effected their return in safety, though Lieutenant Arnold received a second wound through the thigh while in their arms."

All the day and night through did these brave men stand by their officer and the rest of the wounded, attacked continually; but at 2 a.m. they heard heavy firing and hope of relief rose in their hearts; then there was again silence. "The last gleam of hope vanished away. To attempt to carry away the wounded was hopeless. They resigned themselves to their fate. Soon after they heard firing in the distance. . . . Nearer and nearer it approached. Then Ryan, suddenly jumping up, shouted, 'Och, boys! them's our own chaps!'" And so it was, and that day all the guns and the surviving wounded were brought into the Residency, though many of the injured later succumbed.

It was during the operations for the withdrawal of the guns that Private Duffy of No. 10 Company of the Regiment, specially distinguished himself, and his exploit is thus described in the report of his commanding officer :—"One of our 24-pounders which had been used on the previous day against the enemy, but the working of which had ceased owing to the musketry fire poured upon it, was

* Vol. II, p. 59 *et seq.*

left in an exposed position, but it was extricated in a very daring and dexterous manner by Captain Olpherts, aided by Captain Crump (killed) and Private Duffy of the Madras Fusiliers. Captain Olpherts recommends Private Duffy for the Victoria Cross for his gallantry in extricating the 24-pounder under a very heavy fire of musketry and I beg to second the recommendation."

Sir George Forrest gives a more detailed account; he says, "When it grew dark Private Duffy, acting under the directions of Olpherts, crept out unobserved by the enemy and succeeded in attaching two drag-ropes to the trail of the gun. They were fastened to the limbers, the bullocks were yoked, and the gun was fortunately drawn in. Whilst aiding in the operations, Captain Crump, a quick and daring soldier of great intellectual power, was killed.

As soon as Colonel Napier and his party had returned in safety, the Madras Fusiliers were ordered to parade for a sortie under Major Stephenson with a view to capturing the Cawnpore battery and of bringing in or destroying some guns which had been causing the garrison no little annoyance. The following account is taken from Captain Galwey's account of all that occurred this day.

"The Regiment was told off in three divisions, the strength of it not admitting of a large number. Captain Fraser had command of No. 1, Captain Galwey No. 2, and Captain Raikes of No. 3 Division. Lieutenant and Adjutant Gosling, Lieutenants Beaumont and Cleland, and Lieutenant the Hon. J. Fraser, 1st Bengal Native Infantry and Lieutenant Huxham, 48th Bengal Native Infantry doing duty with the Fusiliers, fell in with the Regiment. The party proceeded in strict silence out of the Bailey Gate to the garden opposite, and passed through a door to the right about half-way down the garden, which led through bye-paths till it reached the road, at which place there was a considerable fire from loopholes, and from the tops of houses and from guns of the enemy in position. A charge was made at the nearest gun . . . our men entered by the embrasure and the enemy immediately abandoned this gun." (The gun having been spiked efforts to burst it were unsuccessful.)

During this time a party of No. 1 Division under Captain Fraser, proceeded to reconnoitre a little further, when they came on another battery of the enemy, consisting of a 24-pounder and an 18-pounder. These were abandoned, but the enemy being all round and keeping up such a fire on his party, Captain Fraser sent back to say he required a reinforcement. On this Captain Galwey proceeded with a few men, but on reaching the spot he found . . . that the position could not be held without a further reinforcement. . . . It was now discovered that we had with us no means by which we could destroy or dismantle the gun, so Major Stephenson directed the advance party to fall back on him, which, however, they did not then do. Captain Fraser spoke in the highest terms of the gallantry of Sergeant Lidster, Madras Fusiliers, who spiked the 24-pounder, and of Corporal William Dowling, H.Ms. 32nd, who spiked the 18-pounder gun, being at the same time under a most heavy fire.

" Finding it impossible to burst the first gun, Major Stephenson left a party under a subaltern to protect that gun, and proceeded with Captain Raikes' division to the advanced battery, which was surrounded by high walls. . . . No one knew the way or seemed at all aware of our locality, and at this time firing being heard in our rear, Major Stephenson was compelled to retire by the way we came, it being quite impossible to go forward without guides. The three guns were left spiked. . . . On the return of the party it was exposed to a very destructive fire from the tops of houses and loopholes, and from want of means it was most difficult to take away our killed and wounded. One sergeant (Lidster), severely wounded and since dead, must have been left on the ground had not a private* (Smith) of the 32nd in the most gallant manner, with the assistance of Captain Galwey, taken him up and carried him to a place of safety." Private Smith was killed later.

The following were the casualties this day sustained by the " Blue Caps " :—

Killed and died of wounds: Sergeants Lidster and Edwards, Corporals Barrett and Shannahan, Privates Gibbons and Hayes.

* Another account says that Captain Galwey, Lieutenants Mecham, 27th Madras Native Infantry, and Warner, 7th Light Cavalry, and Private Smith all helped.

Wounded: Corporals Flegg and Traynor, Privates Charles Brown, Quinlan and McCarthy.

Lieutenant Cleland of the Madras Fusiliers was mentioned in despatches in connection with this sortie.

A private of the Regiment had a remarkable escape this day. He was missing after the action and for three days nothing was heard of him, when a party of his comrades, passing near the place where the engagement had taken place, was attracted by his cries and found him in a hidden well.

The original garrison and the relieving force were now shut off from all communication with the Alam Bagh and the outside world generally, and arrangements were made for withstanding a further siege. It was ascertained that with care the available supplies would last about ten weeks, but all would have to be placed on short rations. In Captain Spurgin's diary at this time he wrote:—" Instead of affording any great relief to this unfortunate garrison of Lucknow—I am writing one week after our entrance—we are almost as badly off as the garrison, cut off from our baggage, no communication with Cawnpore, and with few supplies left—daily fighting, daily loss. Arnold has lost his leg and is in a dangerous state; poor Bailey is badly wounded and I fear the spine is touched, as he has lost the use of his arms; a frightful number of the men and sergeants, nearly one hundred, are also wounded. We are now living in a part of the palace of Lucknow; but such a scene of filth, mixed up with costly things, it is impossible to imagine. The finest china, stools, shawls and ornaments intermingled with dead bodies of sepoys, horses, camels, until the stench is so great we can scarcely sit—and no one to remove all this filth."

In the meantime parties had been sent out to open up the Cawnpore road. On September 29th three columns moved out simultaneously, from the Brigade Mess, from the Sikh Square and from the Redan. With the first column were 20 of the 32nd, 140 of the 78th, and 90 of the Madras Fusiliers under Captain Galwey. In this affair Sergeant Higgins and 4 men of the Regiment specially distinguished themselves. They accompanied Lieutenant

Ouseley, 48th Native Infantry, through a number of houses and narrow passages, climbed a high and steep bastion and captured a gun. Several other guns were also here taken and sent into the Residency. On this occasion the Fusiliers had Sergeant Drury, Privates Peard and Sowden killed, while Private McGill was wounded and Privates Young and Parker died of their wounds.

Again on October 1st Colonel Napier took out a column to attack a building known as Phillips' Garden, where there was a powerful battery facing the Cawnpore Battery, already previously captured. The infantry of this column numbered 568, drawn from six different battalions including the 1st Madras Fusiliers, the party supplied by which was commanded by Captain Raikes. The houses surrounding the objective were successively attacked, the enemy driven out, and occupied, Lieutenant Groom, with 50 Madras Fusiliers, particularly distinguishing himself by advancing, as stated by Colonel Napier in his report, "in a very spirited manner under a sharp fire of musketry." Napier further states that "the conduct of the whole of the officers and men was in every way deserving of commendation. They were most eager to assault the battery on the night of the 1st, but I restrained them"; and on the morning of October 2nd the troops forced the enemy's stockade, occupied the battery and burst the guns.

On the same day 15 men of the Regiment formed part of a small detachment detailed under Lieutenant Hardinge to capture the guns to the right of the Cawnpore road. Only one gun was by them found intact, but the party burnt the batteries, blew up a large mosque and fell back without loss.

During the 3rd and 4th the operations for the clearing of the Cawnpore road were continued, and by the last-named date the different parties had reached the Yellow House, not far from the Alam Bagh. Near the Yellow House Major Stephenson, of the Madras Fusiliers, was struck in the stomach by a partially-spent bullet. He suffered great pain, but the bullet did not penetrate, unfavourable symptoms, however, set in, and the wound kept on sloughing until he died seven weeks later; by his fall, wrote General

Outram in a despatch dated November 25th, "the Country and Service have sustained a very heavy loss."

In these days there were no antiseptics and the want of chloroform was much felt. Many of the wounded fell victims to gangrene and only one officer of the relieving force survived amputation. Scurvy too was rife in the hospitals, for fresh meat was scarce and there were no vegetables obtainable. Spurgin writes of these days in his diary:—"The scenes in this hospital are past belief. Two hundred and upwards lying side by side, sick and wounded, and our poor good ladies are walking about bathing the heads of the sick and soothing the dying. God bless them for it!"

The heavy losses sustained in the capture of the Yellow House had obliged the party engaged in it to fall back, but on the 5th a party of the Fusiliers, supported by another of the 78th, was sent to reoccupy the place. With the "Blue Caps" were Captains Galwey (in command) and Fraser, Lieutenants Groom and Dale. The road was now found to be barricaded, and the loss in the forcing of it was heavy. Spurgin writing this day said:—"Three more of our officers wounded—poor Groom very severely, thigh bone broken by a round shot and I fear he will lose his leg; poor Fraser badly hit in the shoulder and Galwey slightly in the neck. Several of the men also were wounded." Lieutenant Dale got off with a bullet through the fly of his cap. The enemy's fire was very heavy and the Fusiliers were ordered to retire. As they fell back, with some men under Lieutenant Dale bringing up the rear, "Private Ryan," so Dale relates, "came up to me and said, 'Sergeant Campbell's left behind. If you will come with me, Sir, we'll fetch him off.' We were then alone. We got the Sergeant off and Ryan would then have earned the Victoria Cross had he not already got it for saving Arnold."

The number of officers in the garrison was now so greatly reduced that the besieged were obliged to remain mainly on the defensive, the enemy in his turn making several determined attacks, which were, however, all successfully repulsed.

Lieutenant Dale with No. 7 Company was now posted in the Throne Room of the Palace, while Captain Grant and his Company occupied the Mosque Picquet which formed a pronounced salient of the defences. Both these posts were under constant fire from the enemy batteries, and Dale recounts how one day a round shot entered the Throne Room, rolling across the floor like a cricket ball until stopped by the body of the Colour-Sergeant, whose leg it ripped up and whose ribs it smashed in before going on its way. The Sergeant was dead before they could get him to the hospital. It was in the Mosque Picquet that on November 2nd Captain Grant was wounded by a musket bullet. "They brought him down," so Dale tells us, "and Dr. Kerry of the 64th cut out the bullet with a knife as blunt as a table knife, while I held his head between my knees. He had been wounded once in Burma, once on the road to Cawnpore, and now again, but he recovered and lived to the age of 85."

Of Grant, Colonel Napier wrote :—" He has commanded the post of the Mosque from the 11th October to the 2nd November, when he was severely wounded. He maintained the post under a constant and close musketry fire and repeated attacks by mining, with cool courage and judgment; both these qualities were required to avoid real and disregard the imaginary dangers of mines, and Captain Grant has displayed them in an eminent degree."

The following extracts from Captain Spurgin's diary give a good idea of the life of the besieged garrison of the Residency in the four weeks between October 16th and November 14th, when the advance of the new Relief Force was drawing daily nearer.

"October 16th.—Well, another week has passed and we are still shut up in this wretched place, and from all accounts that reach us no prospect of getting out for the next three weeks at least. Fortunately our provisions, such as they are, last out well, but these gun bullocks are rather tough. . . . Bailey and Fraser are doing pretty well, Galwey all right again, Groom very bad and I much fear will not recover. Stephenson's hurt has also turned out badly and he looks very ill. No medicines, no wine, no comforts of any kind, no clean rags even to dress wounds, so but few can recover. The enemy still determined, mining and throwing shells all about us.

"October 19th.—Three of our men have had the Victoria Cross awarded them by General Sir James Outram, and had Galwey's name been sent in he would, I am sure, have had it too, for he gallantly threw a wounded sergeant over his shoulder, and brought him out of the most murderous fire of grape and musketry. Grant was the first man into the garrison of Lucknow on September 25th, and General Outram mentioned his name in orders. In fact, both officers and men have behaved most splendidly, but all are sadly reduced in numbers, poor Groom is very bad and I fear cannot recover, Fraser and Bailey are doing better.

"October 22nd.—Groom died yesterday. What a blow for his wife, his child he had never seen. No sooner was his body removed from the hospital than Barclay was put in his place, badly wounded. We have now lost 6 officers killed and 7 wounded—13; but other regiments are equally unfortunate, especially the 78th Highlanders. Our poor horses are now without grain and little grass; some are starving.

"October 27th.—At last we have heard of a chance of relief A column from Delhi is now on its way to join another force at Cawnpore and we may now expect them here in a few days, so we are all in high spirits. . . .

"October 29th.—Stephenson sent for me yesterday, he is very unwell, his wound doing badly. We expect our relief by November 10th.

"November 2nd.—Another sad morning. My friend, Ned Grant, is very seriously wounded. I have just returned from his side. He was shot in the stomach and the ball must have touched the liver. It was cut out of the right side. I was with him soon after he was hit, but I am very uneasy about him, and he thinks badly of himself. Stephenson is, I think, much worse to-day, and, judging from his appearance, I don't think he can recover.

"November 11th.—Our relief is assembling about three miles distant and between this and the 20th I suppose it will take place. . . . Our sick and wounded are doing very badly and the whole garrison is looking thin and wretched. Ned Grant is doing pretty well, though not out of danger; Fraser, Bailey and Barclay doing well, Stephenson sinking from weakness, I think, though his wound, they say, still looks healthy.

"November 14th.—Sir Colin Campbell and our relief is advancing; they commence their operations to-day, and we are to assist them to-morrow. We are very badly provided with men and they are very weak from living so long on half rations and without grog. But I trust all will be well and that the relief of Lucknow will be effected this time."

Something should now be said about the arrangements for and the operations connected with the Second Relief of Lucknow, and of the part played in the latter by individuals of the Regiment both within and without the garrison.

On August 13th, 1857, General Sir Colin Campbell, who had been appointed Commander-in-Chief in India, landed in Calcutta, but his departure up-country was delayed for various reasons, so that it was not until November 1st that he arrived at Allahabad. Here he learnt that Lucknow could hold out until the end of the month. On the 3rd Sir Colin reached Cawnpore, and now he realized how critical was the position since the whole province of Oudh swarmed with rebels, while the trained soldiery of the Gwalior Contingent was only some 50 miles distant, a menace to his communications. The Chief did not, however, lose any time in preparing for an advance upon Lucknow and on November 9th he left Cawnpore, that day covering 35 miles. Next morning he received Outram's suggestions for his line of advance to the Residency, and Sir Colin now perfected his plans so as to avoid the city and the losses which Havelock had experienced in traversing its narrow and tortuous streets; he decided then to move across country to the Dilkusha Park, marching then on the Martinière and the line of the canal, keeping thereafter to the more open ground near the

OFFICERS PRESENT 25TH SEPT 1857

river. The proposed operation was an extraordinarily difficult and dangerous one, for with a force not exceeding 4,500 men of all arms the General had to rescue Outram from the midst of 60,000 trained soldiers occupying strong positions; he had to keep open his communications throughout; he had to bring out of the leaguer women and children, sick and wounded; retire then to the Alam Bagh, leaving there a force to hold that post while he hurried back again to Cawnpore and its slender garrison—and all this had to be achieved within a very limited period.

On November 13th Sir Colin's little army halted at the Alam Bagh, and henceforth the account of his operations will be drawn, so far as these concern the Madras Fusiliers' share in them, mainly from the narratives of Lieutenants Woods and Jones-Parry. The former had been left behind at Cawnpore, while Parry, who had been serving with the Turkish Contingent in the Crimean War, had been recalled from leave in England on the outbreak of the Mutiny.

Lieutenant Woods' reminiscences will first be drawn upon. "Leaving Cawnpore at length," he writes, "with detachments of 'Ours,' the 5th and 90th, this time I was under the command of Major Roger Barnston of the 90th. . . . Advancing in the direction of Lucknow the enemy was rarely seen for the first few days except at a very safe distance from the road. When half-a-mile or more from the walled enclosure, Alam Bagh, we were attacked in pretty strong force by intermingled cavalry and matchlockmen with a small gun. . . . Arrived at the Alam Bagh the officer in command, Major McIntyre of the 78th became our chief. The Residency was about 4 miles off, and we could see the smoke of the shells bursting over it and of the guns firing from both sides."

The garrison of the Alam Bagh was now further reinforced by the men of the Madras Fusiliers who had been left at Allahabad under Captain Harris.

Lieutenant Jones-Parry now takes up the story, tells us of his voyage out from England, of his arrival at Madras where he found all " singing the praises of our Regiment, Neill a sort of demi-god; money was pouring in on all sides in aid of the families of the killed, already Rs. 25,000 had been collected. The newspapers called Neill 'the Saviour of India,' for had it not been for his promptness Allahabad would have been lost. . . ."

On arrival at Cawnpore Jones-Parry, with Taylor of the Madras Fusiliers, was attached for duty, and until arrival at the Alam Bagh, to the 75th Foot, which, having been engaged in the siege and capture of Delhi, was very short of officers; and he appears to have come up with Sir Colin's force soon after it marched Lucknowwards from the Alam Bagh. "Here," he says, "met many of our brother officers, and about one hundred of our men. I was on picket that night with Taylor and Dobbs, an awful place, a ruined village in a clump of trees, with high elephant grass growing close up. . . . The Pandies came very near us and fired all night, but did not hit any of us. In the morning having had our dram and some biscuit, we started off to join the column."

The force must have presented a somewhat motley appearance; the Madras Fusiliers, 160 strong, were dressed in red quilted tunics, blue cap-covers and blue trousers; the 5th were in red with white trousers; the 90th wore white helmets and white trousers tucked into half-Wellington boots; the 93rd were dressed as on home service with bonnet and kilt; while the Sikhs were clothed from head to foot in khaki.

"The first night" (of the advance from the Alam Bagh), writes Lieutenant Woods, "we bivouacked under a *tope* of mango-trees, the canal dug by Ghazi-u-din Haidar being the only obstacle visible between us and the enemy. . . . Next morning, the 14th November, we advanced through a park called Dilkusha. Emerging from the park, whence the enemy were driven, we came to the immense building and grounds of the Martinière College. On the top of the college Sir Colin Campbell caused a semaphore to be erected so that he might signal his advance to the Residency."

Here Jones-Parry takes up the story:—"Our regiment of details, which numbered some 700 men, was ordered to occupy this building" (the Martinière), "but just as we had got comfortably settled an order came for a further advance. The object in view was the capture of a strong position known as Banks' Bungalow. The 93rd and ourselves got into column and advanced under cover of a heavy fire from Peel's guns. The storming party lay down behind the guns until a final salvo had been fired; they then rushed on, but found that in consequence of the canal having been dammed lower down, the water was so deep it was impossible to cross, and as it was getting dark we retired. . . . We now bivouacked in a large clump of trees near the Martinière and awaited further orders. We remained there that night and were much harassed by the continuous fire from Banks' Bungalow. Luckily the shots were high and did us but little damage. . . . All next day, Sunday, we lay in this wood more or less under fire. . . ."

At daybreak on November 16th arrangements were made for the final advance on Lucknow. Lieutenant Woods thus describes what he saw of the day's operations:—" The way lay through orchards with occasional greensward. The Chief waited till our battalion, the 93rd, the Sikhs and the guns had closed up; evidently more serious work was to commence. . . . When we turned out of the orchards into a lane, at right angles to our line of march, the lead began to whizz across from the loopholed walls of the Sikandra Bagh, a high-walled enclosure, though the hedge on our right afforded pretty good shelter. From a large gap, however, about five yards wide, we could see one end of the building whence came spluttering smoke, fire and bullets. One or two wounded men, and a sentry posted here to warn all comers, were scarcely necessary to make us scuttle across this opening, for the invisible enemy behind loopholes were close to our flank.

" Continuing to the end of the lane, I was with the last section of the Fusiliers when we reached an open broad road leading towards the Residency. Here Sir Colin had ordered a gun to breach the wall of the Sikandra Bagh, about 200 yards off. To effect this it was necessary to drag the gun above a smooth mound forming an abrupt termination to the hedges, at right angles to the open roadway. The Chief turned to me and gave his instructions, whereupon my men, scarcely waiting to hear the order, slung their rifles and pulled up the gun in about 15 seconds to his evident and expressed admiration. There was absolutely no cover for the gun nor for those who worked it, and bullets rained like hail on the metal. . . . The Chief . . . sent us to join our comrades across the broad road where we got under cover of some huts in front of the building about to be assaulted. He kept the 93rd in the lane where we had all been temporarily jammed. . . . After about half-an-hour's pounding, Lieutenant Lawrence Graeme of 'Ours,' orderly officer to Barnston, came to say the 93rd were about to assault by the breach at the corner and we were to force the gateway if possible.

"I went towards the gateway with Lieutenants Dobbs and Duncan and a few of our men. Not a soul was visible between us and the reddish walls pierced with loopholes. Peeping through the cracks of the gate, I descried, 50 yards in front of me, a 6 or 9-pounder pointing, with a company of red-coated sepoys drawn up in good order behind it. I said to Graeme who was close at hand—'Look out for grape, there is a gun in front of us.' Irish and Scotch sergeants and privates now came and crowded the gateway, the only place not loopholed inside. The circular towers on each side of it were full of holes, however, so I ran round that on the left to examine an iron grating which I hoped might be pulled out and then the bricks knocked away to gain an entrance. But I found the masonry too strong. Darby Cronley, a Madras Fusilier, who had followed me, said it was an impossibility. I turned back to the gateway again, and as we passed the loopholes my comrade fell stone dead like a dropped handkerchief. . . .

"I now pushed the double gates with all my strength but they merely swung back a few inches. A gun had been sent for, but before its arrival one of our men placed his Enfield against what seemed to be the rivet of the obstructing bar of the gate and blew it away in a moment. Without further loss of time the hive was broken into, and three or four Fusiliers bayoneted every sword-bearing and shield-carrying Ghazi who resisted. . . ."

Privates Leahy and J. Smith of the "Blue Caps" were the first men through the gateway, the latter gaining the Victoria Cross.

STREET FIGHTING: MADRAS FUSILIERS LEADING TO THE RESIDENCY.

FIGHTING AT THE SHAH NUJJEF

The story is taken up at this point by Lieutenant Woods :—
"Bullets were raining in every direction and these soon made the gateway a kind of target for the enemy who were now in the further turrets. I saw a man shot through the ankle; a private of 'Ours' told me his bayonet had stuck in a Ghazi's breast bone and he could scarcely pull it out again, and one had his finger chopped off while pushing open the gate. . . . Once inside the place was like a shambles. . . . Resistance had now ceased and all around lay dead or mortally wounded men. In the evening I computed the number of the enemy killed and placed it as 1,800 within the mark; really over 2,500 were counted and buried.

"The great slaughter completed, we moved on just off the left of the road, and waited while guns from across the river continued to annoy us and shells burst all over the plain. . . . We now made further progress for about a quarter of a mile, and then sat down while the sailors attempted to breach the thick outer walls of the Tomb and Mosque known as the Shah Nujjef. . . . The pounding seemed interminable, but the sailors seemed to enjoy the fun and did not suffer much owing to a belt of undergrowth or plantation obstructing the enemy's view. Before long, however, from the Mosque itself, from the 32nd Mess House, and from the other bank of the river that ran close by, missiles of all sorts began to shower, bullets predominating. . . . The fire from the mosque became rapidly fiercer, and Jones-Parry and Dobbs were sent under Taylor to a still more dangerous spot close to the rebels, in order to keep down their musketry fire and protect the sailors."

Jones-Parry now states that "Sir Colin called for a party to go and burn down a row of mud huts which served as a cover to the enemy's skirmishers. I was near at the time and asked for volunteers; nine of my men came out. . . . The distance we had to traverse was insignificant. As soon as I got into the first hut I put the port-fire to the roof, fired the grass and then went on to the next. But unfortunately no sooner was a blaze well established than my men seized lighted brands right and left and set fire to every hut round. We were instantly in a circle of fire. The dry material blazed like tinder, one of my men's pouches blew up, so that between fire and smoke it was impossible to go further and I ordered a retreat. . . . Up to this time we had acted simply as a gun guard, we had now to join the remainder of the regiment of details and take part in the forward movement. . . . The whole force was on the outskirts of a plain, when the 93rd, covered by our battalion as skirmishers and protected by the incessant firing of the heavy guns, were ordered to form line. My company, under Captain Taylor and Lieutenant Dobbs, was in support. Then with a cheer the Highlanders, led by Sir Colin himself, advanced with a rush. . . . The fire was hellish. In a second every field officer was dismounted, either wounded or with his horse shot under him. We just reached the half-burned huts. To have advanced further would have been madness, so we were ordered to lie down under such cover as we could find. . . . In this advance Lieutenant Dobbs was mortally wounded; a bullet went clean through his leg, shattering the bone and piercing the other leg. We carried him under cover and left him in charge of a sergeant, having said goodbye for ever. . . .

"On entering the Shah Nujjef I saw what a strong place it was and how small our chances of breaching it were. A party of the 93rd was told off to hold the place, and the remainder of the force retired to bivouac near the Sikandra Bagh. The loss in this one operation was 150 out of 800.

"We were scarcely settled down when Sir Colin came up. He asked for Captain Taylor and congratulated him on the work done by the detachment, making special mention of the burning of the huts by the party under my command, and as a compliment said he wished the company to form his guard that night."

Woods supplements Parry's account of the attack on the Shah Nujjef by saying "I only saw the results a little later, for though I was at the assault, I was not in the actual mêlée, being stationed by orders a little distance off. Captain Taylor's party of Fusiliers was for hours in more dangerous proximity to the Shah Nujjef than any of the force, and, though few in number, they irritated the

[*Photo, Gale & Polden, Ltd.*

LUCKNOW PICTURE AND DRUM.

The drum was used to beat the Reveillé of the "Blue Caps" all through the fighting, culminating in the Relief of Lucknow, September 25th, 1857.

enemy by drawing down his fire upon themselves, as was intended. . . . We slept on the open maidan under the stars, in a frost, four of us beneath one military cloak.

"Next day our attention turned to the 32nd Mess House on the right-hand side of the road, up which we were progressing towards the Residency, our goal. This was a building of modern architecture, like a large three-storied London house After it had been bombarded for a time by Peel's guns, a message came from Sir Colin at 2 p.m. that he wanted volunteers for a particular service. Taylor called his company out with Jones-Parry, Reginald Parry and myself. We were drawn up in the road when Sir Colin rode up. He said he was pleased to find we were for this duty and told us that before leaving England he had dined with Her Majesty, who had spoken to him particularly of the gallant deeds of the Madras Fusiliers. He then asked for volunteers to carry two beams and six planks across the open to the Mess House, which he told us was surrounded by a moat. He wanted four men for each beam and two for each plank, which made twenty men, and an officer for each party of four, that is five officers. Their duty would be to place the two beams across the moat and the planks across the beams, each set of men to jump into the moat for protection as their work was accomplished. A firing party would blaze at the windows to assist and he would " recommend the two seniors of the survivors to Her Majesty for the honour of the Victoria Cross." A bugler was to accompany us at whose signal a general assault was to follow. As he uttered this long drawn out speech I watched his wrinkled old face scanning each of us minutely, probably recalling his own youthful sensations when leading a forlorn hope in the Peninsular War when in the 9th Foot.

"He had scarcely come to a pause in his harangue when a batch of officers and men stepped out. . . . It is difficult to describe the mingled disappointment and relief when Sir William Peel came up and suggested that he might be allowed to put a few 68-pounder shells through the windows of the building. He pierced the place through and through in such a way that the enemy fled.

"Almost the last building now separating us from Havelock's command was the Moti Mahal, a palatial residence close upon the river whose walled gardens extended to the road up which we were going. This place was taken by Captain Wolseley and his company of the 90th."

Meanwhile in the beleaguered city the generals had not been idle. Sir Colin had signalled his advance from the Martinière and Outram and Havelock had immediately made their plans of action. As soon as the relieving force approached the Sikandra Bagh, the mines laid under the outer walls of the palace garden were exploded, the walls were shelled, and by nightfall on November 16th the whole of the palace buildings were in the hands of the Lucknow garrison.

Corporal Hosey, Madras Fusiliers, was particularly mentioned for this mining work by Captain Crommlin, R.E.; Lieutenant Hargood, A.D.C., was also mentioned in despatches.

After the capture of the Mess House and the Moti Mahal on the 17th, the relieving force and the garrison were only separated by a narrow open space, and here, " on the sward sloping down from the Mess House stood Sir Colin Campbell, and a blaze of shot and musketry from the Kaisar Bagh rose upon them as the three veterans met. This was a very happy meeting and a cordial shaking of hands took place. On Sir J. Outram privation had not told so heavily, but the hand of death* was on General Havelock, though he lighted up a little on being told for the first time that he was Sir Henry. Loud rang the cheers as the news sped along from post to post that the three Generals had met. ' The relief of the besieged garrison had been accomplished.' In these few terse words the Commander-in-Chief announced the accomplishment of a brilliant achievement, guided by a master hand, and brought to a successful close by the pluck of the British soldier. ' Every man in the force,' wrote Sir Colin, ' had exerted himself to the utmost, and now met with his reward.' "†

* He was seized with dysentery on November 21st.
† Forrest, Vol. II, pp. 166, 167.

OFFICERS PRESENT SIR COLINS RELIEF 16TH TO 22 NOV 1857

EVACUATION OF THE RESIDENCY

"Thus" says Jones-Parry, "after three days' continuous fighting, our object had been accomplished!"

Sir Colin's immediate task was indeed accomplished, but another, equally difficult and dangerous, awaited him. He had certainly suffered fewer casualties in his force than had Havelock, but his numbers were still far too few to hope successfully to cope with the huge and well-trained rebel armies still in the field. It was therefore decided as speedily as possible to evacuate the Residency, to remove all non-combatants to a place of safety, and to destroy everything that could not be carried away. Of the part taken by the "Blue Caps" in the events of the five days that elapsed between the entry of the relieving force into Lucknow and the successful withdrawal of the garrison, Lieutenant Woods' narrative supplies some interesting details. He says:—"Captain Taylor and his company occupied the 32nd Mess House for a time, very near the walls of the Kaisar Bagh, within which walls the enemy's hordes were gathered, guarding spoil and expecting us to attack. But though this was not our intention, we fostered their mistake by threatening to assault for the next three days, while preparations were made to withdraw the supplies in the garrison to the Dilkusha Park, 2 miles in our rear. On one occasion Taylor's men were rather startled to see a large body of the rebel troops emerge from their post through a gap in the walls. They expected an order to retire immediately from such superior force, but the Captain merely said to one of them in his usual slow drawl—'Lend me your rifle,' and shot one of the leaders. Then 'lend me another,' and a second fell at the head of the advancing column. The previous cries of 'Chalo Bahadur!' (Come on, my brave fellow!) were now altered to 'Bhago, Bhai' (run away, brothers), and were obeyed in confusion, accelerated by the fire of the Fusiliers who now crowded the large unprotected windows. . . . During this time the way was being prepared for the unobserved exit of the women and children. All existing cover was made use of and a covered way was erected wherever necessary. The greater number passed out of the Residency on the night of the 19th November through the Moti Mahal garden on their way to the Dilkusha. . . . On the 22nd we were told that we were to return to the Martinière as soon as no one was left between us and the enemy. In the middle of a dark night the naval guns were withdrawn as quietly as possible, and we made a slow retrograde movement for hours, when at length, tired out, we halted and lay down among some bushes."

The original garrison marched out the first, and the Madras Fusiliers, in recognition of the services of General Neill, and of the part they had taken in the first relief and subsequent defence of Lucknow, were allowed to cover the retirement. They were reduced to less than a quarter of their original number, only Captains Galwey and Raikes, Lieutenants Cleland and Dale and Surgeon Arthur, with 80 men being fit for duty. "When I told off my men," so Dale records, "one man was missing and could not be found. Later on, when I went back with my Colour-Sergeant, Cunningham, to withdraw the sentries who had been left behind, and to fire dropping shots to deceive the enemy, we still could not find him, but eventually he turned up before we left. He had got into some corner and gone to sleep."

The retreat was carried out with wonderful skill and without molestation, the enemy being quite deceived, and the whole of the troops had reached their allotted posts at the Dilkusha and Martinière before dawn on November 23rd. Three days earlier General Havelock had been carried to the Dilkusha in a dying condition and on the 24th his body was borne to the Alam Bagh and there buried, he having died that morning. "Nobler life had never happier close," writes Sir George Forrest. "Never was a man more widely mourned or more honoured in his death. On Christmas Day, 1857, news reached England of the Relief of Lucknow, and on January 7th the joy of a nation was turned into mourning by the tidings of Havelock's death. . . . But Havelock belonged to a race that is not confined to a small island, and wherever our English is spoken the news of his death brought sorrow, and men said, 'I am of Havelock's blood.' Let us never forget that the flags in New York were hung at half-mast high when Havelock died."

THE ALAM BAGH

Major Stephenson of the Madras Fusiliers had also been brought from the Residency on November 20th and died from the effects of his wound on the following day.

On November 24th Sir Colin Campbell moved on to the Alam Bagh where Sir James Outram joined him next day, and on the 27th the Commander-in-Chief with 3,000 men set out for Cawnpore, taking with him the women and children brought away from Lucknow, and the wounded of his own and Outram's forces; Sir James was left to hold the Alam Bagh until Sir Colin Campbell should be free to complete the conquest of Oudh.

The troops left at the Alam Bagh constituted the 1st Division of the Army and were made up as follows :—

Artillery	Europeans 332	Natives	108
Military Train	,, 221		
Volunteer Cavalry	,, 67		
12th Irregular Cavalry	,, 3	,,	40
Oudh Irregular Cavalry	,, 1	,,	37
5th Fusiliers	,, 526		
75th Foot	,, 355		
78th Highlanders	,, 439		
84th Foot	,, 431		
90th Light Infantry	,, 591		
Madras Fusiliers	,, 411		
Ferozepore Regiment	,, 5	,,	295
27th Madras Native Infantry	,, 9	,,	457
Madras Sappers	,, 4	,,	110
Total	Europeans 3395	Natives	1047

"As the Alam Bagh was capable of accommodating only a small garrison, he (Outram) had, after establishing a strong picquet there, encamped his main force a mile in rear of the building itself, in the open plain across the Cawnpore road, and he protected his camp by batteries and *abattis*, and by judiciously turning two or three swamps into account. . . . These defensive works, not connected by a continuous trench, occupied a circuit of about

11 miles which extended from a village to the left of the main road to the old and tumbled fort of Jellalabad on the extreme right, in which was placed a sapper picquet and part of the park, the rest being in rear of our camp. The advanced posts were within gunshot range of the outposts of a vast city. Such was the position which for three months Outram held against 120,000 organized troops with more than 30 guns, besides the armed and turbulent scum of a population of 700,000 souls. His force amounted to considerably less than 4,000* of all ranks. Of these the forts of Alam Bagh and Jellalabad absorbed about 600 men; brigade and camp duties 450 more. And thus, after deducting sick and wounded, there remained of all arms and ranks, European and Native, little more than 2,000 available for action during the absence of the convoys, averaging 450 men, which we had fortnightly to send to Cawnpore."†

Extracts may here be given, in concluding this chapter, from the despatches written at this time by the Commander-in-Chief and by General Outram. In one dated Headquarters, La Martinière, November 23rd, Sir Colin wrote:—

"*The Commander-in-Chief has reason to be thankful to the force he conducted for the relief of the garrison of Lucknow. Hastily assembled, fatigued by forced marches, but animated by a common feeling of determination to accomplish the duty before them, all ranks of this force were compensated for their small number in the execution of a most difficult duty by unceasing exertions. From the morning of the 16th till last night, the whole force has been on outlying picquet, never out of fire, and covering an immense extent of ground, to permit the garrison to retire scatheless and in safety covered by the whole of the relieving force.*

"*That ground was won by fighting as hard as it ever fell to the lot of the Commander-in-Chief to witness, it being necessary to bring up the same men over and over again to fresh attacks; and it is with the greatest gratification that his Excellency declares he never saw men behave better. The storming of the Secundra Bagh and the Shah*

---

* From the foregoing " State " this seems an under-estimate.
† Forrest, Vol. II, pp. 272-273.

Nujeef has never been surpassed in daring, and the success of it was most brilliant and complete. The movement of retreat of last night by which the final rescue of the garrison was effected was a model of discipline and exactness. The consequence was that the enemy was completely deceived, and the force retired by a narrow tortuous lane, the only line of retreat open, in the face of 50,000 enemies without molestation. . . ."

Sir James Outram, in a despatch, dated Alam Bagh, November 25th, said:—

"*I cannot conclude this report without expressing to His Excellency my intense admiration of the noble spirit displayed by all ranks and grades of the force since we entered Lucknow. Themselves placed in a state of siege, suddenly reduced to scanty and unsavoury rations, denied all the little luxuries, such as tea, sugar, rum and tobacco, which by constant use had become to them almost necessaries of life, smitten in many cases by the same scorbutic affections and other evidences of debility which prevailed amongst the original garrison, compelled to engage in laborious operations, exposed to constant danger and kept ever on the alert, their spirits and cheerfulness, zeal and discipline, seemed to rise to the occasion. Never could there have been a force more free from grumblers, more cheerful, more willing or more earnest.*

"*Amongst the sick and wounded this glorious spirit was, if possible, still more conspicuous than amongst those fit for duty. It was a painful sight to see so many noble fellows maimed and suffering, and denied those comforts of which they stood so much in need. But it was truly delightful, and made one proud of his countrymen, to observe the heroic fortitude and hearty cheerfulness with which all was borne. . . ."*

In these despatches Major Stephenson, Captain Galwey and Lieutenant Hargood were mentioned.

The following are those of the Madras Fusiliers upon whom the Victoria Cross was conferred, with details of their special acts of bravery:—

London Gazette of June 18th, 1858.—Sergeant Patrick Mahoney. For distinguished gallantry (whilst doing duty with the Volunteer

Cavalry) *in aiding in the capture of the Regimental Colour of the 1st Regiment Native Infantry, at Mangulwar on the 21st September, 1857.*

Private John Ryan.—In addition to the above act (assisting Pte. McManus, 5th Fusiliers, to save Captain Arnold) Private Ryan distinguished himself throughout the day by his intrepidity, and especially devoted himself to rescuing the wounded in the neighbourhood from being massacred. He was most anxious to visit every doolie. Date of act of bravery, 26th September, 1857.

Private Thomas Duffy.—For his cool intrepidity and daring skill, whereby a 24-pounder gun was saved from falling into the hands of the enemy. Date of act of bravery, 27th September, 1857.

London Gazette of December 24th, 1858. Private J. Smith.— For having been one of the first to try and enter the gateway on the north side of the Secundra Bagh. On the gateway being burst open he was one of the first to enter and was surrounded by the enemy. He received a sword-cut on the head, a bayonet wound on the left side, and a contusion from the butt-end of a musket on the right shoulder, notwithstanding which he fought his way out and continued to perform his duties for the rest of the day. Date of act of bravery, 16th November, 1857.

CHAPTER V

1858.

DEFENCE OF THE ALAM BAGH AND RE-CAPTURE OF LUCKNOW—THE END OF THE MUTINY AND RETURN TO MADRAS.

DURING the comparatively long period that elapsed before Sir Colin Campbell was ready to undertake the re-capture of Lucknow, the small force stationed at the Alam Bagh under Outram remained constantly on the alert; and here the position occupied by the Madras Fusiliers in the general scheme of defence was beside the road in the rear of the second line of batteries.

A few days after the Commander-in-Chief had left with the main force for Cawnpore, Lieutenant Dale was sent with a party of 50 Fusiliers to a light gun battery on the left of the main road, which was armed with two 9-pounders and manned by a detachment of gunners under a sergeant. The enemy came out in great force, masking the fire from the Bagh on their left; the heavy guns opened fire and the two 9-pounders replied most effectively, the trails being depressed until a range of 1,900 yards was obtained—an unorthodox procedure in gun practice of that day which seriously aroused the ire of Colonel Napier, the Chief of the Staff!

Skirmishes were of very frequent occurrence, and between December, 1857, and the end of February, 1858, no fewer than seven unsuccessful attempts were made by the rebels to take the British position by assault; in the first of these, on December 22nd, 4 guns, several elephants and much ammunition were captured.

Christmas Day passed undisturbed and the Fusiliers found they had not been forgotten by their friends in Madras, many useful and acceptable presents having been sent them, including many bales of much-needed clothing.

On January 12th, 1858, there was a second serious attack on Outram's position, and in this action the Madras Fusiliers played a prominent part. Captain William Down, who had been on furlough when the Mutiny broke out and had now rejoined, commanded at this time the left-centre outpost and was successful in dislodging the enemy from a grove of trees with his skirmishers, while from the Alam Bagh itself the enemy was driven back by the fire of Maude's guns and the rifles of 200 Madras Fusiliers there stationed. Of this affair Jones-Parry gives the following account:—

"We breakfasted at daybreak and then quietly waited for events to shape themselves. The enemy evidently had good information as to our movements for they generally selected days for an attack when our force was weakened by escorts for convoy duty. On such occasions we used generally to send over 500 men, consequently our absolute fighting force, irrespective of picquets, was only 1,500 men; with this we resisted an attack along the whole of our front by 30,000 men. The attack commenced on the left and was brilliantly overcome by the left brigade; at the same time a very strong force advanced to the half-way picquet between the right brigade and Jellalabad. Our two weak regiments went to the relief with 2 guns and obliged them to retire. In so doing they were exposed to a heavy fire from the Alam Bagh.

"No sooner was this action over than a new attack was made on the left, chiefly by cavalry, and was only discontinued at 4 p.m. Then news arrived that our bridge post, 12 miles in rear, was threatened, and 100 poor worn-out fellows had to march out to reinforce the troops there. So serious was the attack this day, and so completely did it show the power of the enemy to annoy us, and the force at their disposal to bring against us, that Sir James asked for one, or even half a battalion more to reinforce us and save us being left so weak when convoy duty was imposed on us."

It is evidently of this action, though his letter is undated, that Lieutenant Hargood of the Madras Fusiliers writes; he was now A.D.C. to Outram:—"Yesterday," he says, "the enemy made an attack on our camp; they came out between 30 and 40,000

DEFENCE OF THE ALAM BAGH

strong, and made a simultaneous attack in four divisions, but wherever they attacked we had guns placed and they were driven back with the loss of 400 killed and wounded. The casualties on our side—2 Sikhs slightly wounded, and 2 men of my Regiment also wounded, one of which will lose his leg. The casualties in my Regiment the last six months have been—dead, killed and wounded, 401. It is a very severe loss considering we landed in Bengal 842 strong. Captain Spurgin is quite well."

On January 16th the enemy made an attack on the Jellalabad picquet, near which was an outpost of 200 of the Madras Fusiliers under Captain Grant. Lieutenant Dale, with 100 men, was immediately detached to cover the right in a concealed position, but things at one time looked so serious that parties were detailed to be ready to cut the tent ropes and so let the tents fall flat in case the enemy should try to fire them. This attack, like the preceding ones, was beaten back. In an affair on January 28th Privates Warthen and Finnis of the Madras Fusiliers were wounded, but for some weeks now there was no very serious fighting.

Jones-Parry's "Memories" give some interesting details of the life led by the "Blue Caps" while wearily waiting for Sir Colin Campbell's return.

"The right brigade to which I belonged consisted of H.M's. 5th, 84th, and ourselves. . . . The left brigade comprised H.M's. 75th, 78th Highlanders and 90th L.I. In the centre were the artillery and headquarter staff, while in addition to these infantry regiments we had four squadrons chiefly composed of mounted men of the Military Train fresh from England, who had been hurriedly put through some sort of drill. Add to this three field batteries, only one of which was horsed, the other batteries, together with a garrison battery, being drawn by bullocks; we also had a company of Madras Sappers. . . . Luckily we had on our flanks certain impassable swamps, which protected us in a measure; we had well-seasoned men with stout hearts, and, above all, a General in whom we had confidence and who never let anyone feel that there was the slightest cause for anxiety. . . . The first thing to be done was to make ourselves as safe as we could. After the positions of picquets had been selected by the general and his able chief of the staff, Colonel Napier, we were told to use the pick and shovel as much as the rifle and bayonet, so with earthworks, trenches, *abattis*, etc., we entrenched ourselves much after the fashion of Zulus and soon got to understand our duties. We had about a dozen picquets in posts to hold and to man; these required about 800 men by day and over 1,000 by night. . . . It must also be mentioned that we were absolutely devoid of means of transport, we were consequently immobile, and, had any disaster occurred, we could have done nothing but relinquish our camp and retire on Cawnpore fighting every inch of the way. So great was our paucity of officers, owing to deaths, that mere lads just from school had to be put on duty before they had learnt their drill, and often these public-school boys commanded parties which, in ordinary circumstances, would only have been entrusted to officers of great experience. . . . It must not be supposed that we were ever free from annoyance at the hands of the enemy; they kept up a fire more or less day and night, but we were absolutely indifferent to it. . . ."

On February 15th, 16th, 17th and 21st the enemy renewed his attacks upon Outram's position, but was each time repulsed with loss. Of the attempts on the 16th and 17th Jones-Parry writes :—

"On the 16th in the morning they sent out cavalry to try and cut off a convoy, and in the evening about 6 o'clock they commenced a regular attack. It started on the left and the firing was very heavy. Being beaten back there they tried the Alam Bagh, and we were obliged to reinforce it; finally, they retired amid a shower of shell. The firing ceased, that is as much as it ever ceased, about 9.30 p.m. and then we were all able to get a little dinner. . . .

"At 10 a.m. on the 17th they began an attack on our right at Jellalabad, but were driven back; we remained under arms until 1 o'clock. It was a cool day so it did not much matter. In the evening they tried to turn us out again, but we fired lazily at them with big guns and that disheartened them. Our losses as usual were very slight. . . ."

On February 26th a final determined assault was made on the small British force. The Jellalabad picquet was first attacked, but after a sharp struggle the enemy was routed with the loss of 2 guns. Three hours later they again moved out and again suffered severely, while Outram's loss was only 5 killed and 14 wounded. There were no casualties this day among the 132 Madras Fusiliers under Major Galwey, and this was the last attempt made at the capture of the Alam Bagh position, for, on hearing of the near approach of the force under Sir Colin Campbell, the enemy began to confine his energies to extending and perfecting the defences of the city of Lucknow. Of this day's action Jones-Parry tells the following :—

"We fought this battle out during a most awful dust storm, it was simply blinding; both sides ceased firing for neither could see a yard. We piled arms and stood easy. During this interregnum a very funny fellow of my company, named Jimmy Hurd, professionally a dog-stealer in Whitechapel, went up to a very zealous newly-promoted Corporal and said :—' Come, Corporal, own you're a damned coward and would like to run away out of this?' There was something irresistibly comic in Hurd's face, and I am sure that most of us felt he had pretty nearly hit off our sentiments. The Corporal did not see the joke, and said ' Back to the ranks, Sir ! ' "

"For more than twelve weeks he" (Outram) "had with a small body of British soldiers gallantly held the extended position which he was by circumstances compelled to take up, against 120,000 rebels, mainly disciplined soldiers, and had repulsed their fiercest attacks. . . . Outram's success was due not only to his quality as an able and daring commander, but also to his all-enduring fortitude, his unflagging cheerfulness, and all-embracing sympathy as a man. . . . Full justice was not done by Sir Colin Campbell or the Chief of the Staff to Outram's defence of the Alam Bagh, which must be viewed as a fine example of courage and good conduct, and will always stand out as a glorious episode in the annals of the Indian Mutiny."*

* Forrest, Vol. II, pp. 290–292.

In a despatch dated February 28th, 1858, General Sir James Outram wrote :—" From first to last, all alike, officers and men, have acquitted themselves most admirably, and I cannot therefore refrain from this recapitulation of the services of my comrades, and that before the commencement of the approaching operations, lest it may be out of my power to testify hereafter to their devotion, discipline and bravery. I am certain that neither His Excellency nor their country will forget the heroic troops whom it has been my proud privilege to command, and to His Excellency's kind consideration I now commend them."

While in later letters, dated Calcutta, May 11th and 24th, to the Chief of the Staff, General Outram expressed regret at the accidental omissions of the special services of certain regiments and individual officers. Herein Sir James expressed his deep regret at having unintentionally done injustice to the 1st Madras Fusiliers, " a regiment which had by its unvarying zeal, steadiness and bravery placed me under the deepest obligations "; and he specially mentioned Major Galwey, Captains Raikes, Grant and Spurgin.

While the enemy was occupied in strengthening his position at Lucknow, Sir Colin Campbell was arranging measures for the reduction of the city, and the force at the Alam Bagh was anxiously awaiting his arrival, and that of the reinforcements which from time to time were sent thither.

On February 14th Jones-Parry wrote :—" Two companies of the Royal Sapper Corps arrived this morning, they will be very useful in getting things ready for the siege. All the rest of the force is ready and only awaits Sir Colin's order to move on this place. Three infantry divisions have been told off, and they consist of 21 regiments numbering, say, 15,000 Europeans; then there are the artillery, engineers and cavalry. . . . We shall have plenty of men for fighting, but not enough to invest the place properly, that is, so as to let no one escape . . . our division is the 1st and is commanded by Sir James Outram. It consists of three Brigades, viz. :—

" 1st Brigade, under Colonel Russell, composed of H.M's. 5th Fusiliers, 84th and 1st Madras Fusiliers.

ADVANCE ON LUCKNOW

"2nd Brigade, under Colonel Franklyn, consisting of H.M's. 78th Highlanders, 90th Light Infantry, and the Ferozepore Regiment of Sikhs.

"3rd Brigade, under Colonel Hamilton, with the 38th, 53rd and another Queen's Regiment.

"Stores and munitions of war are arriving daily, commissariat stores are literally pouring in, and the engineers are hard at work making up pontoons, etc. February 19th.—We have had a good reinforcement of officers to our Regiment. Young Seton, who was A.D.C. to Havelock and who was wounded at Cawnpore, has returned. February 24th.—The Bengal Fusiliers came in all right and are a great addition to our force. Sir James Outram told us yesterday that he expected Hodson's Sikh Horse, two squadrons of H.M's. 7th Hussars and a troop of Horse Artillery in to-day, and then if these rascals dare to leave their entrenchments they will surely catch it. . . . We have got our carriage issued so that our move must take place soon. General Franks has gained a victory at Tanda and captured 6 guns. . . . Brigadier-General Hope Grant gained a victory to-day and took 2 guns, and Sir James has gone out to-day with all his cavalry and a horse-battery to try to intercept the fugitives escaping into Lucknow after being beaten by General Grant. Nothing could be more cheering than the news from all sides."

On February 28th Sir Colin, having seen the last of his troops start, left Cawnpore and marched to Buntheere, where the whole army was encamped, and on March 2nd he set out with a portion of his force across the level, well-cultivated plain that stretched towards Lucknow; on the same day he occupied Dilkusha House and Park and thus secured a base for further operations. On the 3rd and 4th the remainder of his troops arrived, while on the 5th he was joined by a column under General Franks from Sultanpore. His army now numbered 20,000 men with 180 guns—a more powerful British Army than had ever before been seen in India. For the third time since the outbreak of the Mutiny Lucknow was the scene of fierce encounters and desperate conflicts, which lasted for nearly three weeks. On March 14th Sir Colin regained possession of the Kaisar Bagh and on the 21st the rebels were driven from their last position.

The Madras Fusiliers were not engaged in the main struggle to recover the different fortified posts in the city, but they none-the-less played their part in the conflict. At the outset of the new campaign the troops at the Alam Bagh remained stationary, being employed in keeping open the communications with Cawnpore; but on March 15th the "Blue Caps" marched to the Dilkusha and took up ground near the Martinière, not far from the spot where the Battalion of Detachments had come under fire on their previous entry into Lucknow in November. On the 16th "we got an order," writes Jones-Parry, "to proceed to the 32nd Mess House, near the Kaisar Bagh, which, though very strongly fortified, had fallen into our hands without any trouble. We had scarcely got up to the place when we found the 23rd Fusiliers following us, so our Major (Galwey) imagining something was in the wind, halted on the main road instead of going up to the Mess House.

"It appeared that the Residency was to be attacked that day and we hoped to have formed part of the attacking column, but we were ordered to remain as a reserve. . . . From the Mess House tower we could see the advance admirably and a very pretty sight it was. . . . The column wound through the different buildings till they came to the Residency and then the guns opened fire. The effect of the shot was soon evident for the Pandy Cavalry and Infantry began to swarm on the Iron Bridge in full retreat. They were apparently headed on the other side of the river, for they began scampering back again, and then our fellows gave chase and they dispersed far and wide. The column continued to push on until it had taken the Residency, the stronghold known as the Machi Bhawan and the stone bridge, thus capturing quite half of the city without losing a man. . . .

"That evening the Fusiliers were ordered to take the palace of the ex-minister of Oudh. It was exciting as we were now advancing on a part of the city hitherto unknown to us. . . . We advanced

OFFICERS PRESENT DURING THE MUTINY, 1857-58.

to the large mosque in the centre of the bazaar and then halted for the column to form up; we were this time placed between the 79th and the 23rd and at last started off. We went winding through several streets. Suddenly we halted, the order was passed down for water-carriers to go to the front, and just as they were going a dull, heavy noise was heard and we were enveloped in smoke. A mine had been discovered and before the engineers could damp the powder some lurking blackguard had sprung it. The cry was then raised for doolies and stretchers. I am sure that no one ever saw such an awful sight. . . We finally got on, passing through narrow lanes, where one might be shot any moment from a loophole. Our destination was the palace of the ex-Grand Vizier; on arrival I was left with half a company to hold a gateway at the end of one of these lanes, whilst the others went on and got into the palace without any opposition. . . . The main body of the Regiment occupied the Minister's palace. Ours was not a very disagreeable post, but it was a nervous one, for I knew that the place was infested by *budmashes*, and we were in a labyrinth of narrow lanes and alleys, unlike anything ever seen in a European town. . . ."

The capture of the city and its environs once complete, the Madras Fusiliers were posted to the Begum Kothi, where they remained for three months.

At the end of March General Sir James Outram returned to Calcutta to take his seat as Military Member of the Supreme Council, but before leaving Lucknow he addressed the following letter to Major Galwey, commanding the Madras Fusiliers:—

"My Dear Major,

"*In the prospect of a speedy removal to Calcutta whither I proceed in a few days to assume my seat in Council, I would fain in my farewell order to the Division have given expression as well of the gratitude I feel towards yourself and the officers and men of your noble Regiment for the valuable services they have rendered while under my command, as of my intense admiration of their heroic courage in the field and their good conduct in quarters. But my official order is necessarily of too general a nature to admit of particularizing individual officers and corps; I can do no more therefore than beg you to accept this private expression of the esteem in which I hold you, and request you to inform your officers that I shall ever retain them in grateful and affectionate remembrance. That every blessing may attend you all is the heart-felt wish, my dear Major,*

"Of yours, etc.,
"James Outram."

General Outram's goodwill for the "Blue Caps" found further and outward expression after he had left Lucknow, for in a letter dated May 16th Jones-Parry records that "Sir James Outram has sent up £300 worth of books, racquets, cricket bats and balls, etc., to the Regiment, and has ordered all the leading papers to be sent regularly to the sick. He says in his letter to the Commanding Officer that he is only too glad to be able to record his admiration and appreciation of the services of the Regiment."

The "sick" above alluded to were now very numerous, small-pox was rife among the force and claimed many victims. Jones-Parry, writing on May 15th, tells how he had been sent for to hospital to make a will for Private Daniell of his company who died two days later from this fell scourge; while on the 29th he says:—

"Poor Hargood died a few days ago of a severe fever, he was only ill two days. He was a lion of a soldier, and had been in everything from the first to the last; he had been Havelock's A.D.C. and was then made Outram's; Havelock loved him and gave him as a dying charge to Outram. Poor boy, bullets are charmed, but the unerring finger of sickness was pointed too surely at him. Another good soldier gone!"

Lieutenant Hargood had only lately returned to regimental duty from service on the personal staff of General Outram.

On June 12th General Hope Grant attacked a body of some 16,000 rebels who had taken up a strong position at Nawabganj, about 16 miles from Lucknow, gaining a decisive victory and capturing 6 guns. Four days later, on the 16th, the Madras

Fusiliers were ordered to join the force at Nawabganj, and here they spent the following month in some discomfort owing to the heavy rain which fell. On July 22nd Sir Hope Grant moved out towards Fyzabad to relieve a local raja, one Man Singh, who having at one time taken part with the rebels had later returned to his former allegiance and was now suffering from the enmity his action had aroused among his friends, and was actually besieged in his fort at Shahganj. General Grant took with him the 7th Hussars, 500 of Hodson's Horse, 12 light guns, the 2nd Battalion Rifle Brigade, the Madras Fusiliers and the 1st Punjab Infantry, and the approach of this column was sufficient to cause the dispersal of Man Singh's attackers.

Sir Hope Grant now marched on Fyzabad, which was occupied without loss. Here the force was reorganized and the Madras Fusiliers were placed with the 7th Hussars, the 5th Punjab Infantry, a troop of Horse Artillery, and some Madras Sappers, under command of Brigadier-General Horsford, and this small column was on August 9th directed to march on Sultanpore, where the rebels, lately engaged in besieging Raja Man Singh, were said to be assembling in some strength. Rain had been falling for some days, the track was very heavy and the sun strong, and some of the troops newly arrived from England suffered severely. "Not so the seasoned old Madras Fusiliers to any extent worth mentioning," so Lieutenant Woods hastens to assure us!

On August 13th Horsford encountered and defeated the rebels, drove them across the Gumti and occupied Sultanpore, but was unable to follow up his success as he had no bridging material, and the enemy had destroyed or removed all the boats. On the 22nd General Grant came up with reinforcements, rafts were constructed and preparations made for transporting the force to the right bank. By the 24th all was in readiness, and early on the next morning Lieutenant Dale with 50 men was sent across the river to cover the passage of the rest of the Regiment, afterwards pushing on and taking up a position as advanced picquet. By 4 p.m. the "Blue Caps," the 5th Punjab Infantry, 2 guns and some of Hodson's

Horse had been passed over, and these then advanced and occupied two villages in the front.

Two officers of other corps who were present on this occasion have thus described the passage of the river and the subsequent advance. One says :—*" There were no losses from the enemy's fire in crossing. The heavy battery had opened as soon as it was light enough, and had swept the enemy from the opposite bank so the landing was unopposed. . . . The Madras European Fusiliers and the Punjab Battalion having gone over on a raft, formed rapidly in column of companies for the advance, and were not kept long waiting by the gunners. Twenty minutes after the last horse had scrambled up the bank with his Sikh rider hanging on to his tail, the teams were harnessed and the guns advanced into action at the steady trot peculiar to field batteries."

The other writer was then serving with the 5th Punjab Infantry and writes :—" †Grant, after some delay, had got his troops across the river and was about to attack the rebel force opposed to us. My regiment was skirmishing to the front to cover the crossing when, looking to the rear, I saw that renowned old regiment, the 1st Madras Fusiliers, advancing towards us in line with its Colours flying and band playing. The effect was heightened by a grand sunset just behind the regiment and the sight altogether was most soul-stirring. I need hardly say how heartily the Fifth joined in the advance and how quickly the enemy judged discretion to be the better part of valour."

On August 29th the whole force under Sir Hope Grant advanced and occupied the cantonments of Sultanpore, the enemy having retreated, abandoning his position ; and on the following morning early the force moved out in pursuit, the skirmishers of the Rifle Brigade and Madras Fusiliers covering the advance.

Scarcely had the deployment commenced when a heavy fire opened on the whole line of skirmishers ; the regular cavalry attempted a turning movement, but the advance was temporarily

---

* Bland Strange, *Gunner Jingo's Jubilee*, p. 239.
† Vaughan, *My Service in The Indian Army and After*, p. 82.

CAMPAIGNING IN OUDH

checked by one of the guns of the Horse Battery being overturned, with horses and men, into a ravine. It was at this juncture that Lieutenant Strange, R.A., executed a daring coup, chasing with his own gun detachment the last two guns of the rebel battery and capturing them with guns and limbers. The Fusiliers also played their part in this action and when they finally returned to camp they had marched 36 miles in 22 hours.

Lieutenant Woods contributes some account of the events of the next two months:—" In the great horse-shoe bend of the river at Sultanpore—like the Thames between Kew and Richmond—we encamped for some time. . . . Our camp was eventually joined by more troops and formed a large force. On October 5th the Madras Fusiliers received a draft of 229 recruits. On the 7th I went on an interesting and important raid under Brevet-Major Raikes with the Right Wing and No. 6 Company of ours, 2 R.H.A. guns, a Troop of the 7th Hussars, some of Hodson's Horse under Palliser, 300 of the 5th Punjab Infantry and 25 Sappers and Miners. It was a military picnic in lovely weather and in a beautiful country. Marching about a dozen miles a day, in a week we came suddenly one forenoon upon the object of our search. Our cavalry scouts reported a force was then half-a-mile in front, and we came upon the enemy eating their breakfast in fancied security, a few hundred of them on our side of a river, the bulk not having yet crossed.

" The whole of our little cavalry force charged down upon them at once, closely followed by the 2 guns and the greater part of the infantry. Fifty yards on our side of the river was a ditch concealed by long grass; this was crossed by the Horse, including the artillery, at full gallop; a few Hussars and one of the guns came to grief here, they were all mixed up together but emerged undamaged. The rest profited by their warning and stopped at the brink of the ditch, the guns pounding the flying rebels at short range. A score or more of them were drowned while crossing by the narrow ford. . . .

" This place was close to Shahpore, a village of one large and a few small houses. Here we encamped. . . . A few days later found us near a typical Oudh fortified village." Many concealed arms and the remains of a rebel gun were discovered here and the petty fort was blown up, after which the force returned by easy stages to Sultanpore.

On October 20th Brigadier-General Horsford, having heard that the enemy had taken up a strong position at Daudpore, 11 miles distant, marched out to engage them, his column including 321 men of the Madras Fusiliers under Lieutenant-Colonel Galwey.* The force set out at 2 a.m. and marched 26 miles before it returned to camp at 9.30 p.m. having encountered and defeated the rebels and driven them from their position in great disorder. For their conduct in this action Lieutenant-Colonel Galwey, Lieutenant Sladen and the Regiment were specially commended.

For the next few weeks General Horsford's column moved about the country, meeting with but little resistance and encountering small loss; and on November 23rd the " Blue Caps " fought their last action in Oudh. The Regiment, with two R.H.A. guns and detachments from the 7th Hussars, Punjab Infantry and Hodson's Horse, all under Colonel Galwey, was sent against a body of the enemy in the neighbourhood of Mahona. The fort of Rehora on the right bank of the Gumti capitulated without firing a shot, but many of the rebels managed to get away with their arms and fled to Koili, 2 miles higher up the river, the Punjabees pursuing till they came under the fire of the fort at Koili. Lieutenant-Colonel Galwey hurried up in support, and his offer of terms being refused, a village outside the fort was cleared by the guns and Fusiliers, these latter being left on the bank to see that none of the rebels doubled back. The guns then opened fire on the fort itself, breaching the wall in front of the gate, while two companies of the Madras Fusiliers extended in support of the guns. It was now seen that there was an inner line of defence to the fort and the troops were temporarily withdrawn, when the enemy decamped.

During this action Lieutenant Cleland and Ensign Westerman were wounded; the last-named had been Sergeant-Major of the Regiment, and, with Quartermaster-Sergeant Kelly, had recently

* He had been promoted a Brevet Lieutenant-Colonel on March 24th, 1858.

been promoted to commissioned rank for distinguished conduct in the field.

The Madras Fusiliers now returned with Sir Hope Grant's force to Lucknow, the majority of the mutineers of Oudh having been driven into Nepal, and, leaving a strong brigade to watch the fugitives, the Commander-in-Chief returned himself to Lucknow on January 9th, 1859.

" Thus the long and stern contest for supremacy in Oudh was brought to an end. During the brief winter campaign some hundreds of forts were destroyed, about 150 guns captured, and 150,000 armed men, of whom at least 35,000 were disciplined soldiers, were subdued. The success of the operations was due to the old Chief's capacity for combination and his accuracy and energy of execution. He established a sound system of communication, he had no isolated column, and he insisted on every commander obeying his orders to the letter."*

The Madras Fusiliers did not remain long in Lucknow, for they were very shortly sent to Cawnpore where they arrived on December 9th only some 300 strong, in spite of the large drafts of recruits which had joined the Service companies during the past few months.

It was here decided that the Regiment, now the mere skeleton of a battalion, should return to Madras, but before leaving Cawnpore it was inspected, on January 7th, 1859, by Brigadier the **1859** Hon. Percy Herbert, Commanding the Cawnpore Division.

On the 18th the Fusiliers arrived at Allahabad whence it appears initially to have been intended that they should start upon the weary march to railhead ; Sir Colin Campbell, however, was not unmindful of all that he, and the country, owed to the " Blue Caps," and he wrote a letter to the Governor-General of which the following is an extract, insisting that the Regiment should be saved the long march and should be sent down to railhead by river :—

" The Madras Fusiliers have a right to every indulgence that can

* Forrest, Vol. III, p. 539.

be invented for them. It will be quite right that they should travel down in boats like gentlemen."

Prior to the arrival of the "Blue Caps" in Calcutta, the following had been published in Bengal General Order No. 176 of February 12th. "Notification. On Monday, the 14th inst., the 1st Madras Fusiliers will arrive at Calcutta to embark for Fort St. George.

"It is due to this distinguished Regiment that it should not leave Bengal without receiving from the Government of India a marked acknowledgment of its eminent services.

"Led by their able and intrepid commander, the lamented Brigadier-General Neill, the Madras Fusiliers were the first to carry relief and security to Benares and Allahabad. They formed a part of the force which, under Major-General Sir H. Havelock, first penetrated to Cawnpore and Lucknow. They shared in the long-sustained occupation of Alam Bagh under Lieutenant-General Sir J. Outram, and in the reduction of Lucknow by H. E. the Commander-in-Chief, and they have borne an active part in the final and complete re-establishment of the Queen's authority in Oudh.

"After twenty months of arduous service, the Madras Fusiliers are about to return to their Presidency, their work fully accomplished and their high character as soldiers enhanced.

"His Excellency the Viceroy and Governor-General of India in Council will receive the Regiment with public honours.

"The Regiment will arrive at the terminus at Howrah about 4 p.m. and will be paraded at 5 o'clock before the stairs of the Great Entrance of Government House, there to be received by His Excellency.

"The troops in town and garrison will be paraded in front of Government House at half-past 4 o'clock p.m.

"All the Civil Officers of the Government, the officers of the Garrison and General Staff and other Military and Naval Officers at the Presidency, except those on duty, are requested to be in attendance at the Great Entrance of Government House at 5 o'clock.

"All ships of war and Government vessels in the river will be dressed in honour of the occasion.

"After their reception by His Excellency the Governor-General, the Madras Fusiliers will march out by the west gate and by the river side to the dockyard beyond Hastings' Bridge, where they will immediately embark on board their ships. On their march the Regiment will be saluted by the Fort and by Her Majesty's Ship *Pearl*."

The first party of the Fusiliers left Allahabad on January 22nd, and by February 14th the whole Regiment was concentrated in Calcutta, where a welcome awaited it such as few Corps can ever before have received. On the afternoon of this day the "Blue Caps" were marched down to Government House, while as Lieutenant Woods proudly relates, "Royal Salutes of 21 guns from the Fort and the *Pearl*, man-of-war, were fired; all the troops in garrison paraded on the line of route and in front of Government House, and received us with presented arms. Our little remnant of 300 men, dressed in slate-coloured khaki and very dilapidated clothing, some of us without peaks to our caps or scabbards for our swords, drew up in line at the foot of the white stairs in front of the Grand Entrance. Thus we were in conspicuous relief, since every other person was in full dress, scarlet and gold, or blue uniforms. At the top of the steps were the grandees of Government round the Governor General—Members of Council, Judges, the General of the Division, the Archdeacon of Calcutta, military and naval officers, civil servants etc. The whole of Calcutta appeared to be in the area below and as far as the eye could reach beyond."

Lieutenant Dale adds to the above:—"I don't know what the rest felt, but I know that there were great lumps in my throat as I realized that all this honour was being bestowed on a Regiment to which I had the honour to belong, and on whose rolls were also inscribed the names of Clive and Stringer Lawrence, to say nothing of Neill—right worthy successor of the giants who had gone before."

When the Regiment was drawn up, the Governor-General, Lord Canning, came to the head of the steps and addressed the Madras Fusiliers as follows:—

"COLONEL GALWEY, OFFICERS AND SOLDIERS OF THE MADRAS FUSILIERS!

"*I am glad to have the opportunity of thanking you publicly in the name of the Government of India for the great services which you have rendered to the State. More than twenty months have passed since you landed in Calcutta. The time has been an eventful one full of labours and perils and in these you have largely shared. Yours was the first British Regiment which took assistance to the Central Provinces and gave safety to the important posts of Benares and Allahabad.*

"*You were a part of that brave band which first pushed forward to Cawnpore, and forced its way to Lucknow, where so many precious lives and interests were at stake.*

"*From that time you have, with little intermission, been in the front of danger.*

"*You are now returning to your own Presidency, your ranks thinned by war and sickness, but you return crowned with honour, carrying with you the high opinion of every commander who has led you in the field; the respect of your fellow soldiers in that great English Army in which from the beginning you have maintained a foremost place; and the gratitude of the whole community of your fellow-countrymen of every class. Further, you have the satisfaction of knowing that you do not leave behind you a single spot of ground upon which you have set your feet, where peace and order have not been restored.*

"*When you reach Madras tell your comrades of the Madras Army that the name of the 1st Fusiliers will never be forgotten on this side of India.*

"*Tell them that the recollection of all that is due to your courage, constancy and forwardness will never be effaced from the mind of the Government under whose orders you have served.*

" Tell them especially that the memory of your late distinguished leader is cherished and honoured by every Englishman amongst us, and that though many heroic spirits have passed away since the day he fell in front of you in the streets of Lucknow, not one has left a nobler reputation than General Neill.

" I now bid you farewell, Fusiliers, and I wish you a speedy and prosperous voyage to your own Presidency. You are indeed an honour to it."

That day the " Other Ranks " of the Regiment attended a dinner given to them by the people of Calcutta, while the officers dined with General Sir James Outram, and then, forming up again, the " Blue Caps " marched to their transports amidst the cheers of a very large concourse of people, and, under the command of Colonel Thomas James Fischer*, who had recently assumed command, embarked—Nos. 1, 2, 4, 5 and 9 Companies in the *Tubal Cain*. Nos. 3, 6, 7, 8 and 10 in the steamer *Sydney*, the transports proceeding down the Hooghly in company with H.M.S. *Pearl*, Captain Sotheby, on the following day.

On February 22nd the Regiment landed at Madras and was again received with signal honour. A Royal Salute was fired from Fort St. George, a dinner, at which both the Governor and Commander-in-Chief were present, was given to the non-commissioned officers and men by the people of Madras; the day was observed as a general holiday; while the following address, unanimously agreed on at a public meeting held on February 17th, was presented to the " Blue Caps " by the European inhabitants :—

" FUSILIERS,

" Accept the welcome of your grateful and admiring countrymen assembled to greet your return to Madras.

" Summoned from these shores 21 months ago to meet a crisis unparalleled in the history of British India, when the treason of an army had shaken the Empire to its centre, you hastened to the scene of danger, where your opportune arrival, and the promptitude and energy of your

---

* Lately commanding 18th Madras Native Infantry.

gallant leader, rolled back the tide of successful mutiny and saved Bengal.

"*From that hour to the day you left the field on your return home, you have taken a prominent part in every operation and shared in every feat of arms of the divisions who have borne the brunt of the contest.*

"*And well have you maintained the honour of the First Fusiliers, already distinguished by achievements of no common fame. Nobly have you upheld the indomitable character of the British soldier under circumstances most trying, against appalling odds, when support and succour seemed well nigh hopeless, amid rain and storm, under the withering rays of a deadly sun, in hunger, thirst and exposure.*

"*But while we joyfully hail your return, we cannot forget the heavy cost at which so much glory has been purchased.*

"*We mourn the many gallant men who have sealed their devotion to their country with their blood. We sympathize with the mourners who look in vain for the loved faces which shall greet them no more. Above all we grieve for him, the historian of your military renown, the gallant Neill, whose own achievements in the field at your head, distinguished by every attribute of the great and gifted commander, have added a deathless page to the imperishable record of the Regiment's fame.*

"*But we would not confine our welcome to words of congratulation and sympathy only.*

"*We desire to leave with you some more lasting proof of our admiration and regard, and hope at no distant period to repeat our welcome to our gallant Fusiliers in a more welcome shape. Till then, farewell.*"

But the tributes to the valour of the Madras Fusiliers were not forthcoming only from men of their own blood and speech, for the following unique address was presented to the Regiment by the Hindu community of Madras:—

"GLORIOUS AND HONOURED SOLDIERS OF THE FIRST MADRAS FUSILIERS,—

"Allow the grateful and admiring Hindu community of this your own Presidency to offer you their warmest welcome on the happy

NEILL CENTREPIECE.

Presented to the Officers' Mess of the 1st Madras Fusiliers by their Madras friends in token of their admiration of the gallant achievements of the Regiment during the Mutinies of 1858. Placed by the Officers' Mess of the "Blue Caps" in the Royal United Service Institution.

occasion of your return to it, after an absence of so many long and anxious months, during which you have rendered to Her Majesty and to all your fellow-subjects, both European and Asiatic, services which could not possibly be surpassed either in brilliancy or importance.

"*We all know how great have been your previous achievements, alike within the Presidency and in foreign parts, but even they fall far short in our estimation of the glorious and foremost part which you have taken in the operations necessary to crush the late awful mutiny and rebellion in Bengal and the North-West.*

"*Your splendid exploits in those Provinces have been heard of by us with the highest admiration and the warmest gratitude, which we now desire to express to you from the fulness of our hearts.*

"*Suddenly summoned from the shores of Madras, and single-handed, to stem the flowing tide of revolt, you left all that was most dear to you in the world with the alacrity and ardour of true soldiers, and hastened eagerly to the scene of unparalleled treason, murder and outrage, where, under the leadership of the noble and ever-to-be-lamented General Neill, you at once turned the current of affairs, and became the saviours of Bengal, on which the ferocious mutineers were precipitating themselves. Having thus stemmed the torrent in the very crisis of the fate of the Empire, you followed up the work so grandly begun, by a long series of heroic deeds wherever you came in contact with the foe; taking a leading part in all the most sanguinary and hard-fought engagements which occurred, from the time of your arrival in Bengal down to that of your setting forward on your return to this Presidency.*

"*Never were the loftiest characteristics of the British soldier more strikingly displayed under circumstances of the greatest hardship, difficulty, privation and disproportion of numbers, than in every case by you.*

"*When you were but a handful of men, opposed to hosts, you manifested unvarying courage, endurance and devotion to the cause of your Sovereign and Country, cheerfully disregarding hunger, thirst and exposure, sometimes to the burning heat of India, and at others to the stormy winds and heavy rains.*

"*When nothing but death looked you in the face, you still pressed forward unshaken in confidence and with ardour undiminished, surpassing, if that were possible, and this in seasons of the greatest extremity, the heroism for which your Regiment was ever remarkable when before a foe.*

"*Whenever victory, under the blessing of Providence, crowned the British arms during the late terrible conflict with mutineers and rebels, the Madras Fusiliers, if present, were second to no part of Her Majesty's forces engaged in aiding to secure it, and we may say, without for a moment wishing to depreciate the gallant and noble achievements of other British regiments—all of whom employed against the common foe have crowned themselves with immortal honour—that your services have in the highest degree contributed to the restoration of tranquillity in the disturbed provinces.*

"*Dauntless soldiers and true-hearted fellow-subjects of our beloved Queen, while we thus warmly and joyfully hail the return to our shores of those of you who are now present, we remember and most deeply deplore the heavy price paid for the accession of glory which has been won by the Fusiliers in the deaths of so many of the brave comrades who went hence with you to the scene of strife. The memory of those heroic men who have fallen in their country's cause, will ever be affectionately cherished by our community, and we heartily sympathize with the mourning relations who survive to lament their irreparable loss. Most particularly do we grieve for and venerate the name of your late incomparable commander, General Neill, whom you all loved so well and followed so proudly to the fights in which, under his leadership and example, so much additional renown has been secured for the Regiment.*

"*It is not our intention to honour you in the words only; we sought the privilege of entertaining you as our guests before departure from Madras, but were informed that time would not admit of this intention being carried out. We shall, however, beg your acceptance of a tangible and lasting proof of our grateful regard and admiration as soon as the same can be prepared.*

"*And now, faithful, gallant and highly distinguished men and officers of the Madras Fusiliers, allow us to wish long life, health and prosperity to every one of you and heartily to bid you farewell.*"

THE OLD SILVER ORIENT BOWL OR SOUP TUREEN.
Presented by the Hindoo community of Madras in 1859 to the Sergeants' Mess.

THE NEILL MEMORIAL FUND

The above address was signed on behalf of the Hindu community of Madras by 110 of its principal members.

The above did not exhaust the feelings of intense admiration felt by all ranks and classes of the people of Madras for the splendid services of what they regarded as *their* Regiment; a very large sum of money was raised and the amount subscribed was expended as follows :—

A statue of the late General Neill was procured from England and erected on the Mount Road in Madras, opposite to the entrance to the Club.

A sum of money was set aside and invested in Government securities to give the following gratuities to the best-behaved men, annually discharged from the Service, except those discharged by purchase :—

    To one sergeant a gratuity of one hundred rupees.
    To one corporal a gratuity of seventy rupees.
    To one private a gratuity of fifty rupees.
    To one private a gratuity of thirty rupees.

The selection being made by the Commanding Officer.

A magnificent silver centre-piece, with equestrian statuette of General Neill, was presented to the Officers' Mess, while a very large silver tankard was presented to the Sergeants' Mess; the receipt of these two last-named gifts was acknowledged by Colonel Fischer in the following letter :—

"*I have the honour to acknowledge the receipt of the testimonials— the silver centre-piece intended for the Officers and the silver tankard the gift to the Sergeants' Mess presented by the inhabitants of Madras to the First Madras Fusiliers, in recognition, as you are pleased to say, of its gallant services during the Mutinies in Bengal in 1857–58.*

"*In the name of the officers and non-commissioned officers of the First Madras Fusiliers, I beg to tender, through you to the inhabitants of Madras, our heartfelt acknowledgments and thanks for these noble testimonials, and to express to them the proud gratification we—one and all—feel at the high appreciation by the inhabitants of Madras of the services it has been the good fortune of the First Madras Fusiliers to render to their Government and country.*

"*The magnificent silver centre-piece for the officers, and the handsome silver tankard for the Sergeants will be religiously guarded, and handed down as heirlooms in this Regiment, and whatever may be its future designation, the testimonials will remind us that we are 'the First Madras Fusiliers'—a designation endeared to us by the recollection of the flattering addresses, splendid banquet, pecuniary assistance, and rewards and noble testimonials that have marked the appreciation of our service by the inhabitants of our own Presidency of Madras.*

"*In the name and on behalf of the officers, sergeants and men of the First Madras Fusiliers, I beg you will convey to the inhabitants of Madras the expression of our sincere thanks and acknowledgments for these flattering testimonials, which reached us yesterday in a state of perfect preservation.*"

The casualties sustained by the Regiment during service in Bengal were:—

Killed or died of wounds: Colonel (Brigadier-General) Neill, Majors Renaud and Stephenson, Lieutenants Richardson, Arnold and Groom, and Second-Lieutenant Dobbs.

Died of disease: Lieutenants Chisholm (cholera), and Hargood (fever).

Wounded: Lieutenant-Colonel Galwey; Captains Fraser (twice), Grant (twice); Lieutenants Barclay, Bailey and Cleland and Ensign Westerman.

Three hundred and fifty-two non-commissioned officers and men fell during the campaign and about 200 were wounded, of whom many died of their wounds.

The following officers received decorations or promotion:—

Major and Brevet Lieutenant-Colonel Neill, A.D.C. to the Queen, C.B., promoted Brigadier-General.

Majors Stephenson and Galwey, promoted Brevet Lieutenant-Colonels and C.B.

Captain Spurgin, brevet majority and lieutenant-colonelcy.
Captains Raikes, Grant, Taylor, Fraser and P. A. Brown, brevet majorities.

This last-named officer served in Central India with the Madras Sappers in the force under General Sir Hugh Rose.

CREST OF MADRAS FUSILIERS, 1856.

CHAPTER VI

1859—1870.

THE TRANSFER FROM THE COMPANY TO THE CROWN—THE 102ND REGIMENT (ROYAL MADRAS FUSILIERS) PROCEED ON THEIR FIRST TOUR OF HOME SERVICE.

IMMEDIATELY on conclusion of the dinner given to the " Blue Caps " in Madras, the Regiment left *via* Vellore for Bangalore, where by the end of the first week in March it was established in barracks, and here in the same month a draft of 127 recruits from England joined the Service companies.

The time has now come to give an account of the great changes which were instituted in the government of India and of the effect which these had upon the lives and fortunes of the soldiers of the Honourable East India Company.

Already in many of the letters written to their friends and relations at home by officers of the 1st Madras Fusiliers during the progress of the great Mutiny, there are not wanting signs which show that some at least of the writers had come to the conclusion that when peace again descended upon the troubled land things could not ever again be as they were before the rebellion broke out ; more than once do we find even junior officers expressing the opinion that the rule of " John Company " was at an end, that the government of India and the administration of the army would be assumed by the Crown ; though it may perhaps be conceded that few of those who expressed these opinions had really fully realized all that these vast changes might mean, how the Company's regiments, its officers and men, would be affected.

With the very commencement of the Mutiny the people at home in England began to think that some very drastic steps ought to be taken for the reorganization of the methods whereby India was governed; and before long this vague impression crystallized into a conviction that England must take Indian administration into her own hands, and that the time had come for the fiction of rule by a trading company to be absolutely given up.*

Already as far back only as 1852 Lord Ellenborough had recommended that the government of India should be transferred from the Company to the Crown; but the time was not then ripe, mainly perhaps for the reason that at that date, and for some years previously, Indian affairs had been regarded in England with something like absolute indifference. "India was to the ordinary Englishman a place where men used at one time to make huge fortunes within a few years; and where lately military and civil officers had to do hard work enough without much chance of becoming nabobs. . . . It was associated in the minds of some with tiger-hunting; in the minds of others with Bishop Heber and missions to the heathen. . . . The Indian Mutiny startled the public feeling of England out of this state of unhealthy languor."†

It was therefore almost in consequence of popular clamour, aroused by perfectly natural feelings of passion and panic, that the Imperial Government decided upon a change of system, though it is quite possible that neither the people nor their representatives realized that the "administration of India had long ceased to be under the control of the Company as it was in the days of Warren Hastings. A Board of Directors, nominated partly by the Crown and partly by the Company, sat in Leadenhall Street, and gave general directions for the government of India. But the Parliamentary Department, called the Board of Control, had the right of reviewing and revising the decisions of the Company." In the beginning then of 1858 Lord Palmerston brought in a bill " for the better government of British India," the avowed object of which was the transference of the authority of the Company formally and absolutely to the Crown. The Court of Directors had learnt in the

* Justin McCarthy, *A History of Our Own Times*, Vol. III, p. 125.
† *Ibid.*, p. 115.

previous December that such a Bill was proposed, and on the last day of the year they addressed a letter to the Premier expressing their surprise at a move so hasty, founded, moreover, on no previous inquiry; and that even before the Mutiny was quelled, whilst the excitement in India was at its height, the Ministry had resolved upon the downfall of the Honourable East India Company.

When Parliament met this letter was followed up by a solemn petition, but a huge majority of the House of Commons was in favour of the Bill, the passage into law of which was, however, delayed by the sudden overthrow of Lord Palmerston's government. But his successor brought in a similar Bill which passed into law in the autumn of 1858, and one of its provisions enacted that the military and naval forces of the Company were to be deemed the forces of Her Majesty. On September 1st, 1858, the Court of Directors held their last meeting in the India House in Leadenhall Street, and "thenceforward the old Company of Merchants trading to the East passes out from the high road of history into the homelier by-ways of commercial life, from the task of ruling a world-famous Empire to the game of drawing half-yearly dividends on capital guaranteed by an English Parliament. . . . The Feringhie triumphed, but the assailants had their revenge; for while the last of them were yet fighting, the old 'Koompanie Bahadoor' vanished out of the political world."*

In 1857 the army of the Honourable East India Company numbered 237,476 soldiers, of whom 15,207 belonged to the European regiments and corps in the Company's service, while in that year there were also in India upwards of 24,000 men of the Queen's Army in receipt of pay from the Company.

The Act of Parliament passed in August, 1858, contained among other provisions, one by which it was enacted that the military services of the Company should be deemed to be those of Her Majesty, and to be under the same obligations to serve the Queen as they would have been to serve the Company, while continuing to enjoy all their former emoluments and privileges. This change was

* Trotter, *History of the British Empire in India*, Vol. III, Chap. VIII.

TRANSFER TO THE CROWN

publicly made known in India by a Proclamation of Her Majesty the Queen, published at Allahabad on November 1st, 1858, and re-published at Madras on the 13th of the same month; but in this proclamation the only reference to the army of the Company appears to be contained in para. 4, which runs :—

"And we hereby confirm in their several offices, civil and military, all persons now employed in the service of the Honourable East India Company, subject to our future pleasure, and to such laws and regulations as may hereafter be enacted."

Immediately on hearing of this proclamation the men of the 4th Bengal European Light Cavalry, then stationed at Lucknow, declared that they did not consider themselves bound to serve the Queen until and unless they should be re-enlisted for that purpose, receiving fresh bounty; and on November 8th, 1858, Major-General Sir Hope Grant reported that certain men of the Madras Fusiliers, then serving under him in Oudh, were unwilling to serve Her Majesty on the grounds that they had been enlisted solely for the services of the Company.

When these facts came to the notice of the Commander-in-Chief, Sir Colin Campbell addressed a letter on November 10th to the Governor-General, pointing out that the men had at least a certain amount of reason on their side; that the Company's European soldier was asked in his attestation whether he were willing to serve the *Company*, and that there was therein no alternative of service to the *Crown* so much as suggested; and that although the soldier was certainly sworn to be "faithful" and bear "true allegiance" to the Queen, this was merely as a British subject, that it was in fact a mere oath of allegiance. Further, the Commander-in-Chief pointed out that in the Queen's regiments a man was enlisted to serve in a particular regiment, that he could not be transferred without his consent, and that consequently when for any reason a regiment had to be brought up to unusual and sudden increase of strength, *volunteers* were called upon for the purpose.

Sir Colin then suggested that, in order to allay a feeling of injustice and irritation which certainly existed and which might easily become inconvenient and even dangerous, the men of the Company's European Forces should immediately be given the option of re-enlistment.

The Governor-General, unfortunately, did not concur in this view, and his opinion appears to have been supported by his legal advisers, while he considered that to permit certain men to take their discharge and to re-enlist the remainder would have a bad effect on the native troops. The Viceroy's view was upheld by the Secretary of State in two letters dated December 31st, 1858, and February 24th, 1859, and the Government of India was directed to inform the European soldiers of the East India Company's Army that their claim to discharge or re-enlistment with bounty was inadmissible, and this was accordingly done in a General Order dated Fort William, April 8th, 1859.

This General Order created great and general dissatisfaction, culminating at certain stations in acts of insubordination amounting almost to mutiny; at Meerut especially was there a good deal of trouble, the men, while generally respectful to their officers, maintaining that virtually they were now out of the service and no longer amenable to military law. Later the spirit of discontent extended to Gwalior, Lahore, Agra, Berhampore, Dinapore and Allahabad.

The Governor-General now amended his views and at his instance a General Order was published on June 20th, which maintained that every European soldier on enlistment *had* undertaken to serve the Crown equally with the Company, that the only change made by the Act lay in the designation of the troops, henceforth called " the India Military Forces of Her Majesty "; but it was admitted that the men did honestly believe that their rights had been overlooked, and the soldiers were informed that those who had enlisted for the Company's forces might now take their discharge, should they so desire, with free conveyance to England, but it was decreed that no hope could be held out that the Home Government would recede from the decision already come to in regard to re-enlistment and bounty.

Then on July 9th an order was published which concluded

with the words :—" The Commander-in-Chief hopes that the old soldiers of Her Majesty's Indian Army will be wise enough not to throw away, without due reflection and in a moment of excitement, the advantage of former services. They are precisely in the same position as regards pay, clothing, pension and other regulations as the men in Her Majesty's Regiments of the Line."

The discontent engendered by the Act and the proclamation does not appear to have been so apparent, or at any rate so articulate, in Madras as in Bengal, and other parts of Northern India. But when on May 24th, 1859, at Bangalore there was a parade for the celebration of Her Majesty's birthday, it was noticed that the Madras Fusiliers did not join in the cheering, and on inquiry by the Lieutenant-General commanding the Division the men stated that they considered themselves entitled on re-enlistment to bounty, or to discharge, since they were bound to serve the Company only and were not liable to transfer to the Queen's service without their own consent.

In a letter from the Commanding Officer to the Military Secretary to the Commander-in-Chief, dated May 25th, 1859, he stated the men declared that " they were Englishmen, but had been transferred like guns and bullocks to the Queen, and they might be transferred again to the Americans to-morrow. They were no longer men, but cattle or goods transferable without their consent obtained, or even asked for, from one party to another."

The demeanour of the men of the Madras Fusiliers on this parade was quiet and subordinate, but it was very evident that it was their pride that was hurt by the *manner* of their transfer.

1860 The number of men of all ranks of the Madras Fusiliers who took their discharge was 298, leaving 56 sergeants, 46 corporals, 40 drummers and 430 privates, but some at least of those who accepted discharge re-enlisted in the British Army in England during 1859-60.

Since the year 1800 the system of promotion of officers in the Company's infantry had been by regimental rise, but this came to an end on December 31st, 1858, and it was then laid down that officers joining were not to be posted to regiments as heretofore, but were to be entered in one infantry general list according to seniority, thus reverting to the system which had been in force during the eighteenth century.

1861 "On the 26th February, 1861, a special Commission was appointed to consider and report upon the arrangements necessary for carrying out the amalgamation of the European troops of the Indian Army with Her Majesty's British Forces in accordance with the Royal Warrant, and the orders of Her Majesty's Government, and on the 10th April the European officers and men of the Indian Service were informed of the conditions of their amalgamation with Her Majesty's general forces, ' whereby two armies will be united which severally have rendered the most signal services to their Queen and country.' The order then went on to say that ' Her Majesty's Government have expressed an anxious desire to preserve the proud recollections of distinguished service which belong especially to the older regiments of each Presidency, and to incorporate, with Her Majesty's Army, corps which have so greatly contributed to the acquisition and maintenance of Her Majesty's Dominions in the East.'

"The following were the principal features of this comprehensive measure :—

"All warrant officers, non-commissioned officers and men of the European branches of the Army were offered the option of accepting general service on the ordinary conditions, with a bounty to all below warrant rank. All soldiers so volunteering to have the privilege of counting their past service towards pension, either under the regulations of the Queen's or the Company's service as they might choose."*

The Warrant was re-published in a General Order dated Fort William, April 10th, 1861, and the following specially affected the regiments of European Infantry :—Para. 11 ran : "It is desired by Her Majesty's Government to maintain as integral regiments, the three oldest European infantry regiments of the Bengal Presi-

* Wilson, Vol. IV, p. 453 *et seq.*

dency, and all of the three regiments of the Madras and Bombay Presidencies, and to keep the men who are now in each corps, and who may volunteer for Her Majesty's general service, in the regiments which, when transferred to the Line, will represent those to which they now respectively belong."

Para. 13. "Her Majesty having graciously determined to mark her estimation of the services of the Indian armies, by conferring the designation of ' Royal ' upon three of the European regiments, and by selecting for this honour one regiment from each Presidency—the selection of which has been left by Her Majesty to the judgment and discretion of the Government of India—the Viceroy and Governor-General in Council has much gratification in announcing that the following regiments will henceforward bear the honourable designation of ' Royal ' :—

"The 1st Bengal Fusiliers.
"The 1st Madras Fusiliers.
"The 1st Bombay Fusiliers."

Para 14. "The three older regiments in the several Presidencies will thus be converted into regiments of Her Majesty's general army and will be numbered and designated as follows :—

* * * * *

"The 102nd Regiment of Foot (Royal Madras Fusiliers).

* * * * *

Para. 15. "The corps transferred to Her Majesty's service will retain all honorary distinctions which they have won. These will be borne on appointments and Colours, or in the Army List, in such manner as Her Majesty's Government may think best suited to the arm of the Service to which the corps belongs."

The establishment of each of the nine new regiments as regards officers was fixed at 1 Colonel, 1 Lieutenant-Colonel, 2 Majors, 12 Captains, 14 Lieutenants and 10 Second-Lieutenants or Ensigns; and the officers now serving were given the option of joining the new regiments in the same position as that held by them in their old ones; of continuing to be borne on the cadres of their old regiments and being employed locally ; or of entering the Staff Corps then about to be formed.

In the following letter H.R.H. Field-Marshal the Duke of Cambridge, the Commander-in-Chief, welcomed the old Company's regiments to the brotherhood of the British Army :—

"*The General Commanding-in-Chief has received Her Majesty's commands to make known to the British Army serving in India that the arrangements for consolidating the European forces of the Crown in that country have now been completed.*

"*His Royal Highness hails with satisfaction an event which he trusts may be conducive to the best interests of the Empire, whilst it will be of advantage to the troops whom it may concern.*

"*He feels persuaded that the glorious deeds of arms for which the Line and Local Troops have ever been conspicuous will not be forgotten by them now that they are about to join one united Army, and that the only feeling of rivalry which will henceforth exist between the various Corps will be a high spirit of emulation as regards discipline and good conduct during peace, and of gallant bearing and devotion, should their services be hereafter called for in the field.*

"*In the name of the Army, the Commander-in-Chief most heartily and cordially welcomes to the ranks of the general service of the Crown, the officers, non-commissioned officers and soldiers of the local services of the three Presidencies in India.*"

1862 The 1st Madras Fusiliers came into their new title of the 102nd Regiment of Foot (Royal Madras Fusiliers) on July 30th, 1862, when the following officers were gazetted to it, and their names appear for the first time in the Army List for November, 1862. Colonel, Major-General Sir R. J. Hussey-Vivian, K.C.B.; Lieutenant-Colonel T. Raikes ; Majors J. B. Spurgin and H. J. Jepson ; Captains E. S. Daniell, P. A. Brown, Brevet Major, G. F. Gosling, S. H. Jones-Parry, G. J. Harcourt, C. E. Lennox, E. Dunbar, J. L. Seton, A. D. Gordon, L. A. M. Graeme, H. F. Hornsby and W. H. Beaumont ; Lieutenants J. A. Woods, J. J. Barclay, V. C. Bertie, C. H. Dale, J. Duncan, W. Cleland, R. C. Parry, R. F. Burton, N. J. C. Stevens, A. Cuppage, C. L. Oliver, C. B. S. Neill, F. J. Granville, E. J. V.

COLOURS OF 102ND ROYAL MADRAS FUSILIERS.

ROYAL COLOURS PRESENTED

Rogers and T. R. Tabuteau; Ensigns J. H. Waller, J. Maule, St. J. Green, J. Blair, J. C. V. White, C. H. Carr, H. L. Berkeley, A. Hamilton, G. F. Preston and T. B. Turner; Captain F. Samwell, Paymaster; Lieutenant Stevens, Instructor of Musketry; Lieutenant Duncan, Adjutant; Quartermaster Thomas Moore; Surgeon R. B. Smyth, and Assistant-Surgeons W. J. Tyrrell and G. Ashton.

A depot for the Regiment in England does not appear to have been formed until some time early in 1863, when three companies of the 102nd formed part of the 3rd Depot Battalion at Chatham, composed of depots of the 1st Battalion 19th Foot, the 51st, 75th, 81st, 91st, and 102nd. The officers of the Regiment who joined this were Brevet Major Brown, Captain Gosling, Lieutenants Woods and Granville.

1863
1866
At the end of 1862 and beginning of 1863 the Royal Madras Fusiliers left Bangalore and by January 17th the companies were disposed as follows:—Headquarters and 6 companies at Cannanore, 3 companies at Malliapooram and 1 company at Calicut. On January 5th, 1866, 1 company under Captain Lennox was detached to Trichinopoly.

The time was now come when the Regiment was to receive its new Royal Colours, and for this ceremony the troops at Cannanore were paraded on the morning of January 26th, 1866,—the 102nd, on the right, the Artillery and 13th Native Infantry in the centre and the 40th Native Infantry on the left of a three-sided square, the new Colours of the Regiment being on a pile of drums in the centre. The ceremony commenced and the Rev. C. H. Deane, Chaplain of Cannanore, then offered up the customary prayer, after which the new Colours were handed by Majors Spurgin and Jepson to Mrs. de Saumarez, the wife of the Brigadier-General, and by her presented to Ensigns Blair and Hamilton, who received them kneeling. Mrs. de Saumarez then addressed the Regiment as follows:—

" COLONEL RAIKES, OFFICERS AND SOLDIERS OF THE ROYAL MADRAS FUSILIERS,

"*It has been with a feeling not only of great satisfaction but equally of pride, that I have accepted the compliment contained in the request* that I should present these new Colours to your distinguished Regiment. Symbols of adoption into the more immediate service of our Sovereign, I know how deeply prized and cherished they will be by every man of the Corps. It cannot be but that regret should accompany your separation from that Army, in which, and with which, you have so long served and earned so great a portion of glory; but that regret will have merged in the loyal feeling that you only leave the Army of India to become an integral part of the Army of England.

"For about 200 years, side by side with the Madras native soldier, under one form or another, the Corps has taken a distinguished part in the war service of the Madras Army, and, whether serving as independent companies, now in one branch of the Service, now in another, as artillery, infantry, or cavalry as your earliest predecessors did, for the first part of its existence; or, with a more perfect organization, a battalion, known and renowned as 'Madras Europeans,' and subsequently with even still greater distinction as '1st Madras Fusiliers,' the Regiment fighting in every part of India, as well as the more Eastern countries of Asia, has nobly maintained a place second to none in the annals of the British Army. No names are more deservedly honoured than those of its former chiefs—Lawrence, Clive, Barry-Close and Malcolm—in the earlier history of England's victories in the East, none in her late hour of need in India fell with more glory than the gallant Neill, 'though many fell and there was much glory.'

"From Plassey to Lucknow your Colours tell the war history of India. The course of your service will necessarily now soon take you home to our common country, but I am assured that wherever you may serve, your motto still will be 'Spectamur Agendo,' and that, in leaving India, you will only pass to other fields equally fertile of glory.

"With an earnest prayer for your future success, and wishing you God-speed on your approaching return to England, though Renaud and Stephenson, Arnold and many other heroic spirits, both officers and men, have passed away from among you, dying in the service of their country, I would now, with but slight alteration, re-echo the sentiments expressed by the great and good Lord Canning, in his last farewell to the Regiment, and with him would repeat that though you may return

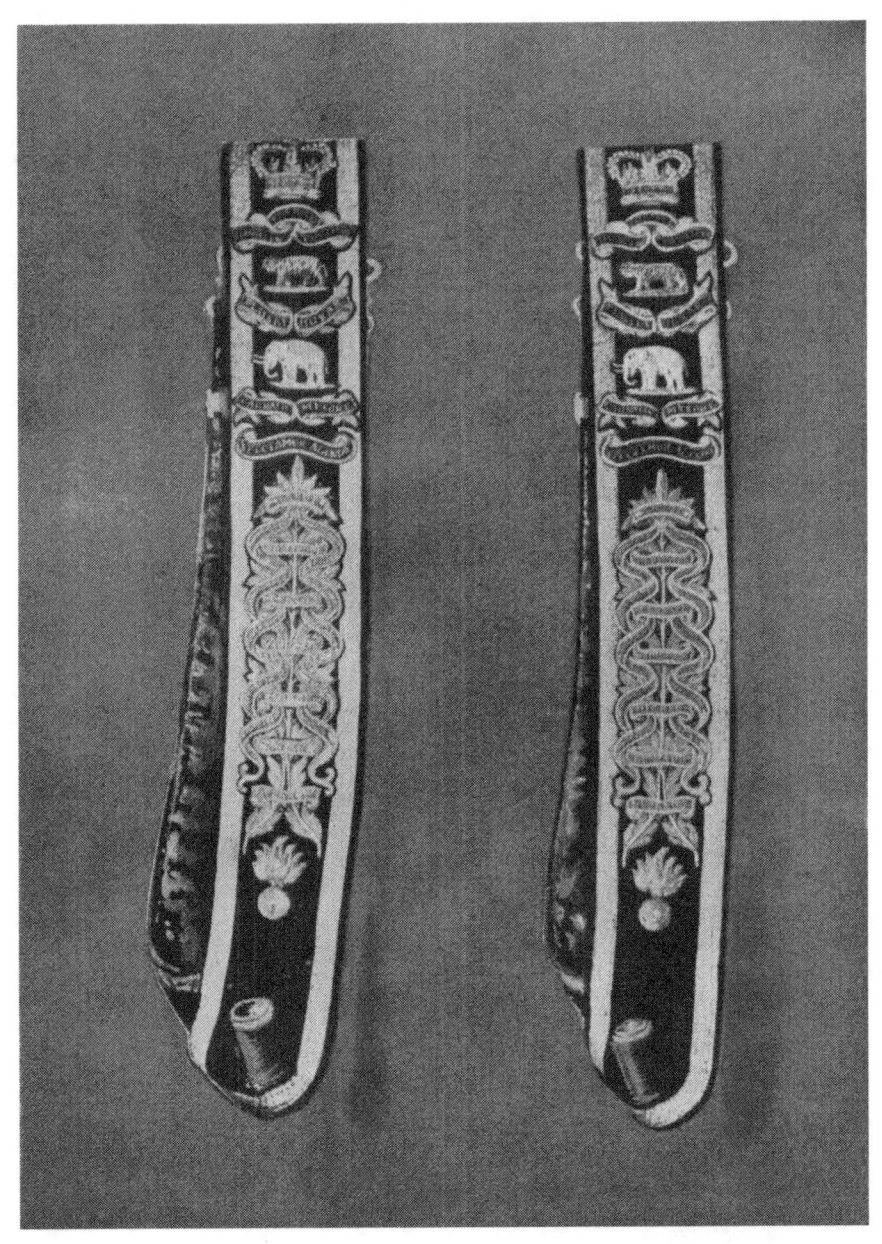

COLOUR BELTS.
Presented by Colonel H. D. Taylor.

to your country with ranks thinned by war and sickness, you return covered with honour, carrying with you the high opinion of every commander who has led you in the field, the respect of your fellow-soldiers in the great English Army, in which, from the beginning, you maintained a foremost place, and the gratitude of your countrymen of every class."

Colonel Raikes now replied in the following words :—

"MRS DE SAUMAREZ,

"*In the name of the Regiment I beg to thank you most sincerely for the honour you have done us in presenting our new Colours, and also for the very flattering terms in which you have so kindly addressed us. You have alluded in a most complimentary manner to our transfer from the Indian to the British Army. I can assure you that there is not a man amongst us who does not look back with pride to the days he served in the glorious Madras Army; and the fact of those Colours being presented by the wife of a distinguished officer of that Army, enhances our feelings of pride and gratification on this occasion. It would be unbecoming in me to expatiate on the services of the Regiment to which you have alluded in so complimentary a manner; but I trust I may be permitted to express my conviction that these Colours will ever be guarded with honour and devotion, and that, when unfurled in the face of an enemy, all ranks of the Regiment will vie with each other in leading them to victory, and adding to the decorations already emblazoned upon them. In conclusion let me again thank you for the very kind manner in which you have addressed the Regiment."*

The ceremony proceeded and was concluded in the manner ordained by old tradition, and on August 28th of this year the old Colours were lodged in St. Mary's Church, Madras, with all possible honour; two Colour-Sergeants came to Madras from Cannanore in charge of the Colours, and the guards which paraded on this historic occasion were furnished by the 3rd Battalion 60th Rifles.

Lieutenant-Colonel H. D. Taylor, formerly of the Madras Fusiliers, presented the Regiment with a very handsome pair of Colour-belts which were used in review order for very many years.

1867 At the beginning of January, 1867, the Regiment left Cannanore by Wings and proceeded via Bombay to Kamptee, where it was concentrated by February 18th.

During the cold weather of this year there were some manœuvres in the vicinity of Kamptee which were attended by the Commander-in-Chief, General Sir William Mansfield, who took the opportunity of addressing the Madras Fusiliers and expressing the pleasure he felt in meeting again a Regiment which had in the past rendered such distinguished service. Sir William then announced that all Presidency distinctions having now been swept away in the British portion of the Army, regiments would serve henceforth all over India, and he hoped therefore that the approaching removal of the Regiment to Lucknow would not be unpopular.

1868 On January 28th, 1868, then, the Madras Fusiliers marched from Kamptee to Jubbulpore and proceeded thence by rail to Lucknow which was reached on February 26th. During this year an expeditionary force proceeded from India to Abyssinia under command of General Napier, who had been chief of the staff to Outram during the operations for the relief of Lucknow at the time of the Mutiny; the Regiment was not employed, but three officers—Captains Seton, Graeme and Beaumont—served with the Land Transport Corps, and Captain Graeme was promoted Brevet Major for his services.

1869 The Madras Fusiliers had been little more than a year at Lucknow when, on May 19th, 1869, orders were received for the Regiment to hold itself in readiness to proceed to England—on its first tour of home service, being the second of the old Company's regiments to leave India. Early in the month following volunteering to other British regiments stationed in the country was opened, when a total of 205 men from the Royal Madras Fusiliers volunteered in varying numbers for 21 different regiments and battalions.

1870 The Regiment remained at Lucknow during the remainder of this year, finally leaving for Bombay on January 28th,

OFFICERS' BUCKLE FOR BELT.

VALEDICTORY ORDERS

1870, and on the next day the following valedictory order was published from Army Headquarters, Calcutta:—

"*The Commander-in-Chief in India has great satisfaction in publishing to the Army the following farewell order of the Right Hon. the Viceroy and Governor-General in Council, which has been issued on the occasion of the approaching departure for England of the 102nd Royal Madras Fusiliers.*

"'*His Excellency, in bidding farewell, feels assured that the Madras Fusiliers will maintain in the new field to which they are called that high character for courage, discipline, and efficiency, which they have gained by more than a century's good service in the plains of India.*

"'*In 1868 The Right Hon. the Viceroy and Governor-General in Council published a farewell order on the occasion of the approaching departure for England for the first time of the 101st Regiment Royal Bengal Fusiliers.*

"'*The 102nd Royal Madras Fusiliers proceeds to England during this cold season, and much that was said in 1868 by His Excellency in Council, in bidding farewell to the 101st Fusiliers is applicable to the 102nd Regiment; while on the other hand there are peculiarities in the career of the 102nd Regiment quite different from those which characterize the services of the 101st Regiment.*

"'*When the order of October 30th, 1868, was issued, the 101st Regiment was quitting its own Presidency, where it was very well-known; while the 102nd Regiment is leaving a Presidency to which it did not belong as a Corps of the Indian Army, though its service in Bengal and in concert with Bengal troops had made its name and reputation at various times, and especially in 1857, almost as well known in the Presidency as if it had been a Bengal Regiment.*

"'*The Government of the Presidency of Fort St. George detailed the services of the 1st Madras European Regiment (now the 102nd Royal Madras Fusiliers) in a General Order of March 12th, 1841, when the motto "Spectamur Agendo" was conferred upon the Regiment, and when it was allowed to bear numerous names of actions and services in which it had been engaged, upon its Colours.*

"'*His Excellency the Governor-General in Council feels that he cannot do better than here give a copy of that order honourable as it is to the 102nd Regiment, though the mere record of names gives no adequate idea of the arduous struggles in which the Regiment was engaged during a period of a hundred years, not only with nations, but also against French troops led by distinguished commanders.*'"

Then followed the General Order of March 12th, 1841, already given in full in a previous chapter, whereafter the Viceroy's farewell continued as follows:—

"'*Since the issue of the above order by the Governor-in-Council of Fort St. George, the Regiment has been employed in the following services:—*

"'*Second Burmese War, 1852, 1853, and 1854, and present at the capture of Pegu, relief of Pegu, investment of Pegu, and operations in its vicinity. A portion of the Regiment was in the expedition from Rangoon to Tonghoo and capture of that place. A detachment at the entering of Beeling by escalade, and another employed in clearing rebels and dacoits from around Beeling in 1854; a detachment subsequently employed with the Special Commissioner for marking the boundary had several encounters with the Burmese. Ten officers and one hundred and eighteen men of the Regiment were killed or died of wounds or disease in this Second Burmese War.*

"'*In March, 1857, the Regiment embarked for Persia, but was shortly after recalled, as the war had terminated. Called to Bengal in consequence of the critical state of affairs in that Presidency, the Regiment landed in Calcutta on May 23rd, 1857, under Colonel Neill, and was at once pushed towards the North-West. A detachment was present at the suppression of the Mutiny at Benares and at the clearing of the rebels from Allahabad in June, 1857.*

"'*The Regiment advanced from Allahabad and formed part of General Havelock's force at the actions of Futtypore, Aoung, Pundoo Nuddee, Cawnpore, Oonau, Bussarat Gunge, Burrakee Chowkee, Bhittoor, Mangulwar and Alam Bagh; and in the relief of the Presidency of Lucknow on September 25th, 1857. Present from that date at the defence of Lucknow (including several actions) till November*

CAP BADGE AND BUCKLE.

22nd, 1857. *A detachment served with Lord Clyde's force at the final relief of Lucknow, including the storming of the Secundrabagh and Shah Nujeef. The Regiment was with Sir J. Outram's force at the Alam Bagh from November, 1857, till March, 1858; at the capture of Lucknow, and subsequently in the various affairs in Oudh until the end of 1858. In this war seven officers were killed or died of wounds, two died of disease, six were wounded, and three hundred and fifty-two men were killed or died of wounds or disease. The Regiment on reaching Calcutta in February, 1859, on its way back to its own Presidency, was received with the highest honours, and was addressed by the Viceroy in the following terms :—'"*

Then followed the Viceroy's speech which is already given on a preceding page.

"'*The Right Honourable the Viceroy and Governor-General in Council wishes this distinguished corps a hearty farewell, and every good fortune in its future career out of India, and entertains no doubt that in other countries it will maintain, as the 102nd Regiment, the high reputation it has won throughout its long and varied service in India as the Madras Europeans and 1st Madras Fusiliers.*'"

On February 20th, 1870, the Madras Fusiliers left India after an uninterrupted service of more than two centuries in the country, embarking in H.M's. Indian troopship *Malabar*.

Although the Suez Canal had been formally opened in the previous November, it does not appear to have been yet available for the passage of ships so large as the Indian troopships, and the Regiment was trans-shipped at Suez. Two companies, containing only 64 non-commissioned officers and men, under Captains Seton and Woods, came on in the *Himalaya*, reached Portsmouth on Monday, March 21st, and proceeded next day to Dover, and, disembarking, the 2 companies took up their quarters in the Citadel. The remaining 8 companies completed their passage to England in the *Serapis* which arrived at Portsmouth on the 25th, and the troops landing on the following day proceeded by rail to Dover. Here the Regiment was joined by the depot companies which during the previous year had been stationed first at Walmer and latterly at Shorncliffe. The following disembarked at Portsmouth with the Headquarter Companies :—Lieutenant-Colonel Raikes, C.B., in command ; Captains Harcourt, Hornsby, Beaumont, Duncan and Cleland ; Lieutenants Parry, Adjutant, Stevens, Rogers, Blair, Carr, Turner and McCaskill ; Ensigns Hornsby and Craig ; Surgeon Smyth ; Assistant-Surgeons Tyrrell and Kirkwood; Paymaster Thomson ; Quartermaster Moore, 437 non-commissioned officers and men, 46 women and 81 children. Lieutenant Tremenhere came on separately in the *Crocodile* troopship.

The officers at the Depot—then with the 6th Depot Battalion—at the time of the arrival of the Regiment in England, appear to have been Captains Daniell and Dunbar, Lieutenants Blunt and Humfrey, Ensigns Elliott and Kerr.

The *Pioneer*, mentioning the departure of the Regiment from India, remarked :—" We lately noticed the farewell order to the 102nd Regiment (the old 1st Madras Fusiliers), which rehearsed the splendid services of the Regiment in generous and lofty language. But an acquaintance with the inner circumstances of the Corps, as to promotion and preferment to staff appointments, shows that the generosity of Government towards it has been strictly confined to words. The Army List shows that this illustrious and unlucky Regiment contains no fewer than twelve Lieutenants who have served more than ten years each. How long will it be before the last of them gets his company ? The first three of those indeed were already lieutenants in the 1st Madras Fusiliers when that corps under Neill came to the rescue of England, and played a foremost part in rolling back the Mutiny from Benares, Allahabad and Cawnpore. This slowness of promotion is a misfortune ; but that Government has neglected all its opportunities of mitigating the misfortune is ingratitude, and belies discreditably the language of Lord Canning—' Tell them ' (alluding to the rest of the Madras Army) ' that the name of the 1st Fusiliers will never be forgotten on this side of India, and all that is due to your courage, constancy, and efficiency will never be effaced from the mind of the Government under whose orders you have served.' An alleviation might easily have been extended to the ill-fortune of the subalterns of this Corps by opening the door of the Staff Corps as widely to them as it had been opened to men with smaller claims. But we are assured that every application for admittance from an officer of the 102nd of more than seven years' service has been refused. In other words, the extraordinary duration of their ill-luck is given as the reason for making it perpetual."

The Madras Fusiliers had now, for the first time in their stormy career, enjoyed more than a decade of peace, but nearly twice that period of time was to elapse before the 102nd Foot—under yet another designation—was to again proceed on active service in the field.

CHAPTER VII

1870—1899.

HOME SERVICE—GIBRALTAR—BECOMES THE 1ST BATTALION ROYAL DUBLIN FUSILIERS—CEYLON—HOME SERVICE AGAIN—THE OUTBREAK OF THE WAR IN SOUTH AFRICA.

1870 THE Madras Fusiliers brought home with them from Lucknow a tiger cub which had been given to the Regiment by the officers of the 5th Lancers. The name of this tiger was "Plassey"; he grew to be a very fine animal, was always quite tame and gentle, and, led by a Fusilier, he was accustomed to march in front of the band, and on guest nights in the Officers' Mess was led round the mess table. On one occasion the soldier who looked after him, having taken more drink than he could carry, took refuge in "Plassey's" cage, and on the arrival of a picquet to remove the incapacitated soldier to the guard-room, the tiger stood over his keeper and showed his teeth to the men of the picquet, who wisely withdrew, leaving the soldier where he was. When sober the man left the cage quite unmolested!

"Plassey" was not popular in Dover, where the civilian population was afraid of him, so in 1871 he was sent to the Zoological Gardens and died there in 1878, his head being mounted for the Officers' Mess of the 102nd.

In May, 1870, fusilier caps were issued to the Regiment, and in the same month the men were re-armed with breech-loading rifles with steel barrels; in August a new valise equipment was introduced.

1872 The establishment of the Battalion was fixed at 700 rank and file, but on February 1st, 1871, this was reduced to 600, while on April 1st of the year following a further change

From the "Illustrated London News" of 30th April, 1870.

A REGIMENTAL PET TIGER.

"The Royal Madras Fusiliers, of which regiment the first detachment arrived at Dover on the 25th ult., have brought home with them from Lucknow a fine young Bengal tiger, presented to them by its captors, two officers of the 5th Royal Irish Lancers, Captains Thackwell and Chaffy. These gentlemen, when shooting in the Terai last hot season, encountered a tigress with two cubs and killed the mother, but not before Captain Thackwell's arm had been severely torn and bitten, so that it was found afterwards necessary to amputate the limb; and this operation, we regret to say, caused his death from exhaustion in a few days. One of the cubs did not long survive its arrival at Lucknow; the other was given to the Royal Madras Fusiliers for a regimental pet, which is the more appropriate since the figure of a tiger has for many years formed the emblem of the Regiment. 'Plassey,' as this young animal is named by its masters, is hardly yet full grown; and, though possessing great strength and a large appetite, has shown no sign of a ferocious disposition. He delights in playing with any men or animals that will go near him. He had a free passage from India to Suez on board the 'Jumna,' and from Alexandria to England on board the 'Serapis,' granted to him by the kindness of Captains Rickard and Piers."

From some paper unknown, probably a Dover paper.

A LOCAL TIGER STORY.

"A singular scene occurred the other day at the citadel at Dover. The 102nd Regiment brought with them from India a very fine young tiger. He is very tame. It is stated that recently his keeper got the worse for drink, and made his way to the den, fearing detection. An officer, seeing that the man lay asleep and the tiger sitting near him, sent for the picquet, who at any other time can do as they please with the beast. The moment they attempted to go near the keeper the tiger growled, and very soon let them see they must keep off. For two hours the tiger kept guard over the keeper, who, on awakening, was surprised to see no one dare come near his charge."

was made and the establishment then laid down was as follows:—
1 Colonel, 1 Lieutenant-Colonel, 2 Majors, 10 Captains, 16 Lieutenants, 1 Paymaster, 1 Adjutant, 1 Quartermaster, 1 Sergeant-Major, 1 Quartermaster-Sergeant, 1 Bandmaster, 1 Drum-Major, 1 Paymaster-Sergeant, 1 Armourer-Sergeant, 1 Orderly-Room Clerk, 10 Colour-Sergeants, 1 Pioneer-Sergeant, 1 Sergeant Cook, 1 Sergeant Instructor of Musketry, 28 Sergeants, 18 Drummers, 40 Corporals, and 480 Privates.

During the two years that the Royal Madras Fusiliers remained at Dover they proceeded each summer to Aldershot to take part in the manœuvres, and at the conclusion of those in 1872 the Regiment marched to Southampton from where it crossed over to the Isle of Wight and was quartered at Parkhurst, sending one company to Marchwood, two to Fort Victoria and one to Sandown.

1873 For some considerable time past a Parliamentary Committee had been in session to consider and report upon "the organization of the various military forces of the Country"; two reports were presented, in February and July, 1872, and as a result on March 3rd, 1873, a General Order, No. 18, was specially issued introducing a new scheme for the localization of the Army. Under this scheme the 102nd Royal Madras Fusiliers and the 103rd Royal Bombay Fusiliers were linked together and formed the 66th Sub-District with a Brigade Depot at Naas, in County Kildare, Ireland. The Counties of Dublin, Wicklow, Kildare and Carlow composed the sub-district, while to the two regular regiments were affiliated the following five Militia Battalions: the Carlow Rifles, the Kildare Rifles, the Wicklow Rifles, the Royal Dublin City (Queen's Own Royal Regiment), and the Dublin County Light Infantry.

The command of the Brigade Depot was bestowed upon Colonel J. B. Spurgin, C.B., C.S.I., who on completing his command of the Royal Madras Fusiliers in 1873 had been succeeded by Lieutenant-Colonel H. J. Jepson, and who had himself taken Colonel Raikes's place in December, 1870.

The Depot does not appear to have been finally formed before the beginning of the winter of 1873, and the following are the names of the officers who in the first instance composed it, with the regiments to which they belonged :—Colonel J. B. Spurgin, C.B., C.S.I. (102nd), Major G. J. Harcourt (102nd), Captains J. J. Barclay (102nd), F. Reeves (103rd), W. H. Brind (103rd) and W. B. Lindsay (102nd), Lieutenants J. Blair (102nd), H. F. Heathcote (103rd) and S. J. Wynne (103rd) ; Paymaster, Hon. Major J. O'Connor and Surgeon-Major J. H. Finnemore. The " other ranks " were made up by 2 Colour-Sergeants, 4 Sergeants, 5 Corporals, 2 Drummers and 20 Privates from each of the two linked regiments—102nd and 103rd.

On June 14th, 1873, the establishment of the Regiment was fixed at 28 Officers, 42 Non-commissioned Officers, 16 Drummers, 40 Corporals and 480 Privates.

1874 In May, 1874, the Royal Madras Fusiliers left the Isle of Wight and sailed in the *Tamar* to Portland, there relieving the 4th Battalion 60th Rifles, and both here and in the last garrison the men made a fine reputation as a grand shooting regiment ; in 1874 " F " Company was the best shooting company in the Army, while in the year following this honourable place was taken by " A " Company, the 102nd being this year the best shooting regiment in the whole of the British Army.

1876 The " Blue Caps " remained something under two years in Portland, and then on April 15th, 1876, embarked in the *Assistance* for conveyance to Gibraltar, which was reached on the 23rd and here the Regiment relieved the 31st Foot, occupying quarters at Europa and Windmill Hill Barracks ; the embarking strength was 20 Officers, 36 Sergeants, 17 Drummers, 39 Corporals and 563 Privates ; the following are the names of the officers accompanying the corps :—Lieutenant-Colonel Jepson, Majors Harcourt and Hornsby ; Captains Cleland, Lindsay, Carr, Turner, Faber, McCaskill and Vetch ; Lieutenants Kerr, Dowdall, Hutchinson, Palmer, Bird (Adjutant), and Oates ; Second-

Lieutenants Hicks, Mills and Shadforth; Paymaster, Captain Thomson, and Quartermaster Stenson.

Gibraltar was at this time by no means a health-resort, the Regiment suffered much from sickness and some 10 men died during the first year there.

1878 In 1878 Russia and Turkey were engaged in hostilities, and at one time it appeared by no means unlikely that the United Kingdom might be embroiled and that it might again be necessary for her, as in 1854, to declare war against Russia; the Army and Militia Reserves were called up and all the regiments on the home establishment were brought up to a war footing; while it was considered by no means improbable that troops might be sent to Turkey from Malta and Gibraltar. The war-crisis did not, however, endure for more than a few weeks and on July 31st the Army and Militia reserves were disbanded and things resumed their normal peace conditions.

1879 At the end of this year the Regiment received orders to prepare for embarkation for Ceylon, and on January 18th, 1879, it sailed from Gibraltar in the *Tamar*. At this time General Lord Napier of Magdala was Governor and Commander-in-Chief of Gibraltar, and he came down to the transport to bid the Regiment farewell, addressing officers and men in the most flattering terms, expressing his sincere regret at losing so fine a set of men from his command, and recalling the days when he had fought alongside the Regiment, then the 1st Madras Fusiliers, round Lucknow.

Ceylon was reached on February 18th and disembarking next day the Fusiliers relieved the 57th Foot and took up quarters in the Fort at Colombo, sending two companies on detachment to Kandy and one company to Point de Galle.

1880 During the year 1880 the British Government had been engaged in hostilities with the Boers of the Transvaal; matters had been going none too well and our troops had suffered some serious checks and even reverses, and the matter of sending out considerable reinforcements to General Sir Evelyn Wood, now in command in the field in South Africa, was considered. On January 2nd,

1881, telegraphic orders were received in Colombo from home ordering the Headquarters and four companies of the 102nd to be held in readiness to proceed on active service to Natal; three days later the order was cancelled, and matters remained as usual until March 1st, when the order was repeated, but directing six companies to be sent now in place of the four originally called for. Headquarters, with "C," "D," "E," "F," "G," and "H" Companies, strength 18 officers and 603 other ranks, embarked in H.M.S. *Euphrates* on March 13th under Lieutenant-Colonel J. Duncan, who had been promoted *vice* Colonel Harcourt in the previous June, and arrived at Durban on March 29th—only to learn that peace had been concluded with the Boers and that the Regiment was to return at once to Ceylon without disembarking. The Royal Madras Fusiliers were joined at Durban on April 8th by a draft from the linked Battalion, and then sailed at once for Ceylon, which was reached on the 29th of the same month.

During this year a change of very great importance was made in the organization, titles, and—in many cases—in the uniform of the regiments of the Line and the Militia, under General Order No. 41 of May 1st, 1881, but which was specially issued on the 11th of the previous month. Under this order the infantry of the Army was for the future to be organized in Territorial Districts, each of four battalions for Great Britain and five for Ireland, the 1st and 2nd Battalions of each being Line and the remaining two or three Militia. The old numbers were to be done away with, and each regiment was to bear a territorial designation corresponding to the particular locality with which it was connected. All honours, etc., hitherto borne by either Line Battalions of the Territorial Regiment were for the future to be borne by both, while the colour of the facings was for Irish Regiments to be green, except that Royal Regiments were to retain blue facings with the national lace, which for Irish Regiments was to be "shamrock."

Then with General Order No. 69 of July—specially issued on June 30th—there was published an Appendix giving the composition and titles of Territorial Regiments, and in this it was announced that the 102nd and 103rd Regiments would form henceforth the 1st and 2nd Battalions respectively of "The Royal Dublin Fusiliers," of which the Carlow, Kildare, Dublin City and Dublin County Militia would form the 3rd, 4th and 5th Battalions. The precedence of the Territorial Regiment was to be 69th, the headquarters of the Regimental District was still, as heretofore, to be at Naas, while the uniform remained unchanged as to colour, being scarlet with blue facings.

In connection with the above the following appeared in regimental orders of June 25th, 1881 :—" In publishing the above extract from General Orders the Commanding Officer desires it to be understood that from the 1st proximo inclusive the Regiment will become the 1st Battalion The Royal Dublin Fusiliers, a title which he feels sure will win the heart of every Irishman under its Colours, as it is one which serves to keep up the memory of home, and of all that is dear to the soldier ; and the Commanding Officer feels confident that under this new title all ranks of the Regiment will strive to uphold and maintain the combined honours and distinctions which bear comparison with those of any other Regiment in the Service, and which point to a history of which both Regiments may justly be proud."

1884 The 1st Battalion of the Royal Dublin Fusiliers, as the Regiment must now and henceforth be called, remained some considerable time longer in Ceylon, but of its stay in the island, there is nothing of special significance to record—the one outstanding event being the replacement in June, 1884, of Lieutenant-Colonel Duncan, on completion of his period of command, by Lieutenant-Colonel Cleland.

1885 On November 27th, 1885, the Battalion left Ceylon, after a stay there of nearly seven years, and embarked for home in the troopship *Himalaya*, at a strength of 18 Officers, 2 Warrant Officers, 44 Sergeants, 37 Corporals, 16 Drummers and 454 Privates.

As an aftermath of the Nile Expedition of 1884 and the withdrawal of a large number of British troops from Upper Egypt, there was at this time a recrudescence of trouble in the Soudan, a large force of dervishes was reported to be advancing against Kosheh and Wady Halfa, and such troops as were adjacent were sent up to meet and check them, while others were needed to take their places in Lower Egypt and on the lines of communication. This was the situation when the 1st Battalion Royal Dublin Fusiliers was passing in the *Himalaya* through the Suez Canal, and it was hurriedly disembarked at Alexandria, as a precautionary measure, on December 13th, and was quartered at Ras-el-Tin Barracks, the married families going on to Malta in the troopship. The stay of the

1886 Battalion in Egypt was not a prolonged one, for in the New Year the prospects of disturbance and the need for more troops up the Nile had passed, and on February 27th, 1886, the Royal Dublin Dusiliers embarked again in the transport *Poona*, arrived at Kingstown on March 13th and proceeded by rail to Mullingar. Here a draft of 4 officers and 208 other ranks was waiting and was taken on the strength; these had been sent from the Depot to Naas to take over barracks and get things in order for the incoming Battalion.

During this year there was a certain amount of rioting in the north and other parts of Ireland and the troops were consequently a good deal moved about—three companies being sent in May to Dublin; in June the Battalion, less one company remaining in charge of barracks at Mullingar, moved to the Curragh; on August 14th six companies returned post-haste to Dublin, Headquarters and about 100 men then returning to Mullingar; and actually it

1887 was not until the early part of the year 1887 that the Dublin Companies gradually returned to headquarters as troops were withdrawn from the disturbed districts, but even then one company, under Major Holmes, was detached to Sligo.

The following were the officers who were serving with the Battalion on April 1st of this year :—Colonel Cleland, Lieutenant-Colonel Vetch, Majors Holmes, Kerr and Morrison, Captains Mansel, Hughes, Oates, George and Scott, Lieutenants Goddard (Adjutant), English, Gordon, O'Neill, Rutherfoord, Sheppard, Bacon, Loveband,

Godley, Bolton and Weldon, Second-Lieutenant Roddy and Lieutenant and Quartermaster Baker.

The Battalion remained in Ireland some five years longer, moving in December, 1887, to the Curragh, thence in September, 1890, to Newry and then leaving in June, 1893, for England, **1890** where it was sent by steamship and rail to Strensall Camp in Yorkshire. While at the Curragh in 1887 a Field Service Cap, Austrian pattern, and of a special shade of blue in memory of the "Blue Caps" of Mutiny days, was introduced for wear by the officers of the Battalion.

In 1893 the Battalion was re-armed with the improved Lee-
1893 Metford Rifle, Mark I, and on February 8th, 1895, Lieutenant-General Sir J. B. Spurgin, formerly of the "Blue Caps," was
1895 appointed Colonel of the Regiment *vice* Lieutenant-General Fraser, transferred to the colonelcy of the Royal Irish Regiment; while in May the Battalion furnished guards of honour on the occasion of the arrival at and departure from Sheffield of their Royal Highnesses the Duke and Duchess of Connaught.

On July 8th the "Blue Caps" moved from Sheffield to Gosport, and in the following month, made up to four companies of a strength of 501 all ranks, left via Netley, Ocknell and Rockford for manœuvres in the New Forest area, returning at their conclusion to Portsmouth and the Anglesey Barracks into which the remainder of the Battalion had moved during the absence of Headquarters. While stationed at Portsmouth the 1st Battalion Royal Dublin Fusiliers was called upon for the performance of many duties of a ceremonial
1896 character. Thus in February, 1896, it furnished a detachment of 3 officers and 100 rank and file for attendance at the funeral in the Isle of Wight of H.R.H. Prince Henry of Battenberg; for a fortnight in the autumn the Battalion furnished the Queen's Guard at Osborne, Captain Chapman, Second-Lieutenant Hudlestone and 44 other ranks being detailed; while later again the officers and men were called out to line the Railway Jetty on the occasion of the embarkation there of H.I.M. the Emperor of Russia.

In this year a new valise equipment was issued and taken into wear; in April Lieutenant Pilson and 30 non-commissioned officers, rank and file of the Battalion were detailed for instruction as a mounted infantry section, and proceeded to Aldershot to join the Mounted Infantry Battalion which had there been formed, and of which Captain Godley, of the Dublin Fusiliers, had been appointed Adjutant; and after the very briefest of training this section embarked on May 2nd for South Africa in the *Tantallon Castle*; Captain Godley also sailed in the same transport.

On December 31st, 1896, the following officers were on the strength of the Battalion:—Lieutenant-Colonel Riddell, Majors Hicks, O'Neill, Shadforth and Gordon (at the Depot), Captains Pearse, Strickland, Chapman, Mainwaring, Smith and Godley (South Africa), Lieutenants Pilson (South Africa), Royce-Tomkin, Fetherstonhaugh, Dibley, Romer, Venour (Depot), and Riccard, Second-Lieutenants Higginson, Hill, Hudleston, Seppings, Watson and Molesworth; Captain Dickinson (Adjutant), and Lieutenant Ward (Quartermaster).

The following were the nationalities in the Battalion at this date:—

English...	...	1 warrant officer and 128 sergeants, rank and file.
Scotch ...	...	0 ,, ,, ,, 4 ,, ,, ,, ,,
Irish ...	...	1 ,, ,, ,, 538 ,, ,, ,, ,,
Born in India ...		0 ,, ,, ,, 2 ,, ,, ,, ,,
Foreigner	...	0 ,, ,, ,, 1 ,, ,, ,, ,,
Total	...	2 warrant officers and 673 sergeants, rank and file.

1897 At the end of April, 1897, the Battalion moved by rail from Portsmouth to Aldershot and on arrival here was quartered in Ramillies Barracks, North Camp, and on June 22nd was taken up to London to take part in the celebrations of Her Majesty's Jubilee, lining Piccadilly from Hamilton Place to the Naval and Military Club, Lord Palmerston's old house.

On the following day the Mounted Infantry Section, which had left England for South Africa rather over a year previously, rejoined the service companies at Aldershot. When the original Mounted Infantry Force was raised, the detachment under Lieutenant Pilson, furnished by the Battalion, formed No. 3 Section of the Irish Company, the force being commanded by Lieutenant-Colonel Alderson, and on the Mashonaland trouble breaking out while the Mounted Infantry were stationed at Wynberg, Cape Colony, the Irish and Rifle Companies were ordered to Mashonaland in June via Beira and Salisbury. The Royal Dublin Fusiliers detachment took part in the action at Makoni Kraal on August 3rd, and in several smaller engagements, and had three men wounded—Privates James Smith, Patrick Colin and Patrick Byrne. When the detachment sailed from Durban on its way home in May, 1897, in the *Dunera*, four men were left behind, having joined the British South Africa Company's Police, while on arrival at Southampton two men remained in hospital at Netley.

When in July, 1896, Captain Godley was appointed Staff Officer to the Mashonaland Field Force, Lieutenant Pilson succeeded him as Adjutant of the Mounted Infantry; both officers received brevet promotion for their services.

Lieutenant-Colonel Alderson made the following report on those who served under him :—

"The detachment under Lieutenant (now Brevet Major) Pilson did their work most excellently at all times, and this was specially the case when they were on active service in Mashonaland. They were always ready and willing to work, cool and handy under fire, and proved themselves good soldiers. Of Brevet Major Pilson I have a very high opinion, and I had much pleasure in reporting on him to Sir Frederick Carrington, K.C.B., K.C.M.G., commanding the troops in Rhodesia, as follows :—' Very cool under fire and with a good knowledge of how to treat men and of professional details ; I consider that Lieutenant Pilson is an excellent officer. As I reported to you in my telegram of September 2nd he commanded a detached patrol with success.' Of the non-commissioned officers and men I would specially bring to your notice the following :—Colour-Sergeant Campbell proved himself a valuable and reliable

Colour Sergeant and did excellent work at all times; Sergeant Dardis did good work as section sergeant; Lance-Corporals Greene and Joyce, Privates Byrne (severely wounded), Chapman, O'Brien (No. 3099), McCarthy and Brown. How much I appreciate the very good work done and the loyal support given me by Brevet Major Godley I think you already know from previous correspondence, and I will only add how much pleasure I had in bringing him to the notice of Sir Frederick Carrington, and subsequently in doing my best to rectify the mistake made in regard to his brevet."

1898 In December, 1898, those officers and men present with the Battalion received their medals for the Rhodesia Expedition at the hands of General Sir Redvers Buller.

During the autumn of this year the Battalion was re-armed with the Lee-Metford Rifle, Mark II, and later a new pattern cap badge was issued—a white metal scroll inscribed "Royal Dublin Fusiliers," surmounted by a brass grenade, on the ball of which was the Royal Tiger and Elephant in white metal.

1899 On May 2nd, 1899, the "Blue Caps," now commanded by Lieutenant-Colonel G. A. Mills, recently promoted from the 2nd Battalion, moved from Aldershot to the Curragh.

During the summer of this year the long-standing disagreement between the British Cabinet and the Transvaal Government led, in the first place, to a situation of extreme tension, and finally to the outbreak of war. The Government of the Transvaal had put forward a claim to be considered as a sovereign State; this claim was refused by the British authorities in September of the year; and on receipt, and largely no doubt in consequence, of this refusal the President and his followers incontinently rejected every one of the counter-proposals which the English Cabinet had earlier advanced. The Government in London now realized that the outbreak of war was by no means impossible, and that our garrisons in South Africa were dangerously weak in face of the warlike and indeed threatening attitude of the Transvaalers and the uncertainty of the action of the Orange Free State. Reinforcements were therefore sent to South Africa from Europe and 5,000 British troops were ordered from India to Natal, these all arriving in the country before the end of September. The 2nd Battalion of the Royal Dublin Fusiliers was already at this time at Pietermaritzburg, Natal. This month had hardly come to an end before the Government of the Orange Free State made it abundantly clear that, in the event of war between the United Kingdom and the Transvaal, their whole weight would be thrown on the side of their sister-state; on October 9th a Proclamation was issued in Great Britain and Ireland calling out the Army Reserves; and on the same day President Kruger presented an ultimatum to our representative demanding an answer within 48 hours. Her Majesty's Government refused so much as to discuss this ultimatum, with the result that on October 11th the Transvaal and the Orange Free State declared war against Great Britain and sent their armed forces across our border from north and west.

On October 7th orders were received for the "Blue Caps" to mobilize and form part of the 5th (Irish) Brigade, commanded by Major-General Hart, in the Third Division under General Gatacre, for service in South Africa. As originally formed the 5th Brigade contained the 1st Battalions of the Inniskilling Fusiliers, Connaught Rangers, and Royal Dublin Fusiliers, and the 2nd Battalion of the Royal Irish Rifles. By October 17th mobilization was completed and the Battalion was then ordered to embark at Queenstown on November 10th; while on the 2nd the following letter of farewell from Lieutenant-General Sir J. B. Spurgin, the Colonel of the Regiment, was published in Battalion Orders :—

"DEAR COLONEL MILLS,

"The time for the departure of the Regiment under your command for active service in South Africa is now at hand. Accept my sincerest congratulations at the prospect of joining the 2nd Battalion in trying conclusion with the Boers, and I know well that the Regiment will fully emulate its predecessors on active service, both in arduous fatigue and in giving hard blows, for it is inherent in every Fusilier.

"My warm and hearty wishes go with you, and with every officer, non-commissioned officer and man, and with God's blessing give you a speedy and successful return."

The advance party, consisting of "B" Company under Second-Lieutenants de Salis and MacLeod, left the Curragh for Queenstown on November 9th, and was followed next day by Battalion Headquarters and the remaining companies, played to the railway station by the bands of the 8th Hussars and 1st Battalion Leicestershire Regiment; by 3.30 p.m. the 1st Battalion Royal Dublin Fusiliers had embarked at Queenstown in the *Bavarian*, and half-an-hour later the ship drew away from the quay and commenced her voyage to South Africa.

The composition of the Battalion was 28 Officers, 1 Warrant Officer, and 921 Non-commissioned Officers, Rank and File, and the following are the names of the officers of the Staff and Companies :—

Lieutenant-Colonel G. A. Mills, in command, Major H. P. Hicks, second-in-command, Lieutenant P. Maclear (Adjutant), Lieutenant H. A. F. Watson (Machine Gun Officer), Lieutenant B. P. Lefroy (Transport Officer), Hon. Lieutenant J. Ward (Quartermaster), Lieutenant L. N. Lloyd, R.A.M.C. in medical charge, and Sergeant-Major T. Hartigan (Sergeant-Major).

"*A*" *Company*: Major A. W. Gordon, Lieutenant J. F. S. Winnington (Worcester Regiment, attached), and Second-Lieutenant A. Brodhurst-Hill.

"*B*" *Company*: Second-Lieutenants E. A. A. de Salis and R. MacLeod.

"*C*" *Company*: Captain A. H. Bacon and Second-Lieutenant J. C. Halahan.

"*D*" *Company*: Captain R. M. F. Swift, Lieutenant J. W. H. Seppings and Second-Lieutenant A. Moore.

"*E*" *Company*: Lieutenants E. A. Molesworth and H. Wethered (East Lancashire Regiment, attached).

"*F*" *Company*: Captain A. J. Chapman, Lieutenant G. Hudleston and Second-Lieutenant J. S. Burra.

"*G" Company*: Captain C. B. J. Riccard, Second-Lieutenants R. G. B. Jeffreys, and R. L. H. Conlan.

"*H" Company*: Major W. H. S. O'Neill, Lieutenant G. D. Ewart (South Lancashire Regiment, attached), and Second-Lieutenant W. F. Stirling.

The troops on board the *Bavarian* were under the command of Colonel Ivor Herbert, C.B., and comprised No. 12 Field Company, Royal Engineers, 1st Battalion Connaught Rangers, 1st Battalion Royal Dublin Fusiliers, No. 15 Field Hospital, No. 8 Bearer Company and other details; while the vessel also carried the following foreign military attachés: Lieutenant-Colonel d'Amade (France), Captain Baron von Luttwitz (Germany), Major Gentilini (Italy), Lieutenant Colonel Stakovitch (Russia), and Captain Slocum (United States).

On November 28th the *Bavarian* arrived at Cape Town where it had been expected that the greater part of the Army Corps and Cavalry Division would disembark preparatory to commencing the advance on the capital of the Transvaal by way of the Orange Free State, in accordance with the general plan of campaign decided upon before General Sir Redvers Buller, the British Commander-in-Chief designate, had sailed from England. When, however, General Buller reached Cape Town on October 31st he was met with a situation which caused him the deepest anxiety. While he and the greater number of the units of the Expeditionary Force had been upon the high seas, the Natal Field Force had fought three comparatively indecisive actions and now lay hemmed in at Ladysmith, closely watched by the enemy in greatly superior strength; the safety of the Natal capital seemed very precarious; strong Boer forces were reported moving down towards the northern border of Cape Colony; Kimberley was threatened, while the absence of news from Mafeking made it at least doubtful whether that township might not already have been overwhelmed. The vanguard of the Army Corps was not due at Cape Town for some ten days and complete disembarkation could not be hoped for until early in December, so that at least a month must elapse before General Buller could begin his advance into the Free State.

"Notwithstanding these anxieties General Buller was at first inclined to adhere to the scheme originally designed, and to wait until he could remove the pressure on Ladysmith and Kimberley by striking straight at Bloemfontein. . . . Yet a few hours later it became evident that the whole case was graver than Sir Redvers had at first conceived"*; and on November 2nd Buller cabled to the War Office: " I consider that I must reinforce Natal, hang on to the Orange River Bridge, and give myself to organize troops expected from England. . . . I shall send Gatacre's Division on arrival to Natal, and with Methuen's and Clery's try to keep the main line open and relieve Kimberley."

As a result of this decision the Army Corps was practically broken up, its units separated and some of their commanders taken from them; thus General Sir W. Gatacre was sent round to East London, whence he moved on Stormberg, taking with him, among other troops, the 2nd Battalion Royal Irish Rifles of the 5th Brigade, while the *Bavarian* left Cape Town on the afternoon of the day of arrival there and sailed for Durban which was reached at noon of December 1st. Here the Battalion was at once disembarked and during the night proceeded to Pieter Maritzburg, arriving there next day and encamping to the west of Fort Napier.

The place of the 2nd Battalion Royal Irish Rifles in the 5th Brigade had now been taken by the 1st Border Regiment, while the 2nd Battalion Royal Dublin Fusiliers replaced the 1st which was temporarily relegated to the lines of communication. General Buller had reached Durban on November 25th and had now something like 19,000 men under his command, exclusive of line of communication troops; the officer exercising command immediately under General Buller was Lieutenant-General Sir C. Clery.

The Battalion spent three or four days at Maritzburg marching and manœuvring in the neighbourhood to get the men into hard condition after their sea voyage; and while here the buttons of the helmets were painted blue to keep up the traditions of the " Blue Caps."

* *Official History of the War in South Africa*, Vol. I, pp. 196, 197.

On the morning of the 6th, in accordance with orders received the day before, " A," " B," and " C " Companies—8 officers and 276 other ranks—left Maritzburg by rail under Major Hicks for temporary attachment to the 2nd Battalion, then at Frere, while later in the day the rest of the Battalion was railed to Mooi River station; on the 8th, leaving " H " Company at Mooi River the remainder were sent to Brynbella Farm, 9 miles north of Mooi River, and took up various positions to protect the railway, " H " Company rejoining headquarters on the 10th.

On November 14th very heavy gun-fire was heard in the direction of Colenso, some 25 miles to the north, and during the forepart of the following day both artillery and rifle fire was distinctly audible; later on news was received of the abortive attempt by Buller's army to cross the Tugela River.

The three companies of the 1st Battalion which had been detailed to join the 2nd Battalion, whose numbers were seriously reduced by losses at Talana and the inclusion of nearly one hundred men among the Ladysmith garrison, had reached Estcourt on December 6th, and marched thence on the next day to Frere as rearguard to a small column composed of a brigade division R.F.A. and the 1st Battalion Connaught Rangers. On joining the Headquarters of the 5th Brigade, then re-forming at Frere, the three companies of the 1st Battalion Royal Dublin Fusiliers attached to the 2nd Battalion of the Regiment, were at first permitted a separate organization, so that the 2nd Battalion had for a time eleven companies.

At Frere General Hart's Brigade formed part of an outpost line, holding a range of kopjes extending in a westerly direction from the railway line about 2¼ miles north of Frere. Here nothing of moment occurred until December 13th when the Brigade advanced 5 miles north to Chieveley where camp was pitched 4 or 5 miles south of Colenso, and well within view of the hills occupied by the Boers on the north bank of the Tugela River, which runs west and east through Colenso, a small straggling village of some 20 or 30 houses. Colenso, though insignificant in size, possessed a considerable strategical importance, as near it the river was crossed by two bridges, a road and a railway bridge, the latter being the largest on the Natal line.

On the south bank of the river near Colenso, the ground towards Chieveley is mostly undulating veldt, broken here and there by dongas and spruits, but in the more immediate vicinity there is much mimosa scrub. About 3 miles east rises Hlangwani Mountain, the western end of a range of hills forming part of the south bank of the Tugela; to the west the country is open and flat almost to the river bank. On the north bank a line of low kopjes follows the course of the river eastward, extending north for about a mile; then begins an open space of country about a mile and a half in width, somewhat broken by dongas. On the north of this again the ground commences to rise towards Grobelaar's Kloof and Onderbrook Mountain which lie north and north-east of the Colenso-Ladysmith road. The country on the north and to the west of the road is very open and flat for from 2 to 3 miles when it begins to rise, culminating in some high broken kopjes forming part of the same range as Grobelaar's Kloof. This range runs in a somewhat circular direction, striking the river east and west of Colenso about 4 or 5 miles apart, thus forming in a measure a horseshoe with Colenso between the two ends. There were three drifts across the river near the village; one about 100 yards north of the road bridge, another some 150 yards south, and a third, a bridle drift, about 2 miles west of the bridge.

To the 5th (Irish) Brigade was allotted the task of forcing the passage of the river by the bridle drift.*

"On the evening of the 14th it was known that the Army was to advance next day and attempt the passage of the Tugela. Colonel Cooper, commanding the 2nd Battalion Royal Dublin Fusiliers, assembled his officers in order to explain the orders. He stated that the 5th Brigade would cross the river at a drift 2 miles west of Colenso, then move down the left bank so as to take in rear

---

* What here follows is taken from Romer and Mainwaring, *The 2nd Battalion Royal Dublin Fusiliers in the South African War*, p. 34 *et seq.*

the Boers defending Colenso Bridge, which would be attacked by the 2nd Brigade. The Brigade Orders detailed the Dublin Fusiliers to lead the advance to the river, and afterwards to cover the rear of the Brigade when it moved down the left bank.

"Everyone was early astir on December 15th. Breakfasts were at 3 a.m., but before that hour tents had been struck and packed in the wagons in which great-coats, blankets and mess tins were also placed, so that the men only carried their haversacks, water-bottles, rifles and 150 rounds. The Brigade fell in at 3.30 a.m. It was still quite dark and . . . the advance was commenced just as the eastern horizon grew grey with the dawn.

"The Battalion, which led the Brigade, deployed into line to the right and then advanced by fours from the right of companies. In front rode the General with his staff and a Kaffir guide; behind came the other three battalions of the Brigade in mass. The deployment of the battalions brought . . . the three companies of the 1st Battalion on the right. In this order the Brigade moved across the broad expanse of veldt leading to the banks of the Tugela. In front, beyond the river rose tier on tier of ridges and kopjes, backed by the towering mass of Grobelaar's Kloof. . . . Only on a spur to the left front could be seen a few black specks, the figures of watching Boers.

"Soon the naval guns in front of Chieveley opened fire, dropping their shells on the horse shoe ridge to the north of Colenso and into a kraal further to the west. But no answer came. The Brigade moved on . . . there was a momentary halt in order to cross a spruit running diagonally across the line of march. The ridges in front grew nearer and plainer; they still seemed deserted although the eyes of many foes might be watching the advancing khaki-clad troops . . . . It was past 6 a.m. Suddenly the hiss of a shell sounded marvellously close, there was a metallic clang, and a cloud of dust arose some hundred yards in front. It was a Boer shrapnel and the battle had begun.

"Each company of the Battalion, without waiting for orders, front formed and doubled forward. The mounted officers at once dismounted, Major Hicks' horse being shot under him as he was in the very act of getting off its back . . . . Another shrapnel burst over the line, and then the enemy's musketry blazed forth, finding an excellent target in the massed Brigade which was deploying as best it could . . . . All did their best, the men rushed forward after their officers and at their signal lay down in the long grass, whence fire was opened at the invisible foe. It was very difficult to discover the Boer positions. There was one long trench near the kraal which the naval guns had been shelling, and further to the west could be seen another parapet from which came an occasional puff of smoke betraying a Martini rifle and black powder. But if the Boers could not be seen, they could be both heard and felt; there was one ceaseless rattle of Mausers, and a constant hum of bullets only drowned by the screams of the shells.

"Short rushes were made as a rule, and the flank companies edged away in order to give room for a more reasonable extension But no sooner had the Battalion opened fire than it was reinforced by companies of the Connaught Rangers, and, later, of the Inniskilling Fusiliers and the Border Regiment. In a comparatively short time after the first Boer shell the 5th Brigade had been practically crowded into one line. Officers led men of all the four regiments, and encouraged them with the cry, 'Come on, the Irish Brigade!' . . . . Small groups of men, led by an officer, jumped up, dashed forward a few score of yards, and then lay down. Nobody knew where the drift was, nobody had a clear idea of what was happening. All pushed forward blindly, animated by the sole idea of reaching the river bank . . . . The centre and right advanced through low scrub into a loop of the river. Some sections of the 1st Battalion on the extreme right came upon a spruit and, under shelter of the banks, pushed ahead of the line.

"Thus by short and constant rushes, the assailants worked their way forward. A brigade of Field Artillery was supporting the attack from behind, but they found it as difficult as the infantry did to locate the Boers, and most of their shells were quite harmless to the enemy, while a few dropped close to the attacking infantry.

They aided the latter indirectly, however, since the Boer guns turned their attention to them.

"General Buller had early recognized the difficulties of the 5th Brigade and sent orders for it to retire. But it is easier to send a force into a battle than to draw it back, and the great difficulty at Colenso was to communicate with the Company Officers, who had to be left entirely to their own initiative. Finally an officer of the Connaught Rangers volunteered to take to the firing line General Hart's written order to retire. He succeeded in reaching the front, and then, thinking that he had struck the right of the line, turned to his left. In reality he had gone to the centre of the attack, and consequently the retirement was carried out partially and by fractions. The left fell back about 10 a.m. in good order, though the Boers, as usual, redoubled their fire when they saw their foes begin to retreat. The centre and right having received no order nor warning, clung to their ground and in some cases even made a further advance. Section after section, however, gradually realized that their left flank was uncovered and that a general retreat of the Brigade was in progress. A score of men, under the command of an officer, would rise up and double back, causing as they did so an instant quickening of the enemy's fire. All round the running figures the bullets splashed, raising little jets of dust. Occasionally a man would stumble forward or sink down as if tired, but it seemed wonderful that the rain of bullets did not claim more victims; they claimed enough, however, of the unfortunate three companies of the 1st Battalion, whom the order to retire never reached. Till 1 p.m. and the arrival of the Boers, they lay down where they were, suffering a loss of some 60 per cent. When at last Major Hicks realized the situation, he touched with his stick the man on his right to tell him to pass the word to retire—but he touched a dead man; he turned to the left only to touch another corpse. One company was brought out of action by a lance-corporal. Then the Boers arrived and began making prisoners; one shouted to Major Hicks for his revolver; he replied that he had not got one—it was in the holster on his dead horse—and stalked indignantly off the battlefield without another question being put to him.

"The Boer heavy artillery pursued the retiring troops with shells, which made a prodigious noise and raised clouds of dust, but seldom did any damage, and gradually a region of comparative peace was reached where the ground was not being continually struck by bullets, and where only an occasional shell fell. The extended lines of the 4th Brigade, ordered to cover the retirement, came into view, and behind them the men of the Irish Brigade collected again in companies and battalions. Then, although the artillery was still roaring fiercely and the Mausers rattled with tireless persistence, the Brigade trudged back to its former camping ground, pitched tents, and began to cook dinners."

The 2nd Battalion, to which Major Hicks's three companies of the 1st were this day attached, suffered a total loss of 219, of whom 52, including one officer, were killed, and of this number the three attached companies contributed more than their full share; for Captain A. H. Bacon and 28 non-commissioned officers and men were killed, Major A. W. Gordon, Second-Lieutenant MacLeod, and 98 rank and file were wounded, while 5 men were missing. Among the killed was the colour-sergeant of Captain Bacon's company, Colour-Sergeant V. J. Magee, while Major Gordon, who was shot through the knee early in the action, was later brought in by Sergeants Keenan and Dillon of the 1st Battalion.

Some of the men of the three companies of the Battalion did not get into camp till 5 p.m., and some of those who were "missing" appear to have been taken prisoners on the very banks of the Tugela. Many fine actions were this day performed, and amongst a host of other older soldiers, who showed their worth under trying circumstances on this somewhat unfortunate day, was Bugler Dunne of the Regiment, a mere boy who did his duty like a man, and had the good fortune to be received by Her Majesty the Queen on his return home. Dunne's father was also in South Africa, a colour-sergeant in the 5th Battalion. The spirit of the men was throughout quite remarkable, and made officers and non-commissioned officers proud to command them. The reverse, so far from depressing them, appeared to have exactly the contrary effect, and merely hardened their determination to succeed.

"The greater part of the 16th December was occupied in burying the dead, and at nightfall orders were received to strike camp, when the Brigade marched back to Frere, which was reached on the early morning of the 17th, and we occupied our former camping ground."

The three companies attached from the 1st Battalion were so greatly weakened by the casualties they had sustained in this action that it was deemed inadvisable any longer to maintain their original separate organization, and they were accordingly now broken up and distributed among the companies of the 2nd Battalion, taking part with them in several of the other actions which finally ended in the relief of Ladysmith early in March, 1900.

While the companies under Major Hicks had been engaged in this first Battle of Colenso, the Headquarter Companies—"D," "E," "F," "G," and "H"—of the 1st Battalion had remained quietly at Brynbella Farm, but on the 21st they were ordered back to Mooi River, as this place was considered to be too weakly defended, and here they were left until early in the new year, guarding the railway line and bridges—a very important but unexciting duty.

The troops in South Africa were not forgotten at Christmas time by their Queen and countrymen, as witness the following telegrams received and published :—

From Her Majesty the Queen :—

"*I wish you all a bright and happy New Year. God bless you all.*
"V. R. I."

From the Lord Mayor of London :—

"*Kindly convey troops front hearty Christmas greetings, admiration, sympathy their struggles.*"

CHAPTER VIII

1900—1902.

THE WAR IN SOUTH AFRICA.

JUST as the year 1899 closed two officers—Captain Chapman and Lieutenant Watson—left the Battalion to join a mounted infantry battalion then being formed at Frere; this corps was officially styled the " Composite Regiment of Mounted Infantry," but was later more generally known to fame as " Gough's M.I."

1890 On January 2nd Major Hicks and Lieutenant de Salis rejoined from the 2nd Battalion, and on the 10th of this month the five companies of the 1st Battalion moved by rail from Mooi River to Estcourt, relieving there a battalion of the Somersetshire Light Infantry. Here for some weeks the men were busily employed in rebuilding the defences and adapting them to the reduced garrison, also in supplying the various posts and picquets required for the protection of the railway line and town of Estcourt; there were occasional alarms, and rumours of impending attack were tolerably frequent, but these were in every case wholly devoid of foundation.

The Headquarter Companies 1st Battalion left Estcourt by rail on March 3rd and proceeded to Colenso, dropping " D " Company, under Captain Swift, *en route* at Frere; while here the following order was published :—

"*In recognition of the gallantry displayed by the Irish Regiments in the Natal Campaign, Her Majesty the Queen has directed that the shamrock be worn by all ranks on St. Patrick's Day.*"

On March 21st the residue of " A," " B," and " C " Companies rejoined from the 2nd Battalion; they had been absent just over four months, had gone away originally numbering 8 officers and 287 other ranks, and of these only 2 officers—Captain Venour and Second-Lieutenant Halahan—and 94 men returned.

Next day Captain Swift's Company came in to Headquarters from Frere.

Several changes occurred among the officers during the month of April; Major Hicks was sent into Ladysmith to take command of the 2nd Battalion in place of Colonel Cooper, who had been appointed to command a brigade; Lieutenants Molesworth, Brodhurst-Hill and Halahan were invalided home; and Second-Lieutenant Lamprey came out from home with a small draft.

At Colenso the 1st Battalion made a stay of just two months, engaged in the usual routine duties of the lines of communication, and seeing the 2nd Battalion pass through on April 10th *en route* for Durban with Major-General Hunter's Division, now composed of the 5th and 6th Brigades and transferred to the western side, where they were moved up to Kimberley and marched thence northward. On the day following orders were received for the Battalion to move at once into Ladysmith, but these orders were almost immediately cancelled, much to the disappointment of all ranks, who were beginning to fear that the war would come to an end without their seeing a shot fired. However, they had to possess their souls in patience until May 5th, when it was announced that the 1st Royal Dublin Fusiliers were to move on the 8th, in order to join at Elandslaagte the 10th Brigade, commanded by Major-General Talbot Coke, in the Vth Division under Lieutenant-General Hildyard.

The Gloucester Regiment relieved the Battalion soon after daybreak on the 8th, and by 8.40 a.m. the last detachment had left Colenso; and on arrival at Elandslaagte the Battalion proceeded to and encamped at Battle Ridge, 4 miles to the west, being played in by the drums of the 2nd Battalion Middlesex Regiment, which, with the 2nd Dorsets, made up the 10th Infantry Brigade, and here the Battalion remained until May 13th. On this date, in consequence of orders received, the Dublin Fusiliers struck their camp at 2 p.m., and sent all tents, extra baggage, and other impedimenta to the rail, then marching off, the destination being a hill commanding the passage of Sunday's River lying to the west of Battle Ridge, and running approximately east and west. The hill to be occupied was about 2 miles north of the river and 5 miles east of the bridge which crossed it.

The Battalion arrived here about 7 p.m., and found the drift absolutely impassable for wagons, and these had to be left for the night 3 miles in rear. The 14th and 15th were passed in extending the position and in improving the drift and its approaches, assisted by the 11th Brigade, which had now arrived, and by this drift the greater part of the Vth Division was put across the river.

On the 15th "B" and "C" Companies moved on to Wessels Nek about 5 miles north, and on the day following the remaining companies moved on to the same place, acting *en route* as escort to some heavy guns. The 17th found the Battalion on the march with cavalry, some guns and ammunition and supply columns for Waschbank, 8 miles further on, and on arrival here the Dublin Fusiliers joined up with the other battalions of the brigade which for the past ten days had been operating in the direction of Helpmakaar. Early on the morning of the 18th—a deviation having been completed at the railway bridge which the Boers had blown up in retreat—the brigade set out to march 20 miles to Hatting Spruit; the first part of the way was through a valley at the head of which, 12 miles distant, was the railway junction of Glencoe; and this was reached at 10.30 a.m. after a steady up-hill march. Everywhere were traces of the hurried retreat of the enemy, live shell in large numbers being found lying by the roadside.

A considerable halt was made at Glencoe, the Brigade not moving on again until 3.30 p.m. Hatting Spruit was entered soon after dark and here the arrival of the 10th Brigade completed the Vth Division, for the 11th Brigade was already encamped here.

The combined division moved off towards Daunshauser at 10 a.m. next day, but had not gone far when it was ordered back to repair the railway line, so, leaving one battalion from each brigade to garrison Hatting Spruit, Hildyard's Division retraced its steps and remained some days at Glencoe engaged in re-establishing the bridges; but by the 24th the remaining units of General Hildyard's command were again at Daunshauser, where the 1st Royal Dublin Fusiliers rejoined their brigade that evening; here Captain Riccard joined the Battalion from Pieter Maritzburg.

Marching early on the 26th, the division reached Ingagana, 15 miles north, after a very hot and dusty march, and the same evening the Battalion was sent on a further 2½ miles to Rooi Pynt, a high hill overlooking the town of Newcastle some 6 or 7 miles distant; this was occupied next day, the troops bivouacking on the north side of the town, which was found to have been greatly damaged by the Boers, many of the houses, the railway station and goods yard having been set on fire, and the water tanks and railway bridge blown up.

The 10th Brigade remained in the vicinity of Newcastle until June 5th, and here two officers joined, Major Shadforth coming out from home on May 31st and taking over command of "B" Company, while Captain Todd rejoined on June 2nd from Mooi River, where he had been for a month in hospital.

June 5th saw the division again on the march, the objective being Ingogo, 11 miles distant; the Battalion halted for the night at De Wet's Farm on the Ingogo Road, about 2 miles south of the drift and close to the junction of the Botha's Pass Road.

During the past week General Buller, in command of the Natal Army since the arrival as Commander-in-Chief of Field-Marshal Lord Roberts, hoping much from the evident demoralization of the enemy forces in his front, had been endeavouring to persuade the Boer leaders in Natal of the futility of further resistance. The local Commandant had agreed to the discussion of terms and had met General Buller, who had propounded certain conditions of surrender, which had been referred to the Boer chiefs. Both sides employed the brief respite from hostilities in bringing up forces to the front, and when on June 5th the British offers were definitely and decidedly rejected by Commandant General Louis Botha,

Buller's plans were prepared for the seizure of the southern side of Botha's Pass.

At 7.45 a.m. on June 6th a battery of Field Artillery, the 2nd Battalion Middlesex Regiment and the South African Light Horse marched off to the west in the direction of Van Wyk which was 5 or 6 miles distant—a high hill, almost a mountain, some 2 miles in extent running north and south, situated at the northern end of the Drakensberg Range and overlooking and commanding the road and valley leading to Botha's Pass. The abovementioned troops very soon came under gun and rifle fire which was maintained the greater part of the day in a desultory manner.

The rest of the brigade left De Wet's Farm at 2.45 p.m. and after a stiff climb reached the top of Van Wyk about dusk, having been detained when half-way up to re-make a road which was impassable for wagons by reason of the very many boulders with which it was covered.

About 5 p.m. the Boers made a very determined attack upon the southern extremity of the mountain where the Middlesex were in position, and five companies of the Royal Dublin Fusiliers were moved up in support and came under fire. The attack was beaten off and the enemy withdrew about 6.15. By this time the remaining three companies of the Battalion, which had been kept back to bring up tools, arrived at the top of the hill, and the men began to entrench; the Battalion furnished the outposts that night holding the whole of the southern end of the mountain. The position was not an especially ideal one; it was open to attack, which was daily expected, the water supply was a matter of great difficulty, rations had to be carried by hand some 3 miles from the wagons, while the cold at night was intense.

On June 8th the 2nd and 11th Brigades, Dundonald's Cavalry Brigade and the guns attacked and captured Botha's Pass, the 10th Brigade remaining on Van Wyk to cover the left of the attack; and on the afternoon of the 9th the Battalion passed over Botha's Pass and entered the Orange Free State, bivouacking that night 2 miles west of the Pass.

The following day General Buller's force moved forward about 10 miles to Gansvlei, the advance being somewhat feebly contested by the Boers who were driven off by the South African Light Horse, these sustaining some 10 casualties, and the Battalion spent an intensely cold night on Tabanyama Mountain. The men fell in at 7 a.m. on June 11th, all cheering, as it was understood that the Battalion would be in action before night set in. The advance was directed towards Alleman's Nek, about 7 or 8 miles north by east of Tabanyama, the brigade halting after marching for a couple of miles about 10 o'clock, when General Coke explained the situation to his subordinates.

" Between Sir R. Buller's Army and Volksrust now intervened but one obstacle. But it was no trifling one, and here again delay, as the lessons of the Natal campaign had more than once shown, might render it all but insuperable. Springing from the Drakensberg Range at Majuba and Iketeni Mountains, a bold spur ran in a north-westerly direction, bridging, as it were, the wide valley which rolled between the Drakensberg and subsidiary range of the Verzamel Berg in the Transvaal. This spur, therefore, ran directly athwart the Volksrust Road, which at the afore-mentioned Alleman's Nek surmounted it by a deep cleft, flanked by almost precipitous bluffs. Here was then a strong position; and Sir R. Buller's information ran that the enemy was now upon it in sufficient force to form a strong detached right flank-guard to the commandos upon Laing's Nek itself."*

At 10 a.m. the 10th Brigade advanced in extended order, passing through the 11th Brigade which was holding a line of kopjes. At noon the line reached a small farm lying in a hollow about $2\frac{1}{2}$ miles from Alleman's Nek, and on the kopje above the farm was a horse artillery battery in action, supported by the South African Light Horse and Thorneycroft's Mounted Infantry. The Battalion now moved to the right or east of the farm and formed up in quarter column some 200 yards in rear of the battery.

* *Official History*, Vol. III, p. 273.

The ground in front of the guns sloped more or less gradually to a farm lying at the foot of the Nek; to the west the ground was undulating while to the east it sloped gently for about 2,000 yards, then rising again to a ridge on which was a sugar-loaf hill; beyond this ridge was a valley on the far side of which was the left of the Boer position. This was on a high and steep ridge of horse-shoe shape, Alleman's Nek being on the north-western end; on the south-eastern extremity was a small Nek carrying a road, and on the south side of this was a strong position which to a certain extent flanked the Boer left. From the left centre of the enemy position two or three spurs jutted out towards the ground where was the battery, and these spurs were pointed out to the Dublin Fusiliers as their main objective in the coming attack.

At midday the 10th Brigade was disposed as follows:—The 2nd Battalion Dorsetshire Regiment lay in extended order near the horse artillery battery and in front of the 1st Battalion Royal Dublin Fusiliers; while the 2nd Battalion Middlesex Regiment was to the left rear of the Dorsets, on the left of whom was the 2nd Brigade, with the heavy naval guns in its immediate neighbourhood.

The action was commenced on the part of the enemy by his opening fire at the horse battery, his shells falling some 30 yards to the left of the Battalion, and as reply was made by every British gun, the Boer fire was quickly silenced.

About 1.30 p.m. the infantry attack began, the 10th Brigade moving off—the Dorsets in the centre making for the conical kopje to the right of Alleman's Nek, the Middlesex moving in rear in support, while the Fusiliers advanced against the two spurs previously pointed out. As the Dublins advanced, Colonel Mills determined to seize a small conical kopje which was in the line of the Battalion advance, and between this kopje and the Boer position was a valley, in the centre of which was a dam; here the " Blue Caps " came under a slight rifle fire and a more or less heavy shelling by pom-poms.

The conical hill was reached at about 2.45 p.m., " A," " B," and " C " Companies being on the left or north of it; " G " and

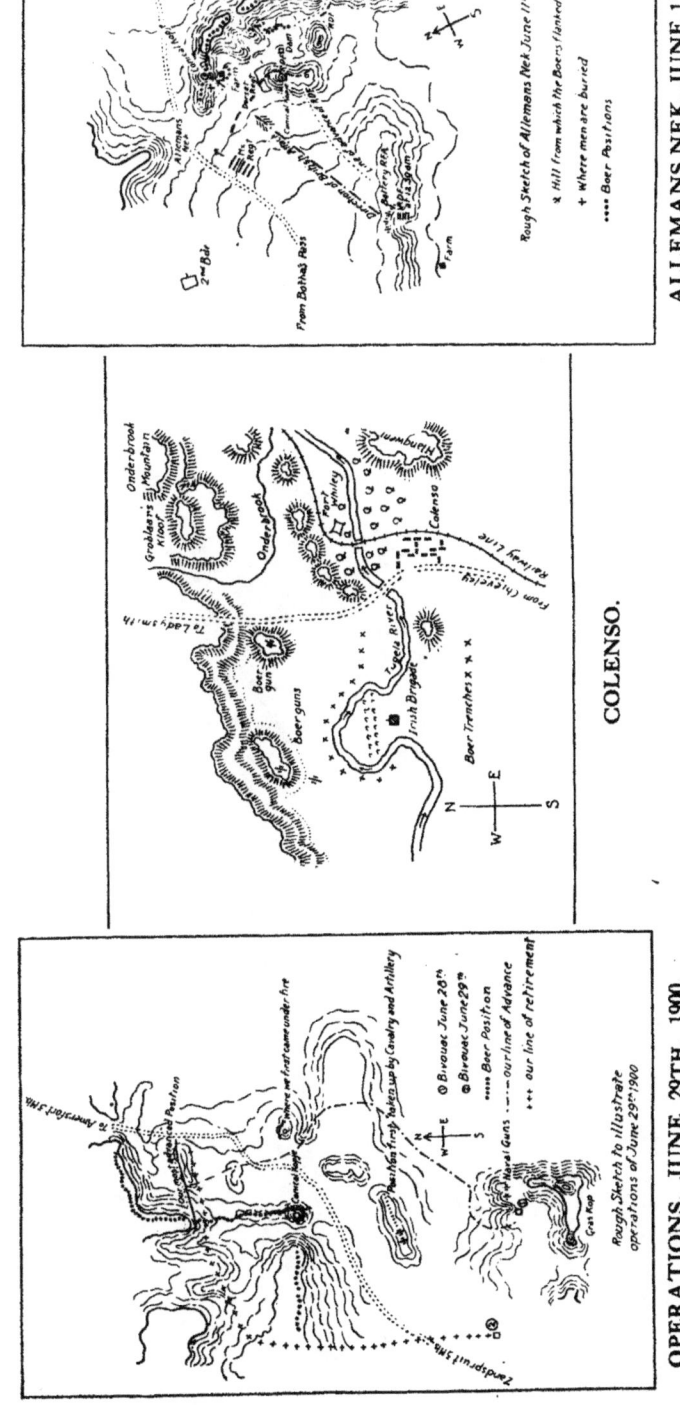

OPERATIONS, JUNE 29TH, 1900.   COLENSO.   ALLEMANS NEK, JUNE 11TH, 1900.

"H" on the ridge to the right or south; while "D" and "E," which had some little time previously been detached, were on the extreme right and near the position taken up by Gough's Mounted Infantry.

"F" Company now advanced into the valley as far as the dam, but could get no further owing to the severe flanking fire by some Boers in a donga 200 yards distant.

A considerable number of Boers could be seen on the ridge beyond the valley, but the Battalion Maxim gun now came into action against them, causing them quickly to get under cover. The action then became general, and about 3.30 p.m. the enemy fire was severe; the range was 1,500 yards, and they had estimated it very accurately, while there was no cover beyond a few ant-hills here and there. "F" Company, under Lieutenant Seppings, was still near the dam, while, though "A," "B" and "C" Companies had advanced slightly, they could get no further.

Shortly after this Colonel Mills was wounded and Major O'Neill assumed command, and by now "D" and "E" Companies had worked round on the extreme right and come into action against the Boer left; but, though reinforced by another half-company, these could not get to the top of the ridge, as the British shells were bursting upon it, while, owing to the dense smoke caused by a veldt fire, communication with the battery was impossible About 4.30 a further advance was made, and it was seen that the enemy was giving way; the British pressed on, and between 5.30 and 6 the top of the ridge was gained and Alleman's Nek was won, the Boers falling back on Volksrust and Zandspruit.

So far the story of the action is taken from Lieutenant Maclear's diary; the *Official History of the South African War** gives a slightly different account of the doings this day of the Royal Dublin Fusiliers. "Their orders had been to work in line with the right of the Dorset Regiment and to threaten the Nek behind the foremost kopje, while the Dorsets assaulted it in front. The Battalion had not advanced far before it found itself enfiladed

* Vol. III, p. 277.

from the right by a warm and increasing fire from that portion of the Boer line opposite Dundonald's Mounted Infantry; and imperceptibly the advance of the Fusiliers deflected eastwards towards the kopje in the valley which faced the enemy's rifles. An interval, therefore, began to open between their left and the right of the Dorset Regiment, and so rapidly did this increase that about 4 p.m. Talbot Coke, having vainly attempted to call up the regiment by flag signal, despatched his Brigade-Major to bring it back to its proper line of advance. The officer did not come up with the Dublin Fusiliers before they, trending still further to the right, had become involved in Dundonald's part of the action, sending, indeed, two companies to the assistance of the 3rd Mounted Brigade It should be stated that the Officer Commanding the 1st Royal Dublin Fusiliers had every intention of resuming his proper direction as soon as he had dealt with the situation on his right. He left orders to that effect, when a wound compelled him to go to the rear. The Boer's fire attack on the right, however, proved more than a momentary demonstration, and, indeed, partook of the nature of a counter-attack, and only one and a half companies of the Dublin Fusiliers were able to rejoin the brigade before nightfall."

The casualties this day incurred by the Battalion amounted to :—*Killed*, 3 non-commissioned officers and men; *wounded*, Lieutenant-Colonel Mills, Lieutenant Seppings and 12 non-commissioned officers and men.

That night the Battalion bivouacked at the foot of the Pass, and, moving off next morning, joined the other regiments of the 10th Infantry Brigade on the far side of the Nek; and then, marching on, passed through Volksrust and arrived on June 13th at Charlestown, where shortly after arrival the Battalion was formed up and addressed by the Brigadier, who thanked all ranks for their services in the capture of Alleman's Nek.

The Dublin Fusiliers remained at Charlestown until the 16th, and were joined here by Lieutenant Hudleston from Maritzburg and by Second-Lieutenant Smithwick from home.

During the next three or four days there were several moves

the Battalion marching on June 16th to Volksrust, thence next day to a position 5 miles away to the east of Houtnek, returning on the 20th to Volksrust, and finding then the eastern line of the outposts round the town, with a guard at the bridge half-way to Charlestown. Here Lieutenants Patey and Hawker, 3rd Battalion, and Jones, 4th Battalion, joined from England on the 24th and 25th, while on the 26th Captain Venour and Second-Lieutenant Lamprey were admitted to hospital, both eventually being invalided home.

On the 27th the Battalion received orders to move next day with a flying column in the direction of Zandspruit. The column—composed of 4 naval 12-pounders, the 19th Hussars, a battery R.F.A., the 2nd Battalion Middlesex Regiment and 1st Battalion Royal Dublin Fusiliers—left Volksrust early on the 28th, and, marching through Zandspruit, moved on to the northern slopes of Graskop, a very prominent mountain about 15 miles north of Volksrust and 5 miles north-east of Zandspruit.

There was some interchange of shots before dark, but this soon ceased and the night passed quietly. On the following morning early the column moved off in battle formation with the intention of compelling the surrender of Amersfoort, a town about 8 miles to the north of Graskop. The 19th Hussars scouted to the front and flanks, supported by the Dublin Fusiliers, who had three companies of the Middlesex Regiment on their left, the remainder of the troops following in rear with the guns and transport. The advance was over undulating veldt, broken here and there by the usual dongas.

The enemy was found to be holding a position on a ridge which ran from west to east, and then turned north almost at right angles for nearly a mile, bending round again to the east, and so forming a sort of natural basin up which the British advanced. At the south-east corner of the ridge was a conical kopje which was strongly held by the Boers. The orders given to the infantry were to advance up the basin, keeping to the east of the conical hill, and about 9 a.m. the fire from the naval guns and those of the field battery caused the Boers to fall back a short distance; but as the

Royal Dublin Fusiliers moved on they came under a smart fire from some Boers posted on the ridge about 700 yards to the left; these, again, retired, but the further advance was contested by other parties of the burghers to the left and front. The firing line was here very extended, being some three-quarters of a mile in extent, and two companies had to be sent to the left to engage the enemy and keep down his fire. By 12.30 p.m. all hostile rifle fire had ceased, and by now the Fusiliers had reached some 3 miles south of Amersfoort and 700 or 800 yards from the ridge, between which and the advance was a small valley; the troops were ordered to halt and allow the baggage to close up, and shortly after the Battalion was ordered back to Graskop, its retirement being at once greeted by shells from four Boer high-velocity guns which dropped near, but did no damage. That night the Dublins bivouacked on the northern slope of Graskop, withdrawing on the next day to Zandspruit.

The casualties on the 29th were 2 men killed and 1 wounded. From Zandspruit 2 officers—Captains Swift and Todd—were admitted to hospital, and the latter was invalided home.

On July 2nd four companies of the Battalion—" A," " B," " C," and " D "—under Major Shadforth left for a farm known as Holfontein, about 3 miles to the north of the town, in order to put a hill near there in a state of defence preparatory to its occupation, and on the following day the remainder of the companies with two 4.7 guns proceeded to the same place and were busily employed during the next few days in erecting defences and putting up gun emplacements; the name of " Dublin Hill " was later given to this post, where the Battalion remained some three weeks, occasionally engaging with rifle fire Boers who were seen in the neighbourhood, while the big guns with the little force now and then opened fire upon parties of the enemy observed on the neighbouring hills.

General Buller was now busy preparing for his advance on Ermelo and Carolina in order to effect a junction with the main army under Lord Roberts which was moving east from Pretoria, and by July 21st a considerable number of troops belonging to the 4th

General De la Rey and R. Schalk Burger, at Officers' Mess, Krugersdorp, May, 1902, en route for Vereeniging Conference prior to declaration of peace.

The Boer Position and Battlefield of Alleman's Nek, June 11th, 1900, taken from the position from which the 10th Brigade advanced and overlooked the farm.

Spion Kop, where the most desperate battle of the war was fought, from Boer trenches on Krantz Kloof, South Africa.
(*Copyright, Underwood & Underwood*)

Boer trenches and crest of Hart's Hill—scene of Irish Brigade's famous charge, Colenso, South Africa.
(*Copyright, Underwood & Underwood*)

and 5th Divisions had been concentrated about Zandspruit and Dublin Hill. The movement by the Natal Army commenced on the 22nd, one column on the right, under Major-General Coke, advancing from Zandspruit towards Graskop; the centre, under Major-General Howard, moving east from Dublin Hill; while the left column, commanded by Major-General Brocklehurst, moved north for 3 or 4 miles, then wheeled to the right and advanced in an easterly direction parallel to the other two columns.

Only one wing of the Battalion was employed in these operations, the right half Battalion remaining at Dublin Hill under Major Shadforth, while the Headquarters and " E," " F ," " G," and " H " Companies were attached to General Brocklehurst's force, which contained also the 18th Hussars, four companies Mounted Infantry, four field guns, two naval 12-pounders, and a Wing of the 2nd Lancashire Fusiliers. This column met with no opposition, the centre column being the one which was chiefly opposed, and that night, the Boers having been driven from their ground towards Amersfoort, the columns bivouacked about Meerzicht, the following days being spent in reconnoitring towards Amersfoort and in entrenching posts upon the neighbouring heights for the protection of Paardekop and Zandspruit stations. During this period the mounted troops were almost daily engaged with parties of the enemy, but the Battalion took no part, and the 4th Division was now ordered to concentrate about Meerzicht, while the 5th was sent back to hold the railway line. As a consequence it became necessary to relieve the posts held by the 1st Battalion Liverpool Regiment, which belonged to the 8th Brigade, 4th Division, and accordingly on July 28th the Headquarters and Left Wing Royal Dublin Fusiliers marched to Zandspruit and thence next day to Laing's Nek, relieving a wing of the Liverpools; while on the 29th the remaining companies marched to Zandspruit and there entrained, two companies going under Major Shadforth to Ingogo, while the two others, commanded by Major Gordon and Captain Swift respectively, were sent to Coetzies Drift, in both places relieving companies of the

Liverpool Regiment. The two companies at Ingogo were moved to Charlestown about a week later.

On the last day of July a draft of 93 non-commissioned officers and men joined the Battalion under Second-Lieutenants Knox and Tredennick; a few days later another arrived in charge of Second-Lieutenants Brown, 4th Battalion, and Henry, 3rd Battalion West Riding Regiment; shortly before this Lieutenant Stirling had left to join the Mounted Infantry of the 4th Division; on August 14th Lieutenants Lefroy and Jeffreys had gone with 75 other ranks to the 5th Division Mounted Infantry, then forming at Charlestown; on the following day Colonel Mills came back to command; on the same day two of the Headquarter Companies were sent away to guard the reversing station under Captain Riccard; while on the 15th "C" Company under Lieutenant Conlan was brought in from Laing's Nek to Charlestown.

During the next two and a-half months the Battalion companies were very frequently moved about as the exigencies of the military situation in the neighbourhood demanded, and were much employed in providing escorts for convoys to and from Wakkerstroom and in patrolling the country round. But finally on October 31st the Royal Dublin Fusiliers were relieved at their various posts and brought in to Volksrust, there taking the place of the East Surrey Regiment. Here the Battalion was very much split up, occupying a large number of small defensive posts and blockhouses, and only some 130 officers, non-commissioned officers and men remained at Headquarters.

On November 24th 100 men of the Battalion accompanied a column, placed under the command of Colonel Mills, and composed of 2 guns, 100 1st Battalion Royal Dublin Fusiliers, 1 Squadron 5th Dragoon Guards, and the South African Horse, which was sent out to hold the ground to the north of Hurrican Hill, some 5 miles north of Wakkerstroom, to cover the emplacement of a 4.7 gun on Hurrican Hill. There was no opposition during the day but when returning in the evening to Volksrust, the column was attacked and persistently followed up by the Boers for several miles. The attack was successfully repulsed and the General Officer Commanding the Volksrust Sub-district, in acknowledging receipt of the reports of the affair, wrote :—" He fully appreciates the activity shown as well as the creditable conduct of Lieutenant-Colonel Mills and Lieutenant-Colonel Law and of the troops under their command."

About this time there were some further changes in the distribution of the officers of the Battalion ; Major O'Neill left to take up the duties of Commandant at Durban ; Captain Le Mesurier—who had arrived from home late in November—Lieutenants Moore and Burra joined a Mounted Infantry Company which was formed ; and Lieutenants Molesworth and Brodhurst-Hill rejoined the Battalion from England.

At the end of the year 1900 a change was made in the command of the British Army in South Africa, for Field-Marshal Lord Roberts had been appointed Commander-in-Chief at home, his presence in the United Kingdom was urgently required, and his departure could not be indefinitely postponed. On November 29th, therefore, he gave up the command of the forces in the field into the able hands of General Lord Kitchener of Khartoum, and sailed from Cape Town on December 11th, receiving on arrival the dignity of an Earldom for the conspicuous services he had rendered his country. Since his arrival at the crisis of the struggle he had occupied the capitals of the two States and had shattered their forces into desperate and scattered fragments ; the issue of the campaign was no longer in doubt even if the length of its duration was still uncertain ; and in the farewell order which he issued to the Army, Lord Roberts, best loved of Commanders, thanked his troops for all they had done, for the successes they had won, and for the humanity and forbearance which throughout had by all ranks been displayed.

1901 The New Year opened, and before a month of it had passed news came from England to the Army which filled the heart of every member of it with sincerest and deepest grief, for on January 24th the telegraph, helio and flag carried to all columns, north, south, east and west, the tidings of the death on the previous evening of the Great Queen, who had followed in so many campaigns with deep and personal interest the achievements and sufferings of her soldiers.

On February 11th, 1901, "D" Company under Captain Swift, Lieutenant Conlan and Second-Lieutenant Hawkes, was sent via Utrecht to Elandsberg, being there attached to a column commanded by General Burn-Murdoch and being employed during the operations conducted by General French in the Eastern Transvaal. The remainder of the Battalion gave some assistance to the execution of these operations without being very actively concerned with them; thus it found escorts for the convoys sent to the Eastern Transvaal; half the Battalion Mounted Infantry Company under Lieutenant Moore, which had been stationed at Wakkerstroom since the opening of the year, was also employed on these convoys and in patrol work; while for a week from February 14th all available men from Headquarters marched to a position at Engelbrecht's Drift, south-west of Wakkerstroom, and acted there as a "stop" to prevent any Boers breaking back during General French's advance. This was a week of intense discomfort for the rain came down in torrents without cessation.

Nothing of importance or interest occurred during March, but on April 1st a small force under Lieutenant-Colonel Mills, taken from the 5th Dragoon Guards, York and Lancaster Regiment, Royal Dublin Fusiliers, French's Scouts and Johannesburg Mounted Rifles, with two field guns, successfully engaged at Laing's Farm, near Mount Prospect, a Boer Commando which had come through from the Free State the evening before, and had on that morning destroyed the railway near O'Neill's Farm. It was during the retirement of these burghers that they were surprised by Colonel Mills's party, which had taken up a position east of Laing's Farm. The British had no casualties, those of the Boers were estimated at some 25, a thick mist favouring their retreat and making their losses fewer than they might well have otherwise been.

Early in May the Battalion again took over the posts at and about Ingogo, Headquarters and some 200 men being at this latter place, while the other posts were :—

The Railway Station and Drift: "G" Company under Captain Riccard.

Gordon Hill: "D" Company under Captain Swift.

Botha's Post: Lieutenant Patey and half "B" Company.

Colisseum: Lieutenant Conlan and half "C" Company.

Reversing Station: Lieutenant Wodehouse and half "A" Company.

Fort Sandy: Major Gordon and half "A" Company.

While other posts such as O'Neill's Farm, Mount Prospect, Inkweld etc., were at different times held by Majors Shadforth and Gordon, Lieutenant Smithwick, and Second-Lieutenant Heys-Thomson.

This distribution endured more or less until the last week in July, when the Battalion changed places with the York and Lancaster Regiment, moving to Newcastle where the companies were thus disposed :—

Windsor Castle and Donga Spruit: "D" Company under Captain Swift.

Signal Hill: "A" Company under Lieutenant Smithwick and Second-Lieutenant Hawkes.

Fort Biddulph: "A," and half "E" Company under Lieutenant Patey.

Fort Biddulph: "B," and half "E" Company under Lieutenant Conlan.

Fort Metcalfe: "C" Company under Lieutenant Wodehouse.

Rooi Pynt: "F" Company under Major Sennett, 4th Battalion.

Ingagane: Half "G" Company under Captain Riccard.

Daunhauser: One section and half "G" Company under Second-Lieutenant Heys-Thomson.

The Headquarters and the remainder of the Battalion remained at the Defence Camp, situated first on the north and later on the south side of the town.

At the beginning of August Major Rutherfoord joined from the 2nd Battalion; on the 15th Captain MacDonnell arrived from home with a draft of 100 non-commissioned officers and men; later in the month Major Rutherfoord formed a second Mounted Infantry

Company, with Lieutenants Brodhurst-Hill and Wodehouse as his subalterns; Lieutenant Patey about the same time left for home; at the commencement of September Captain Riccard was sent to join the 5th Division Mounted Infantry at Eshowe in Zululand; while for some five or six weeks from September 9th Lieutenant-Colonel Mills, Major Gordon, Captain Bromilow and Second-Lieutenant Knox were absent at Maritzburg helping in the mobilization and training of the Natal Volunteers who had been called out to resist a threatened Boer invasion of Natal; during the absence of Colonel Mills, Major Shadforth commanded the Battalion.

1902 On January 7th, 1902, the Dublin Fusiliers received orders to concentrate on Newcastle, and on relief on the 8th and 9th by the Munster Fusiliers, the Battalion—less the two Mounted Infantry Companies, which for the present remained behind—proceeded by train to Krugersdorp there to take the place of the 2nd Battalion Royal Dublin Fusiliers due to proceed to the coast in view of immediate embarkation for Aden. Krugersdorp was reached on January 13th when the two Battalions of the Regiment met again for the third time during the war, and an exchange of drafts took place, the 1st Battalion sending a number of young soldiers to the 2nd, and receiving in exchange men of the Army Reserve and those whose period of army service was nearly completed. The 2nd Battalion left Krugersdorp for Durban on the 21st when the posts it had occupied were taken over as under:—

Randfontein: "D" Company under Captain Swift.
Middelvlei: One section of "D" Company under Lieutenant Whyte.
Bank: "F" Company under Major Sennett.
Welverdiend: "G" Company under Lieutenant Hawkes.
Frederickstadt: "B" Company under Lieutenant Burke.
Potchefstroom: "A" Company under Major Gordon and "C" Company under Captain MacDonnell and Lieutenant Smithwick.

THE PEACE OF VEREENIGING

Lancaster West Mine and South Ridge : " E " Company under Lieutenant Conlan and Second-Lieutenant Knox.

Headquarters was at Fort Kilmarnock, where were the two Mounted Infantry Companies on rejoining, and portions of other Battalion companies ; on the last day of January the two Mounted Infantry Companies were amalgamated, Major Rutherfoord being in command with Lieutenants Moore and Burra.

For some weeks all here was very quiet, but there were always throughout the whole course of the war certain peripatetic bands of stalwarts in the Gatsrand, a range of hills which ran for some distance parallel with the Krugersdorp—Klerksdorp railway, and here in April misfortune overtook two Mounted Infantry patrols of the Battalion on successive days, several men being wounded and taken prisoners on each occasion.

In this month Colonel Mills left for Natal to command a column, taking Captain Bromilow with him as Staff Officer, and Second-Lieutenants Johnson and Hoey joined from home.

It had now for some time past been abundantly clear that the resistance of the Boer forces was weakening and that there was no longer the same *will* to continue fighting which had been so conspicuous in the earlier years of the war ; and after certain preliminary negotiations the leaders of both the Republican Governments were brought together for a conference at Klerksdorp on April 9th. There was a two-days' discussion, and a decision was then arrived at to make certain proposals to the British Government, and a request for a meeting with Lord Kitchener was despatched to Pretoria. The negotiations were protracted for some weeks and then a meeting of delegates from the two South African States was arranged to take place at Vereeniging on May 15th.

On the 14th the Boer delegates from the Western Transvaal— among them De la Rey, Schalk Burger, Celliers, Kemp and Ferreira —arrived at Krugersdorp, lunched and dined with the officers of the 1st Battalion Royal Dublin Fusiliers, the principals then going on the same evening to attend the Conference at Vereeniging. On May 31st peace was finally signed, and next day the wires carried the news to all the troops holding garrisons, blockhouses, and posts all over Cape Colony, Natal, the Orange Free State and the Transvaal.

This was followed on June 3rd by the following message from Lord Kitchener :—"*Please communicate to your troops the following gracious message which I have received from His Majesty the King and for which I have thanked him in the name of all concerned. Begins. Heartiest congratulations on the termination of hostilities. I also congratulate my brave troops under your command for having brought this long and difficult campaign to so glorious and successful a conclusion.*"

Then on June 8th the following cable from the Secretary of State for War to Lord Kitchener was published for the information of all ranks :—

"*His Majesty's Government offers to you their most sincere congratulations on the energetic skill and patience with which you have conducted this prolonged campaign, and would wish you to communicate to the troops under your orders their profound sense of the spirit and endurance with which they have met every call made upon them ; of their bravery in action ; of the excellent discipline preserved ; of the humanity shown throughout this trying period.*"

Finally, Lord Kitchener's Special Army Order of June 23rd, 1902, may well be given here :—

"*Before leaving South Africa the General Officer Commanding-in-Chief wishes to express his best thanks to all General Officers, Officers, Non-commissioned Officers and Men for the excellent services they have rendered since he first took over command some eighteen months ago. The period in question has offered few opportunities for those decisive engagements which keep up the spirit of an army and add brilliance and interest to its operations. On the other hand officers and men have been called upon for unceasing and ever-increasing exertions in face of great hardships and difficulties against a dangerous and elusive antagonist. The conduct of the troops under these trying circumstances has been beyond all praise. Never has there been the smallest sign of slackness or impatience ; and it seems to Lord Kitchener that the qualities of endurance and resolution thus displayed are more valuable to a Commander than any dashing or short-lived effort by which some hard-fought actions may be won in a campaign of ordinary duration. The General Officer Commanding has also special pleasure in congratulating the Army on the kindly and humane spirit by which all ranks have been animated during this long struggle. Fortunately for the future of South Africa the truth in this matter is known to our late enemy as well as to ourselves, and no misrepresentations from outside can prevail in the long run against the actual fact that no war has ever yet been waged in which combatants and non-combatants, on either side, have shown so much consideration and kindness to one another.*

"*This message would be incomplete if reference were not made to the soldierly qualities displayed throughout the campaign by our quondam enemies, and to the admirable spirit displayed by them in carrying out the surrender of their arms. Many of the Boer leaders, who at an earlier date recognized the futility of carrying on a devastating conflict beyond a certain point, have already for some time served with us in the field, and the aid which they rendered us will not be forgotten. Many also of those who continued the struggle to the last have expressed a hope that on some future occasion they may have an opportunity of serving side by side with His Majesty's forces from whom Lord Kitchener can assure them they will receive a very hearty welcome.*

"*In bidding the Army of South Africa farewell it only remains for Lord Kitchener to wish every individual serving therein all happiness and prosperity for the future.*"

The sudden, if on the whole not unexpected, termination of the three years' war did not at once end all the arrangements for reinforcement of the forces in the field, and in May, and even as late as August 22nd, drafts reached the Royal Dublin Fusiliers, 130 non-commissioned officers and men coming out from home in the first-named month under Lieutenant Pakenham, Royal Munster Fusiliers, while the later draft of equal strength was brought out by Second-Lieutenant French.

On June 3rd Captain Swift and ten other ranks left for home to represent the Battalion at the Coronation of King Edward VII—

a ceremony which had to be postponed indefinitely owing to His Majesty's sudden and very serious illness; and towards the end of the month all the blockhouses occupied by the Fusiliers were evacuated, and the defences in and around Krugersdorp were pulled down, with the result that by June 30th all detachments with the exception of those in the Potchefstroom district, were concentrated at Battalion Headquarters. The Potchefstroom companies — "A" and "C," under Major Gordon and Captain MacDonnell—came in on July 3rd.

On the 8th Headquarters moved from Fort Kilmarnock to camp near the Paardekraal Memorial, and now a commencement was made towards the discharge of reservists and time-expired men, while a proportion of officers in each rank was permitted to proceed home on leave. On July 29th Captains Mainwaring and MacDonnell left for home with a party of 150 men; on July 11th Captain Grimshaw, 2nd Battalion, came in from Pretoria, and, accompanied by Lieutenants Moore and Hawkes, took 100 more men to the port of embarkation; while on the 19th the last party of recruits and time-expired men left for England with Lieutenants Frankland, Supple, Weldon, and Burke (4th Battalion). Besides these above-named officers, the following went home at different times after the proclamation of peace :—Captain Bromilow, Lieutenants Taylor, Conlan, Burra, Jeffreys, and Brodhurst-Hill; then, on October 2nd, Lieutenant-Colonel Mills left the Battalion for good, his place being later taken by Lieutenant-Colonel Bird, D.S.O.

Orders had now been received for the 1st Battalion Royal Dublin Fusiliers to leave South Africa, and accordingly, on October 31st, it went by rail from Krugersdorp to Durban, which was reached on November 3rd, and here the Battalion embarked the same day in the *Dominion* for Malta, passing *en route* by Aden, where it received a hearty welcome from the 2nd Battalion there quartered. Malta was reached on November 25th, and, disembarking the same day, the Fusiliers took over quarters from the Royal West Kent Regiment in Fort Manoel.

The embarking strength of the Battalion on leaving Durban

MENTIONS AND REWARDS

was 15 Officers, 1 Warrant Officer, and 671 Non-commissioned Officers and Men; the officers were Majors Shadforth and Rutherfoord; Captains Loveband, Riccard, Maclear (Brevet Major and Adjutant), and Le Mesurier; Lieutenants Burra and Smithwick; Second-Lieutenants Whyte, Brown, Johnson, Hoey, French, and Wodehouse, and Lieutenant and Quartermaster Little.

The following are the names of the officers and other ranks of the Battalion who were mentioned in despatches and received promotion or decorations for their services during the war in South Africa:—

    Lieutenant-Colonel G. A. Mills, " mentioned " four times, awarded the C.B.

    Lieutenant-Colonel H. T. Hicks, " mentioned," awarded the C.B.

    Major W. H. S. O'Neill, " mentioned," awarded the D.S.O.

    Major A. W. Gordon, " mentioned," promoted Brevet Lieutenant-Colonel.

    Captain and Brevet Major A. J. Godley, " mentioned."

    Captain J. A. S. MacBean, " mentioned," promoted Brevet Major.

    Captain A. J. Chapman, " mentioned " three times, promoted Brevet Lieutenant-Colonel.

    Captain H. C. Smith, " mentioned " twice, promoted Brevet Major.

    Captain R. M. J. Swift, " mentioned."

    Captain and Brevet Major A. F. Pilson, " mentioned," awarded D.S.O.

    Captain W. J. Venour, " mentioned " twice, awarded D.S.O.

    Captain P. Maclear, " mentioned " three times, promoted Brevet Major.

    Captain F. N. Le Mesurier, Lieutenants G. Hudleston, A. A. C. Taylor, H. A. F. Watson, R. G. B. Jeffreys, and Lieutenant and Quartermaster J. Ward, " mentioned."

    Lieutenant B. P. Lefroy, " mentioned," awarded D.S.O.

Lieutenant E. A. A. de Salis, " mentioned," awarded D.S.O.
Lieutenant W. F. Stirling, " mentioned," awarded D.S.O.
Lieutenant A. Moore, " mentioned," awarded D.S.O.

Armourer-Sergeant T. Ford (awarded D.C.M.), Sergeant-Major T. Hartigan, Quartermaster-Sergeant J. Little, Colour-Sergeants L. Holloway and J. Campbell, Band-Sergeant A. Virgo, Sergeants J. R. Gittens, E. Proctor, H. Murphy, G. Clarke, and J. Daley, Corporals G. Frost (twice " mentioned," D.C.M.), P. Myron, P. Flannery (D.C.M.), and Moran, Lance-Corporals F. Holloway and P. MacDonnell, Drummer J. F. Dunne, Privates C. N. Wallace (twice " mentioned," D.C.M.), T. Dowling (twice " mentioned," D.C.M.), W. Cullen (D.C.M.), Eston, McCormack (D.C.M.), E. Birmingham (promoted corporal), and T. Gilbert (promoted corporal).

The following were the casualties sustained by the Battalion :— *Killed or died of wounds*—3 officers and 83 other ranks ; *died of disease*—37 non-commissioned officers and men ; *wounded*—7 officers and 257 non-commissioned officers and men ; and *missing*—18 men ; making a total of 10 officers and 395 sergeants, rank and file. The names of the officers who fell were Captains A. H. Bacon and J. A. S. MacBean ; the wounded were Colonel G. A. Mills, Major A. W. Gordon, Lieutenants J. W. H. Seppings, A. V. Hill, A. Brodhurst-Hill, B. P. Lefroy, and Second-Lieutenant R. MacLeod.

The Battalion Mounted Infantry Company in the War.

The 5th Division Mounted Infantry was raised on August 11th, 1900, by Captain (local Major) A. J. Chapman, Royal Dublin Fusiliers, and three days later the contingent detailed from the Battalion—Lieutenants Jeffreys and Lefroy and 75 non-commissioned officers and men—joined the Mounted Infantry at Volksrust, the whole being completely equipped and horsed by the 26th of the month.

During the next ten days the Mounted Infantry were engaged in operations of a wholly minor character against the enemy between Volksrust and Wakkerstroom, but on September 5th the Mounted Infantry Battalion marched to Wakkerstroom with General Hildyard's column, occupying the town the same day; there was a certain amount of opposition, and the Fusiliers' Mounted Infantry Company sustained five casualties. Four days later the column marched on to Utrecht, leaving half the Dublins' Company under Lieutenant Jeffreys at Wakkerstroom, where for some weeks the men were employed in patrolling the surrounding country; the other half-company started for Utrecht with the column, but was left midway at a place called Groenvlei, where there was a smart action; and thus detached and separated, the two halves of the Royal Dublin Fusiliers' Company remained until the end of the month of November, when they came together again, rejoining the Headquarters 5th Division Mounted Infantry at Utrecht, when they took part in the successful repulse of the Boer attack on that town on the night of December 25th-26th.

Very shortly after the 5th Division Mounted Infantry went to Newcastle, remaining there until February 25th, 1901, when it left for Nqutu, Zululand, marching to Vryheid as part of the escort to a convoy for General French's troops, and being thus regularly employed until March 26th, when Captain Chapman brought his command back to his former post in Zululand; they moved again on April 13th, leaving Nqutu on that date, and marching into NKandhla four days later.

On May 20th the Dublin Fusiliers' Company marched with the rest of the 5th Division Mounted Infantry to attack a commando under a Boer leader named Daunhauser. The attack was successfully carried out on the 21st, but on the way back the Mounted Infantry was heavily attacked itself by another enemy commando which was led by Commandant Grobelaar, and had to fight a rearguard action which endured for eleven hours—from 6 a.m. to 5 p.m. From this time on and for more than two months the Mounted Infantry Battalion continued to patrol and raid the Transvaal border, having constant petty skirmishes, but on August 7th the Battalion was moved close up to the Zululand frontier, and did truly magnificent work in the defences of the two posts of Itala and Prospect, for which all ranks merited the high praise they received, and the account of which is taken from the *Official History*.*

"Botha was on the border of Natal with a muster powerful enough temporarily to destroy Natal as a line of communication even if the colony itself were in no danger of being reconquered. . . . Shouldered away from the Buffalo border by the imposing forces therein waiting, Botha, still seeking to achieve his purpose, edged away southward down the long tongue of the Vryheid district which penetrates Zululand between the Nqutu, NKandhla, Entonyaneni, and Ndwandwe districts, its termination pointing close to Melmoth. Near that place, and to the north-west of it, two small posts guarded the British frontier—namely, Fort Prospect and Itala. The former was held by 35 men of the 5th Division Mounted Infantry and 51 men of the 2nd Dorsetshire Regiment, under Captain C. A. Rowley; the latter by 300 men of the 5th Division Mounted Infantry and two guns 69th Battery R.F.A., commanded by Major A. J. Chapman, of the Royal Dublin Fusiliers. Towards these trifling obstacles Botha's commandos converged with the intention of sweeping them both aside.

"Itala had been well fortified, but it possessed a weak spot in the point of the mountain which stood up a mile distant from the entrenchments, and could not be included in them. On receipt of warning of the Boer advance on September 25th, 1901, Chapman manned this pinnacle with 80 Mounted Infantry men under Lieutenants B. P. Lefroy (1st Royal Dublin Fusiliers) and H. R. Kane (1st South Lancashire Regiment). At midnight the sound of an outburst of firing from the advanced post reached the main position; it ceased for a few moments, again broke out, and finally died away altogether. Shortly after Chapman heard that the outpost had fallen to vastly superior numbers, and he took care that his own men were prepared for a conflict. About 2 a.m. he found

* Vol. IV, pp. 219-221.

himself surrounded by 1,500 Boers. Preceded by a whirlwind of bullets, the enemy stormed close up to the stones of the sangars only to be beaten back by the troops who stood immovably and fenced their stronghold with a ring of fire. At 4 a.m. the Boers, their first momentum spent, fell silent, and Chapman, thinking they had given back sent out his scouts to reconnoitre, and also a medical officer to attend to the wounded on Itala Point. But suddenly a fusilade even fiercer than the first broke upon every side of the camp. It seemed as though the defence must be shortly blown to pieces, so heavy was the storm of lead which, coming from all sides, appeared to revolve like a tropical typhoon around the restricted area of the fort. For twelve hours the mausers poured out an unbroken volley, which was answered by Chapman's men as rapidly as the diminishing store of ammunition allowed. Their cover was good; but nothing could have withstood such battering and men fell regularly. The gunners, who had first sent shell with great effect, were ordered by Chapman to leave their pieces and take shelter where their officer and four men had fallen. As day wore on the position became almost untenable; but to retire from it was impossible, for Louis Botha, who directed the attack by signal from a neighbouring height, had drawn an outer ring of investment. One commando lay across the southern roads; General Opperman with 500 burghers stood between Itala and Melmoth and also between that place and Fort Prospect, 15 miles to the east; General C. Botha with 800 barred the west, and 600 riflemen under Commandant Potgieter held the front (north). There was thus no way out; but Chapman had determined already to fight to a finish where he stood, for he knew every moment's resistance was invaluable to Natal behind him. As evening descended over the long day's combat, his firmness began to draw towards its reward. The enemy, disheartened by their losses, which numbered over 300, and astounded at the failure of their apparently irresistible attack, fired more and more feebly. The encircling rifles, ceasing one by one, and group by group, gave the sign, more significant to a veteran soldier than a sudden cessation, of an onslaught which had spent its force. At 7.30 p.m. musketry had died away, and Chapman, having waited an hour in silence, once more felt all around him with scouts. He soon learned that the enemy was retiring in every direction. Then only, his task being accomplished, did he think of retreat. His casualties numbered over 80, the survivors were exhausted, their ammunition was well nigh expended. Loading every wagon with stores he marched away at midnight and at 4 a.m. on the 27th reached NKandhla, deriving the best assurance of his victory from the fact that the slow progress of his weak and weary force had been unmolested by the enemy."

The casualties in the Mounted Infantry Company from the 1st Battalion Royal Dublin Fusiliers amounted to 10 killed and wounded—Lieutenant Lefroy was wounded in four places.

From this date until the end of the war the 5th Division Mounted Infantry remained on patrol in the Nqutu District.

For the war in South Africa the troops engaged were awarded two medals, known respectively as the "Queen's Medal" and the "King's Medal for the South African War." Curiously enough, and the fact seems to have escaped the notice of many regimental historians, no order for the issue of a medal was promulgated during the lifetime of Queen Victoria. An Army Order on the subject was drafted and actually printed, being dated August 25th, 1900, but it never saw the light. In Army Order 94 of 1901 His Majesty King Edward confirmed the order which Her late Majesty had intended to issue, and in several succeeding Army Orders of this year—Nos. 94, 124, 145, 180 and 195—the scope of the medal distribution was widened, and then, finally, in Army Order No. 232 of 1902, King Edward announced the award of a second medal. The Queen's Medal has 26 clasps and the ribbon is red, blue and orange; King Edward's Medal was given only to those who were actually serving in South Africa on or after January 1st, 1902, and had completed 18 months' war service on that date; it has two clasps only, and the colour of the ribbon is green, white and orange.

CHAPTER IX

1903–1913.

SERVICE IN MALTA—THE IONIAN ISLANDS—EGYPT—INDIA—BACK TO MADRAS.

1903 THE Battalion had been little more than two months at Malta when, early in February, 1903, orders were received for the Headquarters and five companies to proceed on detachment to Crete and Cyprus. Prior to departure the "Blue Caps" were inspected, and many flattering things were said to them, by Major-General R. Lane, C.B., Commanding the Infantry Brigade, and by Field-Marshal Lord Grenfell, the Governor; and then on February 27th Headquarters and "A," "B," "E," "F," and "H" Companies embarked in the *Ortona*, the strength being 16 officers and 500 non-commissioned officers and men, of whom 13 officers and 402 other ranks were destined for Crete and 3 officers and 98 men for Cyprus. The following are the names of the 16 officers :—Lieutenant-Colonel S. G. Bird, D.S.O., Major and Brevet Lieutenant-Colonel A. Gordon (Cyprus); Major A. H. Rutherfoord; Captains M. Lonsdale, N. Le Mesurier and E. A. Molesworth; Lieutenants T. C. Frankland, S. G. Smithwick and R. G. B. Jeffreys (Cyprus); Second-Lieutenants E. V. Knox (Cyprus), W. H. Whyte, A. M. Johnson, C. B. R. Hoey, H. C. Crozier and D. French, and Lieutenant and Quartermaster Little.

The *Ortona* arrived at Candia, Crete, on March 1st, and one company with all the baggage was set on shore on the same day, the remainder of the Battalion disembarking on the 2nd and relieving the wing of the 2nd Battalion Cameron Highlanders, while "A" Company under Brevet Lieutenant-Colonel Gordon prosecuted its voyage to Cyprus.

The three companies—"C," "D," and "G"—remaining in Malta, were under the command of Major Shadforth and took over a draft of 216 non-commissioned officers and men who had been brought out from England in the *Ortona*.

On April 23rd Mr. R. Graves, C.M.G., the British Consul-General for Crete, presented 201 Queen's South African War Medals to officers and men of the Battalion, and on June 19th Sergeants Flannery and Crean, Lance-Sergeants Frost and McCormack and Private Dowling, of the Royal Dublin Fusiliers, and Armourer-Sergeant Ford, Army Ordnance Department, received the Distinguished Conduct Medals which their services had won for them in the same campaign.

This year a very great honour was accorded to the Royal Dublin Fusiliers in the following announcement which appeared in the *London Gazette* of February 6th :—

"*Royal Dublin Fusiliers. Field-Marshal His Royal Highness A. W. S. A. Duke of Connaught and Strathearn, K.G., K.P., K.T., G.C.B., G.C.M.G., G.C.I.E., G.C.V.O., Colonel Scots Guards and Army Service Corps, Colonel-in-Chief 6th Dragoons, the Highland Light Infantry, and the Rifle Brigade (Prince Consort's Own), Personal Aide-de-Camp to the King, to be Colonel-in-Chief, 7th November.*"

On the receipt of the *Gazette* containing the above-mentioned appointment, the following telegram was despatched to the "A.D.C. Commander of the Forces, Ireland " :—

"*Please convey to His Royal Highness the great appreciation felt by the officers, non-commissioned officers and men 1st Royal Dublin Fusiliers, of the honour conferred upon the Regiment by the appointment of His Royal Highness as Colonel-in-Chief—Colonel Bird.*"

To this a reply was received in the words that here follow :—

"*Dublin Fusiliers, Crete. Duke thanks you all for your message, he is glad to be associated with so famous a Regiment.—Military Secretary.*"

On December 13th of this year H.R.H. the Duke of Connaught was present at a great reception given to the 2nd Battalion on its return to Ireland after a long tour of foreign and active service,

ROYAL DUBLIN FUSILIERS: THE MEMORIAL ARCH, DUBLIN.
Opened by H.R.H. The Duke of Connaught, K.G., Colonel The Royal Dublin Fusiliers.

and in a speech which His Royal Highness made to the Battalion he alluded to what he described as "the great honour" done him by His Majesty in appointing him Colonel-in-Chief of the Regiment, and he added :—

"I hope that in this you will recognize not only His Majesty's appreciation of the distinguished services you have rendered to his throne and his Empire, but also that you will see in it his wish that you shall have some special mark of distinction, when he has made me, his only brother, Colonel-in-Chief of the Regiment. I hope I shall long have the honour to be your Colonel-in-Chief and to have a connection with a Regiment of which every Irishman feels so proud."

On November 27th Lieutenant-General Sir J. B. Spurgin, K.C.B., K.C.S.I., Colonel of the Regiment, who had served with the "Blue Caps" in Burma and in the Indian Mutiny, died; he was succeeded by Major-General W. F. Vetch, who had served for twenty-six years in the Battalion, from 1864 to 1890, and who at this time was commanding the Dublin Garrison.

The stay of the Battalion in the Ionian Islands was now drawing to a close, but before leaving, a further distribution of South African medals was made to some 200 men of the Fusiliers by H.R.H. Prince George of Greece, High Commissioner of Crete, who also gave to the Officers' Mess a very handsome silver cup in remembrance of the stay of the Battalion in Crete, and in return the officers asked His Royal Highness's acceptance of a gold-mounted regimental cane.

1904 On March 4th, 1904, the Headquarter Companies left Crete in the *Dunera*, picked up "A" Company at Cyprus, and sailed thence to Malta, where the Battalion disembarked—strength, 15 officers and 475 other ranks—and took over quarters at St. George's Barracks, Pembroke, from the 2nd Battalion King's Own Yorkshire Light Infantry.

While stationed this autumn at Malta the Officers' Mess received another silver cup, which was given by twenty ex-officers of the Battalion in commemoration of the South African War; it bears the following inscription :—" Presented to the ' Blue Caps ' by the past officers of the Regiment as a token of appreciation for the old Corps, and appreciation of their gallant services."

On the last day of the year 1904 the following officers were serving with the Battalion :—Lieutenant-Colonel S. G. Bird, D.S.O., Major and Brevet Lieutenant-Colonel A. J. Chapman ; Majors A. H. Rutherfoord and G. Downing ; Captains A. Loveband, R. M. P. Swift, M. P. E. Lonsdale (Adjutant), C. B. J. Riccard, H. J. Kinsman, E. A. Molesworth, and C. T. W. Grimshaw, D.S.O. ; Lieutenants R. G. B. Jeffreys, T. H. C. Frankland, W. F. Stirling, D.S.O., A. Brodhurst-Hill, R. L. H. Conlan and S. G. Smithwick ; Second-Lieutenants A. H. Wodehouse, E. V. Knox, W. H. Whyte, V. B. Brown, A. M. Johnson, C. B. R. Hoey, H. C. Crozier, D. French, C. C. A. Cooper, A. W. Molony and Lieutenant and Quartermaster L. Holloway ; Captain W. J. Venour and Lieutenant J. S. Burra were serving at the Depot at Naas.

On the same date the strength of the Battalion in other ranks was 980, made up of 843 Irishmen, 95 Englishmen, 24 Scotsmen, and 8 others born in India or in the Colonies.

1905 In the spring of 1905 H.R.H. The Duke of Connaught visited Malta in his capacity of Inspector-General, and had an opportunity of meeting the 1st Battalion of his new Regiment, inspecting the Battalion on parade on March 15th, and directing that the following should be published in that day's orders :—

"*His Royal Highness the Duke of Connaught, K.G., desires to express, as Colonel-in-Chief of the Regiment, the great pleasure it has given him in becoming personally acquainted with this Battalion ; and to notify his entire satisfaction with the fine and soldierlike appearance of the Battalion on parade, and the cleanliness and good order of their barracks. His Royal Highness is well acquainted with the fine history of service which the Battalion bears, and he trusts that all ranks will ever strive to maintain that record in peace and war.*"

During the summer of this year the Battalion received orders that in the autumn it would leave Malta for Egypt, and on October 6th Headquarters, with the Drums, " D," " E," " F," and " H " Companies, embarked under Colonel Bird in the s.s. *Dunera*,

SILVER LOVING CUP.
Presented to the Officers' Mess of the " Blue Caps " by Past Officers of the Battalion in commemoration of the South African War.

which had brought out a draft from home of 99 non-commissioned officers and men. The remainder of the Battalion remained at Pembroke until November 16th, when it went on board the *Assaye*, and by the 20th the whole Battalion was united in Alexandria.

1906 The Battalion remained in Alexandria throughout the year 1906 and the greater part of 1907, pursuing the usual routine of peace soldiering of a Mediterranean garrison; in June, 1906, Colonel S. G. Bird's tenure of command came to an end, and he was succeeded by Lieutenant-Colonel A. J. Chapman. In April, 1907, however, there was a very memorable break in the ordinary round of duty, when Field-Marshal H.R.H. The Duke of Connaught visited Alexandria and presented new Colours to the 1st Battalion of the Regiment, of which he had recently been appointed Colonel-in-Chief.

1907 The ceremony took place on the morning of April 5th, 1907, and is thus described in the local newspaper of the day :—

" At 10.30 a.m. on Friday the 5th April, 1907, the 1st Battalion Royal Dublin Fusiliers (consisting of 8 Guards of 35 files each, with Band and Drums) was formed up in line on the Polo Ground, Sports Club, Alexandria, facing south for inspection by Field-Marshal H.R.H. The Duke of Connaught, who arrived on the ground at 11 a.m. and was received with a Royal Salute.

" H.R.H., accompanied by General Bullock and their staffs, inspected the line and then proceeded to the saluting point. The parade was now formed for the trooping of the old Colours, which ceremony having been carried out, the escort for the Colours, accompanied by Major Downing, with Lieutenants Frankland and Brodhurst-Hill carrying the Colours, marched for the last time down the front of the Battalion, the Band playing ' Auld Lang Syne,' and returned by the rear of the line, where the old Colours were left, cased, in charge of two Colour-Sergeants. Three sides of a square were then formed, the drums being piled in the centre, the new Colours were uncased and placed in position on the drums.

"The Reverend F. B. N. Norman-Lee, Chaplain to the Forces, proceeded with the Consecration Service, opening with the hymn, 'Brightly gleams our banner.' On the conclusion of the service the King's Colour was handed by Major Bromilow to H.R.H., who presented it to Lieutenant Frankland; similarly the Regimental Colour was handed to H.R.H. by Major Rutherfoord, and presented to Lieutenant Brodhurst-Hill. Both officers received the colours from H.R.H. on bended knee.

"Field-Marshal H.R.H. then addressed the Battalion as follows:—

"'*Colonel Chapman, Officers, Non-Commissioned Officers and men of the 1st Battalion Royal Dublin Fusiliers.*

"'*As your Colonel-in-Chief, it gives me the greatest pleasure to present you this day with your new Colours to replace those you received in 1866. In confiding to you these emblems of our Sovereign and our Country, I feel that I am entrusting them to those who will know how to honour and respect them in the same way that they have cherished those Colours of which we have just taken leave.*

"'*Fusiliers, you belong to an old and distinguished Regiment who have nobly borne their share in their Country's battles and in the building up of our great Empire. Formed originally from companies that since 1746 had taken their part in the conquests in India under the East India Company, into the Madras European Regiment in 1837, you took part in all the battles in that country up to 1870. You fought with distinction at Seringapatam, at Arcot, the Indian Mutiny, and the Relief of Lucknow, and served under such distinguished men as Havelock, Outram, Clive, Grant, and Neill, who fell at the head of the Regiment at the Relief of Lucknow. It was at that time you received the soubriquet "Blue Caps," which is commemorated to this day by the unique colour of your forage caps. In 1843 the Regiment became the 1st Madras Fusiliers, and in 1862 the 102nd Regiment of Foot (Royal Madras Fusiliers), in 1873 you were linked with the Bombay Fusiliers, and in 1884 the Regiment received its present title of the Royal Dublin Fusiliers.*

"'Since then the Regiment has seen a great deal of foreign service and fought with the greatest distinction in the South African War, and distinguished itself with the Irish Brigade under General Hart in the Relief of Ladysmith, the Tugela Heights and Laing's Nek.

"'Irishmen have at all times shown a dash and bravery that have made them famous in the annals of the British Army. This Regiment has at all times shown such a splendid spirit in many a hard-fought battle, often against the greatest odds, that I feel confident that should you again be called on to fight the enemies of your country, you will respond with the same loyalty and devotion to duty that have at all times been shown by those that have gone before you. Representing as you do the capital of old Ireland I know that you will never fail in the hour of need, and will know how to maintain the noble traditions of your Regiment, and that your King and Country will ever have reason to be proud of your services.'"

"Colonel Chapman, commanding the Battalion, then made the following reply:—

"'*Your Royal Highness,*

"'*On behalf of the officers, non-commissioned officers and men of the Battalion, I offer you our sincerest thanks for the great honour you have done us to-day, an honour doubly appreciated by us in that we have received these Colours from our Colonel-in-Chief. Your gracious and inspiring words will ever be an incentive to us to uphold the traditions of the past and to add fresh lustre to them in the future, and I would ask you, Sir, to convey our homage to His Majesty the King, and to assure him that the Royal Dublin Fusiliers will ever be found ready to uphold his authority and defend his Empire.*'

"The Battalion reformed line and received the new Colours with presented arms; they were marched in slow time to their position in the centre of the line, the band playing 'God Save the King.' The Battalion now marched past and, reforming into line, advanced in Review Order, halting opposite H.R.H., the new Colours being now lowered for the first time to the Colonel-in-Chief in a Royal Salute.

"Thus ended a most impressive ceremony which will remain in the memories of those who were fortunate enough to be spectators."

When H.R.H. the Duke of Connaught left Alexandria the Battalion furnished a Guard of Honour at Sidi Gaber Railway Station —the King's Colour, Band and Drums and 100 non-commissioned officers and men under Captain Swift, with Lieutenant Knox and Second-Lieutenant Wilson.

The following was published in Battalion Orders of April 6th by command of His Royal Highness :—

"It has given me the greatest pleasure to have had this opportunity of presenting new Colours to the 1st Battalion of my Regiment, and to place on record my high appreciation of their smart appearance on parade; their drill, steadiness, and turn-out left nothing to be desired; the barrack rooms and regimental institutes were most satisfactory."

It was further made known that the Duke had graciously consented to receive and take care of the old Colours which he proposed to place in Clarence House, and on July 22nd, 1907, these Colours were handed over to His Royal Highness in London by a deputation of the following officers of the Battalion: Colonel A. J. Chapman, Major E. A. Dickinson and Captain R. G. B. Jeffreys.

Towards the end of September, 1907, orders were received for Headquarters and "A," "C," "F," and "H" Companies of the Battalion to proceed from Alexandria to Khartoum, there to be stationed; the following officers accompanied the Wing :—Colonel Chapman, Majors Downing and Fetherstonhaugh; Captains Riccard, Molesworth, Higginson and Jeffreys (Adjutant); Lieutenants Crozier, Frankland and French; Second-Lieutenants Mood, Wilson, Beresford, Cooper and Preston, and Lieutenant and Quartermaster Holloway. These companies left in four parties between October 13th and 27th and were concentrated by November 5th.

On the departure of the Battalion from Alexandria the following letter was received by the Commanding Officer from His Excellency the Governor of Alexandria :—

"*On the eve of your departure for the Sudan, permit me to say how much I regret to see you leave Alexandria where you have made yourselves so popular. You may be sure that I shall retain for a long time the remembrance of the relations, both personal and official, which have ever existed between us, and which have always been of a most cordial character.*

"*It is particularly agreeable to me to express to you my satisfaction on the subject of the conduct of your men, which has been irreproachable during the whole time the Battalion has been stationed in Alexandria, and which is to their great honour, as well as to their Commanding Officer and officers whom I congratulate most sincerely.*

"*In wishing you, Sir, your officers and men every success wherever you may be, I ask you to accept my most sincere compliments.*"

1908   Early in 1908 Field-Marshal Lord Roberts issued an appeal on account of the necessitous circumstances of certain old Mutiny veterans; the Battalion subscribed £25 which was remitted to Lord Roberts who acknowledged it in the following terms:—

"ENGLEMERE,
"ASCOT,
"BERKS.

"*February 10th, 1908.*

"DEAR COLONEL CHAPMAN,

"*Please accept my best thanks and offer the same to the officers, non-commissioned officers and men of the 1st Battalion Royal Dublin Fusiliers for their handsome donation of £25 to the above fund. I well remember the Madras Fusiliers during the Mutiny, but I did not meet the Battalion until after the time of Neill—it was after they came out of Lucknow in '57 I first came across it. The men were conspicuous on account of the blue cap-cover they wore.*

"*Believe me, yours sincerely,*
(Sd.) "ROBERTS, F.M."

During this month Field-Marshal H.R.H. the Duke of Connaught was again in Egypt and visited Khartoum where he inspected the Battalion, when he caused the following flattering remarks to be published in Orders :—

"*Field-Marshal H.R.H. the Duke of Connaught, K.G., Colonel-in-Chief, desires to express to Colonel Chapman, Commanding 1st Battalion Royal Dublin Fusiliers at Khartoum, his satisfaction at the state in which he has found the Battalion. H.R.H. was particularly pleased at the condition of the barrack rooms, both at Headquarters and at Alexandria. He considers that the appearance of the men on parade, their soldierlike bearing, reflects credit on all ranks, but His Royal Highness noticed a want of uniformity in handling arms, especially at the ' slope,' and more attention must be paid by company officers to the correct position of the soldier when standing in the ranks.*

"*H.R.H. was particularly gratified at the appearance and excellent work done by the Company detailed for training as a Camel Corps, which shows the interest and care taken by all ranks in this exceptional duty. H.R.H. is glad to note the steady progress and good results in both musketry and signalling, and generally is well satisfied with the high state of military efficiency in which he finds the 1st Battalion.*

"*H.E. the Governor-General of the Anglo-Egyptian Sudan has spoken in high terms of the excellent conduct of the Battalion at Khartoum, which H.R.H. is glad to find thoroughly borne out by the Regimental Records, and in conclusion H.R.H. desires to express his personal satisfaction at having this Battalion of his Regiment in the Mediterranean Command.*"

In August of this year an event occurred which cast a gloom over the whole Battalion, Lieutenant C. C. A. Cooper being drowned in the Blue Nile at Khartoum during the night of the 11th–12th when on his way back from North Khartoum. Two of his brother officers, Major Maclear and Lieutenant Crozier, made every effort to rescue Lieutenant Cooper, but in vain. This much-regretted young officer was the son of Major-General C. D. Cooper, who had served for many years in the 2nd Battalion of the Regiment and had commanded it throughout the war in South Africa.

Orders were now received for the Battalion to prepare to leave the Sudan for the Citadel at Cairo; the move commenced about October 18th and the companies left in several parties, the whole Battalion, including the three companies which had been detached at Alexandria, being concentrated in Cairo by November 4th.

When Headquarters left Khartoum General Sir Reginald Wingate, Governor-General of the Sudan, was at home on leave, but he sent the following cable to the Battalion Commander :—
"*On departure of Battalion from the Sudan I wish to express to your officers, non-commissioned officers and men, my great appreciation of the smartness, soldierly spirit and invariable good conduct of all ranks. The Dublin Fusiliers have ever proved themselves second to none when on service, and it is my privilege to have also found them so in time of peace. I shall always look back with the greatest pride on the time when I had your gallant battalion under my command, and I wish one and all a hearty Godspeed.*"

On the whole Battalion coming together again the companies were commanded and officered as under :—

"*A*" *Company*: Captain Frankland, Second-Lieutenant Preston.
"*B*" *Company*: Major Lowndes, Lieutenants Maclean and Johnson
"*C*" *Company*: Captain Riccard, Lieutenant Crozier and Second-Lieutenant Beresford.
"*D*" *Company*: Major Swift, Lieutenant Knox and Second-Lieutenant Grove.
"*E*" *Company*: Captain Grimshaw, Lieutenant Wilson and Second-Lieutenant Carew.
"*F*" *Company*: Major Fetherstonhaugh, Lieutenant Molony and Second-Lieutenant Anderson.
"*G*" *Company*: Captain Smithwick and Lieutenant Hoey.
"*H*" *Company*: Major Maclear, Lieutenants French and Mood.

In the earlier part of this year there had been some considerable trouble in the Sudan. "In April a body of ex-Dervishes under the leadership of one Abd-el-Kader, attacked and killed Mr. Scott-Moncreiff, the Deputy Inspector of the Blue Nile Province, and an Egyptian Police Commandant, at a village near Kamlin. Dickinson Bey, the Governor of the Province, started for the scene with a small force and was attacked by the band which numbered about 150. The attack was repulsed, 35 of the enemy being killed and the leader captured. Dickinson Bey was slightly and Major Logan severely wounded, and 2 native officers and 8 men were killed. This ended the rebellion, which was not general among the people, but confined to Dervishes who had settled in the district after the fall of Khartoum. Abd-el-Kader was tried at Kamlin before the Mudir's Court under the presidency of the civil judge and being found guilty was executed and his property forfeited. Twenty-three other persons were tried, 20 of them being convicted, 12 being sentenced to death."*

Some of the officers and other ranks of the Battalion, who had undergone training with or were attached to the Camel Corps, were employed in the Sudan in connection with these operations, and on March 25th, 1909, Field-Marshal H.R.H. The Duke of Connaught, at a parade of the Battalion at the Citadel, Cairo, presented His Highness the Khedive's Sudan Medals to all those of the "Blue Caps" who were entitled to them; on the same parade His Royal Highness handed to Major Maclear and Lieutenant Crozier the bronze medals of the Royal Humane Society awarded to them for their endeavours to save Lieutenant Cooper when drowned in the Nile the previous year.

1909

The Battalion was about this time placed under orders to embark for India during the ensuing trooping season, but it was not until quite the end of the year that it proceeded to Alexandria and there embarked, reaching Bombay on January 3rd, 1910. The disembarkation was at once effected and the Battalion then entrained for Ahmednagar where it arrived on the 4th of the same month. The Royal Dublin Fusiliers were here

1910

* *Annual Register*, 1908, p. 415.

"G" COMPANY, 1ST ROYAL DUBLIN FUSILIERS.

The first British Camel Corps in the Soudan, taken at Khartoum in 1908. Commanded by Capt. H. W. Higginson, with Lieuts. S. G. Smithwick and E. V. Knox as subalterns

in the Ahmednagar Brigade of the 6th (Poona) Division, the Brigade-Commander being Major-General F. H. Kelly, C.B., while the Division was under the command of Major-General E. A. H. Alderson, C.B. The other regiments in the Brigade were the 1st Battalion Northamptonshire Regiment, the 110th Mahratta Light Infantry, and the 123rd Outram's Rifles. The following are the names of the officers who arrived in India with the Battalion. Colonel Chapman; Majors Downing, Swift, Smith and Fetherstonhaugh; Captains Lowndes (Brevet Major), Riccard, Maclear (Brevet Major), Molesworth, Grimshaw, D.S.O., Jeffreys, Frankland (Adjutant) and Smithwick; Lieutenants Wodehouse, Knox, Johnson, Hoey, Crozier, French, Molony, Mood, Wilson and Beresford; Second-Lieutenants Preston, Anderson, Grove, Carew and Dunlop, with Lieutenant and Quartermaster Holloway.

In June of this year Colonel A. J. Chapman's time in command of the Battalion came to an end and his place was filled by the promotion of Major G. Downing; and on the 9th of the same month Colonel and Honorary Major-General C. D. Cooper, C.B., was appointed Colonel of the Royal Dublin Fusiliers in the room of Major-General Vetch, C.V.O., deceased, dated March 13th, 1910.

While stationed at Ahmednagar the "Blue Caps" more than maintained the reputation they had established when in Egypt and the Sudan as a good sporting Battalion; they always took the lead in anything of the kind that was on foot, boxing competitions were constantly taking place in their own lines in Wellesley Barracks, while when competing in this or other sports with the different regiments of the Poona Division they more than held their own. In a great Marathon race held in November, 1911, out of 76 starters the 1st Battalion Royal Dublin Fusiliers provided the winner in Private Vine, who completed the very punishing course nearly two minutes ahead of the second man, and out of the first ten men in, four belonged to the Battalion.

1911 The Dublin Fusiliers remained on at Ahmednagar throughout 1911 and 1912, and on August 9th of the latter year the Commanding Officer received the following letter from

1912 General Sir Edmund Barrow, which shows how deep was the affection in which the Regiment was held by those who had ever served in it, no matter how many years might have elapsed since they had severed their connection with it:—

"*As the oldest soldier of the Regiment on the active list, General Sir Edmund Barrow desires to bid farewell to the 1st Royal Dublin Fusiliers on his departure from India.*

"*He is glad to think that by their conduct and discipline they have shown themselves worthy successors to that famous regiment, the old Madras Fusiliers, the Regiment which can pride itself on so grand a share in the conquest of India, and which has had on its rolls such soldiers as Clive, Malcolm and Neill.*

"*Splendid though your traditions are, remember, Fusiliers, that your future good name and fame rests on yourselves, your sobriety of life and your discipline in peace and your devotion and valour in war.*

"*General Sir Edmund Barrow looks to his brother officers, many of whom are Irishmen, to set you an example of duty and conduct in all things, and with an honest pride in his connection with the Regiment, he prays for your happiness and good fame wherever you may be.*"

General Barrow left the Battalion to join the Indian Army in 1874, and had held the command of the Southern Army in India since 1908.

On September 10th it was announced in Orders that the Battalion would move during the ensuing cold weather to the Madras Presidency, being quartered at Bellary and Madras, and was due to arrive at those stations on February 1st and 2nd, 1913,
1913 being relieved at Ahmednagar by the 1st Battalion Oxfordshire and Buckinghamshire Light Infantry. These dates suffered, however, some slight change, and the parties of the Battalion for Madras and Bellary respectively did not entrain at Ahmednagar, the Madras or Headquarters wing until the afternoon of February 2nd, 1913, and the Bellary detachment until the evening of the same day. The first party arrived at Madras at 10.30 a.m. on the 4th; the second reached Bellary at 11.45 a.m. on that date. Headquarters, with "A," "B," "F," "G," and

"H" Companies proceeded to Fort St. George, Madras; "C," "D," and "E" Companies to Bellary. The following officers accompanied the two parties:—Headquarters: Lieutenant-Colonel Downing; Major Fetherstonhaugh; Captains Grimshaw (Adjutant), Jeffreys, Brodhurst-Hill and French; Lieutenants Molony, Mood, Grove, Dobbs, and Dunlop; Second-Lieutenants Bernard, Bagley and O'Hara, with Lieutenant and Quartermaster Kennedy. With the detachment were Major Venour; Captains Molesworth, Johnson and Crozier; Lieutenants Floyd, Philby, Shine and Lieutenant Lanigan-O'Keeffe. Captain Anderson was at Poonamallee.

The Battalion was now in the Southern Brigade (Brigadier-General F. G. Bond, C.B.) of the 9th Secunderabad Division, commanded by Lieutenant-General Sir J. B. Woon, K.C.B.

On the departure of the Battalion from Ahmednagar, the following letter was received by the Commanding Officer from the G.O.C. Ahmednagar Brigade:—

"*On the departure of the 1st Royal Dublin Fusiliers from this Brigade, the General Officer Commanding would like to place on record his very great appreciation of the excellent conduct of the men during the time he has been in command here. Not only has there been no instance of misbehaviour in public, but, owing to the proximity of his quarters, the G.O.C. has been able to appreciate very fully their good behaviour in barracks. The physical fitness of the men, too, is, and has been, excellent throughout. Both these reflect the greatest credit on the Battalion, and in wishing them good-bye and good luck the G.O.C. regrets losing such a fine body of men from his Brigade.*"

But if the Royal Dublin Fusiliers were given a good "send-off" from the station they had occupied since their return to India, a wonderful reception was to be accorded to the Regiment on its return to the ancient city of its birth. Already some months before the "Blue Caps" were due to arrive in Madras a movement had been set on foot and had received wide support for welcoming the Battalion; an influential committee was formed, and as early as

October 14th, 1913, the honorary secretary sent the following letter to Colonel Downing at Ahmednagar :—

"SIR,

"I beg to inform you that the residents of the city of Madras have been gratified to learn that the Battalion which you command is shortly returning to Madras after an absence of about half a century. The history of the 1st Dublin Fusiliers for two hundred years was the history of Madras in its making; for, first as the Madras European Regiment and subsequently as the Madras Fusiliers, the Regiment took part in all the campaigns that led to the conquest and pacification of South India under British rule. The part the Regiment played in the Indian Mutiny, as also in South Africa, is none the less distinguished.

"A movement has been set on foot, and has received general support, to give your Regiment a fitting welcome on its return to the city of its birth and the scene of its former glories. An influential committee has been formed, of which H.E. the Governor is President and the Hon. Sir Ralph Benson, the Acting Chief Justice, is Vice-President, to organize measures to this end, and three schemes have been proposed.

"In the first scheme it is suggested that the Regiment, a few days after its arrival in Madras, should march with its old Colours—now hanging in St. Mary's Church, Fort St. George—escorted by a Colour Guard dressed in the uniform of the old Madras Fusiliers—to the statue of General Neill, and there formally salute the distinguished officer who was its Commander and leader in the days of the Mutiny, and place a wreath on the pedestal, and that subsequently the Regiment should march to the Banqueting Hall, where it would be entertained at breakfast, and an Address would be presented to yourself, on behalf of the Regiment, while in the afternoon there might be sports for the men on the Island—which is just outside the Fort—at which prizes would be presented.

"An alternative proposal is that in the morning the Regiment should salute its old chief in the manner proposed, and that in the afternoon a public function should be held at the Gymkhana on the Island, at which an Address would be presented, together with a piece of plate for the Officers' Mess, and perhaps also an Inter-Company Hockey or Football Challenge Cup.

" A third suggestion is that there should be a march to Neill's statue in the morning, and either sports or an Inter-Company Football or Hockey match in the afternoon, with presentation of a piece of plate for the Officers' Mess, if funds suffice for both.

" I am requested by the committee to inquire whether some such public welcome as is proposed would be agreeable to you and to the Regiment, and, if so, I am to ask you to be good enough to favour me with an expression of your views generally on the form it should take, and as to which of the above proposals would be the most suitable, or whether you would suggest any other. Of the proposals I have outlined the committee is inclined to prefer the second or third rather than the first. Our desire is to make your reception as public and as popular as possible, and while commemorating the return of the Regiment to the place of its birth to make a presentation that shall remain with it as a permanent record of what we in Madras like to think will be a landmark in the history of the 1st Royal Dublin Fusiliers.

" I understand that the Regiment will probably arrive in Madras in February next, and I shall be obliged if you will let me know in due course the exact date, and also inform me how many officers and men are likely to be in Madras City on the probable date of the proposed reception.

" I remain, Sir,
" Yours faithfully,
(Sd.) " A. E. LAWSON, *Hon. Secy.*"

The following full account of the welcome given to the Regiment is taken from the *Madras Mail* of February 18th, 1913 :—

" The Public Reception accorded by the residents of Madras to the 1st Battalion Royal Dublin Fusiliers on the Island on Monday morning was a unique function in the annals of this historic city, and one that will doubtless leave a lasting impression on the minds of the thousands of spectators who assembled to witness it.

The ceremony, which had been arranged by a strong committee, with H.E. the Governor as Chairman and Mr. P. L. Moore, C.I.E., as Honorary Secretary, took place on the Island, the spot chosen being most appropriate, facing as it does Sir Thomas Munro's statue. The public were freely admitted to enclosures which had been specially roped off and in which chairs had been provided for their accommodation, and in which one had been reserved for the old members of the Madras Fusiliers and their descendants. There was a goodly gathering assembled, among whom was that veteran officer, Colonel Tabuteau, an old officer of the Madras Fusiliers, who appeared in his uniform, wearing the decorations of the Indian Mutiny. . . . Shortly after 7.30 a.m. H.E. the Governor rode to the ground escorted by the entire squadron of the Body Guard. . . .

"Immediately on His Excellency taking his stand at the Saluting Base, Colonel Downing asked permission to commence the interesting ceremony of the morning, the trooping of the Colours. The Regiment had in the meantime already paraded on the Maidan in front of the line.

"The old Colours of the Madras Fusiliers which were carried by the Regiment all through the Burmese War and in the Indian Mutiny, and which had been taken charge of on the previous morning from St. Mary's Church, Fort St. George, were on parade, while the old Regimental Colour which was to be trooped was carried by Lieutenant R. Bernard; and there was also on parade a side-drum used at the Relief of Lucknow. The present Colours of the 1st Battalion Royal Dublin Fusiliers were also carried on parade by Lieutenants A. B. Bagley and H. D. O'Hara.

"The ceremony commenced by the pipes and drums, which were assembled in front of the ranks, marching past. The present Colours were then taken down to the Regiment by the escort, to the strains of the Band, and were there received with the General Salute. 'A' Company of the Regiment was then detached and marched round the ground, headed by the Band. They received the old Colours, which were taken round the Regiment and saluted. . . . The entire Battalion then marched past in slow time; this movement was then repeated in quick time, which terminated the ceremony of trooping the Colour. The march-past was well executed, and the Regiment being dressed in Review Order in white, the spectacle was most picturesque.

"The Regiment then formed three sides of a square, with the Band in front facing inwards. The members of the Reception Committee advanced to Colonel Downing, and the following address was read by Sir Ralph Benson:—

"*Colonel Downing, Officers, Non-Commissioned Officers and men of the 1st Battalion Royal Dublin Fusiliers.*

"*We, the Citizens of Madras, welcome you on your return to the City after an absence of 54 years. We need hardly remind you that your history as a Regiment was for over two centuries the history of Madras in the making. The Regiment has borne on the roll of its Officers the illustrious names of Stringer Lawrence, Innes, Clive, Sir Eyre Coote, Malcolm, Barry-Close and Neill, and many others which are inseparably connected with the great traditions of the British in the Madras Presidency.*

"*You are now returning to the scenes where your predecessors, fighting side by side with the brave Indian soldiers of the Coast Army, played so distinguished a part in laying the foundations of the British Empire in India.*

"*Here it was that you earned your regimental motto,* SPECTAMUR AGENDO. *This motto was conferred on the Regiment by an order of Government in 1841, and since that date the names which shine forth in the war records of the Regiment—such names as Punjab, Multan, Guzerat, Ava, Pegu, Kirkee, Lucknow, Ladysmith—show how nobly you have sustained that motto.*

"*We again offer you our most hearty welcome on your return to the city of your birth, and our best wishes that the Regiment may long continue to add lustre to its glorious record.*"

"Colonel Downing then made reply in the following words:—

"*Your Excellency and Members of the Executive Committee.*

"*On behalf of the Battalion which I have the honour to command, I desire to tender you our most sincere thanks for the signal honour which the residents of the city of Madras have conferred upon the Battalion in according us a public reception. I know I am but voicing the sentiments of the whole Battalion, present as well as past, when I tell you that it is with feelings of the deepest gratification that we, the present day representatives of the Royal Madras Fusiliers, once again find ourselves in this city of our birth, and our hearts are stirred by the pleasant thought that Madras is as eager to-day to welcome her old Corps as she was on the 22nd February, 54 years ago, on our return from the relief of Lucknow. We hope that the residents of this most historic city will find as time progresses that the change in their Regiment is but in name only, and that we are as jealous of our reputation as the Royal Madras Fusiliers, as of our title of to-day. Could the grave give up its dead, and General Neill of ever-cherished and immortal memory appear amongst us again, we hope we may say without vain boast that he would, on scanning the Regiment's death-roll in the Empire's last campaign—I mean South Africa—rejoice to think that the same gallantry actuated the Royal Dublin Fusiliers as inspired the 'Blue Caps' he led to victory at Lucknow. In conclusion, we beg to assure the residents of the city of Madras of our high appreciation of the welcome they have given us, and of the cordiality of our feelings towards them."*

"His Excellency the Governor then dismounted for the purpose of presenting to the Regiment a cup, the gift of the residents of Madras, and inscribed with the following :—' Presented by the citizens of Madras to the 1st Battalion Royal Dublin Fusiliers, formerly 1st Madras Fusiliers, on the return of the Regiment in February, 1913, to Madras, the city of its birth and its home for 200 years.'

"In making the presentation of this Cup, Lord Pentland said :—

"'*Colonel Downing, Officers, Non-Commissioned Officers and men of the Royal Dublin Fusiliers.*

"'*I should like to express, if I may, how heartily the residents of Madras concur in the action which has been taken by the Committee who are present here to-day to welcome your Battalion back to what Colonel Downing has so aptly called the city of its birth, and it falls*

THE NEW CENTREPIECE.

Presented by the citizens of Madras to the " Blue Caps" on their return to the city of their origin in 1913, and on disbandment was presented to H.M. The King, June, 1922.

to me, and I have the privilege of offering to the Regiment in the shape of this cup a lasting memento of this impressive occasion, in recognition not only of the gallant services of your Regiment to the country, but also in recognition and in memory of your close connection with this city. So close, indeed, is that connection that the history of your Regiment and your Battalion practically is the history of the city of Madras. In its first beginning it takes us back to the time of Charles I, when scattered companies of Europeans defended the trading ports then of the East India Company. A hundred years later, when these companies were formed into the beginnings of the Madras European Regiment, we come to the great days of Stringer Lawrence—the Father of the Indian Army, as he was called—and of Lord Clive, and later on to the days of Sir Thomas Munro, whose statue stands in front of us. Those were great days, and it is difficult in these peaceful surroundings to imagine that in two short months in the winter of 1759— I think it was 1758-59—no less than 26,000 shot, 80,000 shell, and 200,000 rounds of small ammunition were poured into the Fort by the forces who were besieging it. One hundred years later your Regiment was given the title of the 1st Madras European Fusiliers, and— in 1860, I believe—you then became the Royal Madras Fusiliers. And after a glorious record of 200 years' service in India you went home for the first time. Your history is written in the glorious roll of battle honours on your Colours. Since those days, as Colonel Downing has reminded us, the Regiment has sustained its distinguished reputation. With great pride, therefore, and pleasure, the residents of Madras welcome the Battalion here to-day. It is a regret to many of us that the Sheriff of Madras, a high official and a leading member of a distinguished community, is not able to be present to read the address, but we are singularly happy and proud that his place should be taken by Sir Ralph Benson, who has not only acted as Vice-Chairman of this Committee, but is himself an Irishman of whom Ireland may be proud, and who is well known in this Presidency for his long and distinguished services here.

"*Colonel Downing, you will, I am sure, believe that the action taken by the residents and the Committee has the hearty and general concurrence of all the inhabitants. You meet here under the shadow of a distinguished officer of your own Regiment, and you now go to discharge the important and pious duty of marching to the statue of General Neill which stands no great distance away.*

"*The residents of Madras welcome you heartily to their city. They are confident that during your stay here your Battalion will add to its distinguished record and will place the residents of Madras under an increased claim of gratitude by their conduct and bearing during their stay here. I have great pleasure, on behalf of the Committee, to offer to the Officers' Mess as a memento of this occasion the cup which is before you; and I understand that another cup is being presented this evening—a football challenge cup—which will convey to all ranks the heartiness of the welcome which is now tendered to your Battalion.*"

Colonel Downing made a very brief speech in acknowledgment, thanking His Excellency and the citizens of Madras for the great honour done the Battalion, and stating that the beautiful cup would be a lasting reminder of the events of that great day.

The Battalion then marched in fours to General Neill's statue through streets gaily decorated and densely thronged with people, and on arrival formed a hollow square. Sergeant-Major Hosford then handed a beautiful wreath of laurel and Eucharis lilies to Major Fetherstonhaugh who placed it in all reverence at the base of the pedestal. Colonel Downing then spoke these words:—

"*On behalf of the Officers, Non-Commissioned Officers and men of the Royal Dublin Fusiliers, I place this wreath at the foot of the statue of our former Colonel—General Neill—who served in the Royal Madras Fusiliers from 1833 to 1857, and led the Regiment through the Indian Mutiny, falling himself at the Relief of Lucknow, as a token of our ever enduring regard and admiration of his glorious career.*"

A General Salute was then given—the band struck up the Regimental March, and the Fusiliers marched back to barracks, leaving their old leader to maintain the solitary vigil which had endured for half a century.

PLACING A WREATH ON GENERAL NEILL'S STATUE IN THE MOUNT ROAD, MADRAS, FEBRUARY 17th, 1913, ON THE RETURN OF THE REGIMENT TO MADRAS.

APPENDIX

The Victoria Cross was conferred on the following non-commissioned officers and men of the Regiment for their services during the Mutiny:—

SERGEANT PATRICK MAHONEY.—Date of act of bravery, September 21st, 1857. For distinguished gallantry (whilst doing duty with the Volunteer Cavalry) in aiding in the capture of the Regimental Colour of the 1st Regiment Native Infantry at Mangulwar on September 21st, 1857.

PRIVATE JOHN RYAN.—Date of act of bravery, September, 1857. He, in conjunction with Private McManus, His Majesty's 5th, rushed into the street in Lucknow and took Captain Arnold out of a dooly and brought him into the house in spite of a heavy fire in which Captain Arnold was again wounded. In addition to the above act, Private Ryan distinguished himself throughout the day by his intrepidity, and especially devoted himself to rescuing the wounded in the neighbourhood from being massacred.

PRIVATE THOMAS DUFFY.—Date of act of bravery, September 27th, 1857. For his cool intrepidity and daring skill whereby a 24-pounder gun was saved from falling into the hands of the enemy. *N.B.*—Private Duffy was recommended for the Victoria Cross by Colonel Robert Napier and Captain W. Olpherts. The former, as is well known, became Field-Marshal Lord Napier of Magdala, the latter was known throughout the army as General Sir William Olpherts, V.C., G.C.B., and more particularly by his well-earned sobriquet of " Hell Fire Jack."

PRIVATE J. SMITH.—Date of act of bravery, November 16th, 1857. For having been one of the first to try and enter the Gateway on the north side of the Secundrabagh. On the gateway being burst open he was one of the first to enter, was surrounded by the enemy, received a sword cut on the head, a bayonet wound in the left side, and a contusion from the butt-end of a musket on the right shoulder, notwithstanding which he fought his way out and continued to perform his duties for the rest of the day. Elected by the private soldiers of the detachment of the 1st Madras Fusiliers.

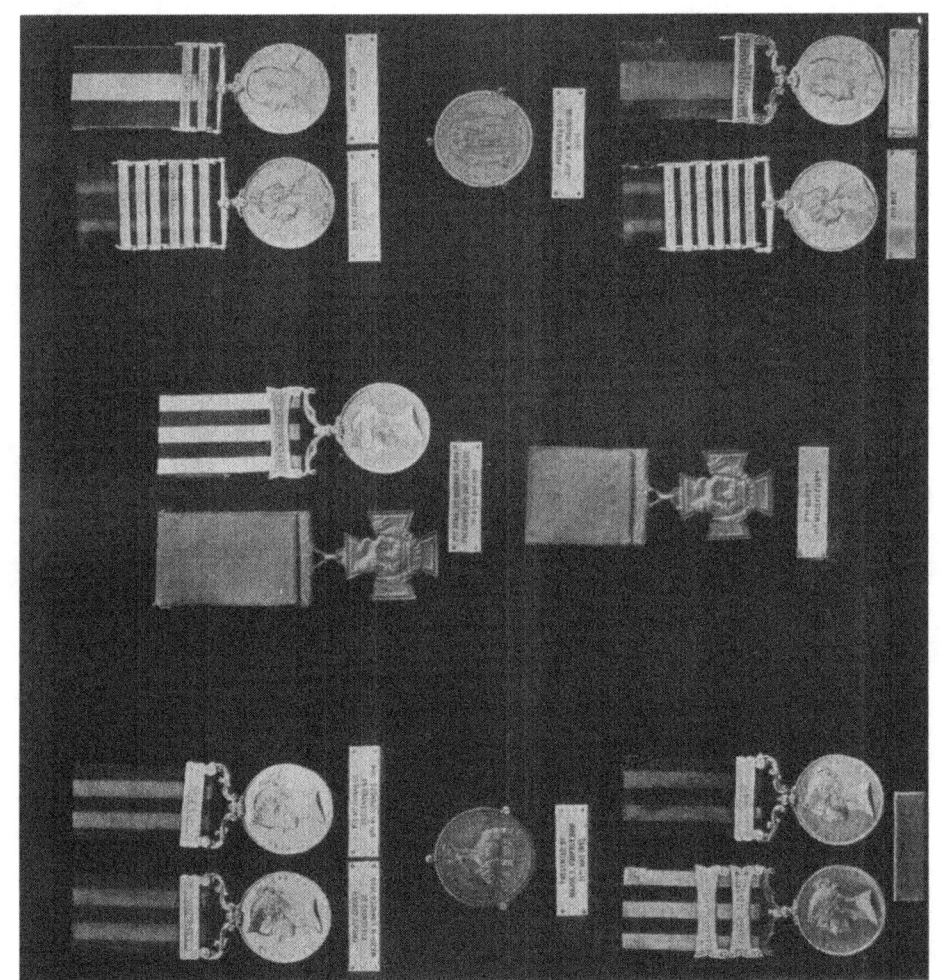

TWO MUTINY V.C.'s AND OTHER MEDALS IN POSSESSION OF THE OFFICERS' MESS.

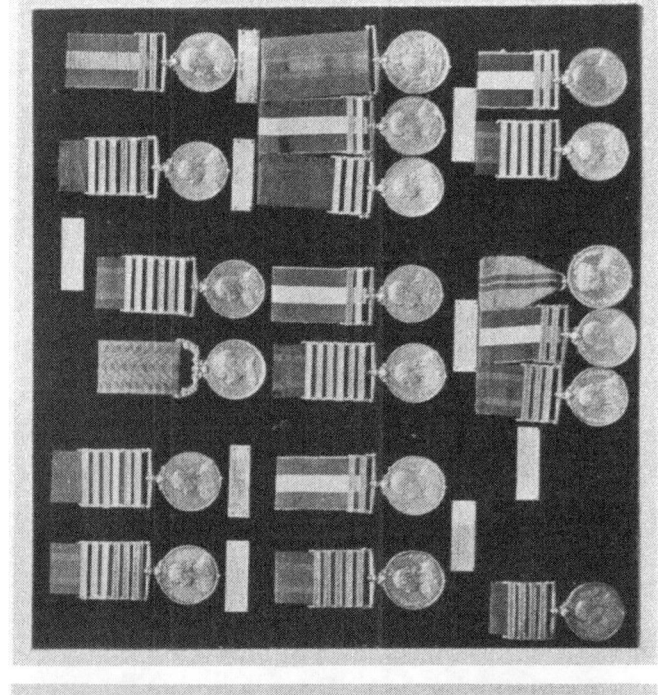
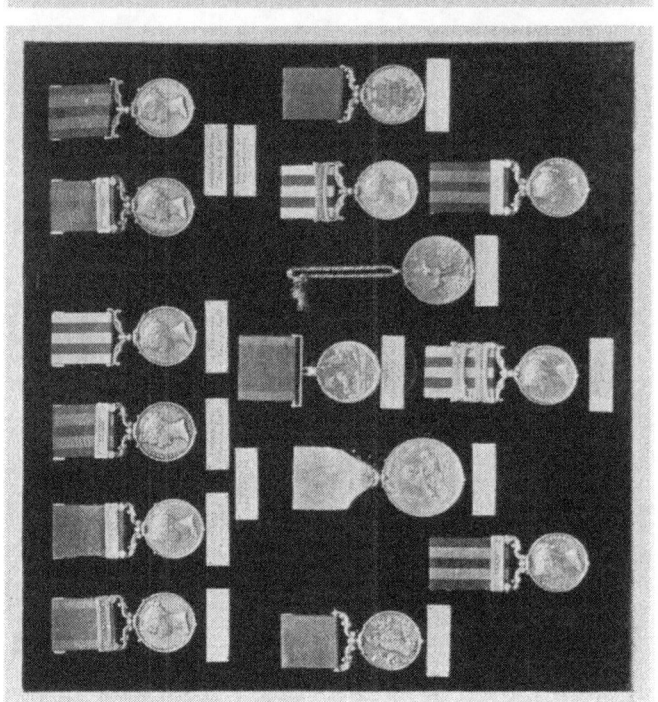

CASES OF MEDALS OF INDIAN AND SOUTH AFRICAN CAMPAIGNS IN POSSESSION OF THE OFFICERS' MESS.

INDEX

ALAM BAGH, 73, 87, 93, 102; garrison of, 103; defence of, 107 *et seq.*
Alleman's Nek, action at, 177–180
Amalgamation of Battalions, 3
Anderson, 2/Lieut., 209, 211; Capt., 213
Anderson, Surgeon W. S., 1, 29, 31
Apthorpe, Lieut.-Col., 30
Arnold, Lieut. N. H., 40, 42, 48, 59, 65, 66, 68, 76–78, 84, 87, 89, 130
Arthur, Surgeon, 76, 102
Ashton, Asst.-Surgeon, 141

BACON, Lieut. A. A., 156; Capt., 162; killed, 170
Babington, Capt., 13
Bagley, 2/Lieut. A. B., 213, 216
Bailey, Lieut. W. S. 40, 44, 48, 76, 87, 90, 92, 130
Baker, Lieut. and Qr.-Mr., 157
Barclay, Lieut. J. J., 40, 71, 76, 92, 130, 140; Capt., 152
Barker, Lieut. H. F., 1
Barker, Ensign A., 1; Major, 14
Barratt, Cpl., 86
Bashiratganj, action at, 60–62
Beaumont, Lieut. W. H., 40, 43, 48, 66, 76, 85; Capt., 140, 144, 148
Bell, Col. J., his memo *re* "Honours," 6, 10, 11
Benares, Neill arrives at, 42
Beresford, 2/Lieut. R. H., 206, 209, 211
Berkeley, Ensign H. L., 141
Bernard, 2/Lieut. R., 213, 216
Bertie, 2/Lieut. V. C., 53; Lieut., 76, 140
Bird, Lieut. and Adjt. S. G., 152; Lieut.-Col., 192, 199, 202, 203
Birmingham, Pte. E., 194
Bithur, action at, 67
Blair, Ensign J., 141; Lieut., 148, 152
"Blue Caps," derivation of title, 51
Blunt, Lieut. J. H., 148
Bolton, Lieut. A. H., 157
Bond, Surgeon T., 6

Bowen, 2/Lieut. C., 14, 17, 20, 21, 29
Boyce, Lieut. G. K., 1
Brice, 2/Lieut. W., 14, 29, 31
Brind, Capt. W. H., 152
Brodhurst-Hill, Lieut. A., 162, 173, 192, 194, 202–204,; Capt., 213
Bromilow, Capt., 188, 189, 192; Major, 204
Brown, Lieut. D., 13, 14; Capt., 30, 31
Brown, Lieut. J. V., 1; Capt., 5
Brown, Lieut. P. A., 14, 17, 19, 20, 25, 29, 30, 31; Capt., 131, 140, 141
Brown, 2/Lieut. V. W., 184, 193
Brown, Capt. W. R., 13, 14, 29, 31
Brown, Pte. Charles, 87
Brown, Pte., 160
Burke, Lieut., 188, 192
Burma War, Second, outbreak of, 14
Burra, 2/Lieut. J. S., 162, 189, 192, 193
Burrard, Lieut. N., 1, 5
Burton, Lieut. R. F., 140
Butler, Major C., 13
Byrne, Pte. Patrick, 159, 160

CALCUTTA, Regt. leaves Madras for, 39; Regt. lands at, 40
Calder, Capt. A., 1
Campbell, Gen. Sir Colin, 65, 92 *et seq.*; meeting with Outram and Havelock, 100; letter about Regt., 121
Campbell, Sergt., 89; Clr.-Sergt., 159, 194
Campbell, Surgeon A., 1
Canning, Lord, 57, 80; his General Order, 122; speech to Regt., 124, 125, 148
Cape Town, arrival at, 163
Carew, 2/Lieut., 209, 211
Carnegie, Asst.-Surgeon, 14
Carr, Ensign C. H., 141; Lieut., 148; Capt., 152
Carter, Lieut., 14
Cattley, Lieut., 13
Cawnpore, arrival at, 55
Ceremony at Gen. Neill's statue, 220

INDEX

Ceylon, service in, 153, 154
Chambers, Major P., 13
Chapman, Capt. A. J., 157, 158, 162, 172, 193-8; Lieut.-Col., 203-6, 211
Chapman, Pte., 160
Charbagh Bridge, action at, 76
Cheape, Brig.-Gen. Sir John, 16
Chisholm, Lieut., 66, 68; death of, 130
Cholmeley, Asst.-Surgeon, 14, 17
Christie, Lieut. J., 14, 29
Clancy, Pte., 19
Clarke, Ensign J., 6
Clarke, Sergt. G., 194
Cleland, Lieut. W., 40, 48, 51, 53, 66, 68, 70, 76, 85, 87, 102, 120, 130, 140; Capt., 148, 152; Lieut.-Col., 154
Coke, Maj.-Gen. T., 173, 181, 183
Colenso, battle of, 165 *et seq.*
Colin, Pte. Patrick, 159
Colours, presentation of, 5, 11, 13, 14; Royal Colours, 141, 142, 203, 204
Conlan, 2/Lieut. R. H. L., 163; Lieut., 184, 186, 187, 189, 192, 202
Connaught, H.R.H. Duke of, appointed Colonel-in-Chief, 200
Cooper, Col. C. D., 173; Maj.-Gen., 208; appointed Col., 211
Cooper, 2/Lieut. C. C. A., 202, 206; drowned, 208
Craig, Ensign, 148
Crean, Sergt., 200
Crete, 199
Cronley, Pte. Darby, 96
Crozier, 2/Lieut. H. C., 199, 202, 209, Lieut., 208-11; Capt., 213
Cullen, Pte. W., 194
Cuppage, Lieut. A., 140
Cyprus, service in, 199

Dale, Lieut. C. H., 40, 64, 66, 68, 74, 76, 80, 89, 90, 102, 107, 109, 117, 123, 140
Daley, Sergt. J., 194
Dalhousie, Lord, 15, 16, 31
Dangerfield, Lieut. E., 14, 17, 18, 30, 31, 60
Daniell, Lieut. E. S., 14, 17, 18, 20; Capt., 140, 148
Daniell, Pte., 116
Dardis, Sergt., 160
Davies, Asst.-Surgeon J., 6
Day, Asst.-Surgeon F., 14, 25
De Salis, Lieut., 162, 172, 194

Despatches, Sir Colin's, 104; Outram's. 105
Dibley, Lieut., 158
Dickinson, Capt. E. A., 158; Major, 206
Dickson, Capt. F., 14
Dilkusha, 102
Dillon, Sergt., 170
Discontent among Company's troops, 136 *et seq.*
Dobbs, Lieut. F. H., 94, 96; killed, 97, 98, 130
Dobbs, Lieut. J. F. K., 213
Doveton, Lieut. F. B., 1
Dowdall, Lieut., 152
Dowling, Pte. T., 194, 200
Down, Capt. W. M., 108
Downing, Major G., 202, 203, 206, 211; Lieut.-Col., 213, 216-220
Drury, Sergt., 88
Duffy, Pte., 84, 85; wins V.C., 106, 221
Duke, Lieut. T., 1; Major, 13; Lieut.-Col., 14
Dunbar, Capt. E., 140, 148
Duncan, Lieut. J., 71, 96, 140, 141; Capt., 148; Lieut.-Col., 154
Dunlop, 2/Lieut., 211, 213
Dunne, Bugler J. F., 170, 194
Dunsheath, Pte., 20
Durban, arrival at, 164

Edwards, Sergt., 86
Egypt, 202, *et seq.*
Elliott, Ensign, 148
Enfield Rifle, Regt. only one to be armed with in 1857, 47
England, ordered to for first time, 144
English, Lieut. F. P., 156
Eston, Pte., 194
Ewart, Lieut. G. D., 163

Faber, Capt., 152
Fetherstonhaugh, Lieut. E., 158; Major, 206, 211, 213, 220
Finnemore, Surg.-Major J. H., 152
Finnis, Pte., 109
Fischer, Col. T. J., assumes command, 125, 129
Fisher, Lieut. G. R., 14

INDEX

Flannery, Cpl. P., 194; Sergt., 200
Flegg, Cpl., 87
Floyd, Lieut. H. M., 211
Ford, Arm.-Sergt. T., 194, 200
Frankland, Lieut. T. C., 199, 202–206, Capt., 211
Franklyn, Capt. E., 1
Fraser, Lieut. J., 14; Capt., 40, 48, 52, 59, 65, 71, 76, 85, 86, 89, 90, 130, 131
Fraser, Lieut. Hon. J., 85
Fraser, Lieut.-Gen., transferred, 157
French, Capt. St. J. B., 1, 4
French, 2/Lieut. D., 191, 193, 199, 202, 206, 209, 211; Capt., 213
Frost, Cpl. G., 194; L./Sergt., 200
Fusiliers, title of, granted, 10

Galwey, Capt. M., 14, 39, 40, 66, 68, 76, 85, 86, 89, 90, 102, 105, 111, 112; Major, 115; Lieut.-Col., 120, 130
Geils, Capt., 14, 29; death of, 31
George, Capt., 156
Gibbons, Pte., 86
Gibraltar, service at, 152, 153
Gibson, Major J. F., 1
Gilbert, Pte. T., 194
Gittens, Sergt. J. R., 194
Goddard, Lieut. and Adjt., 156
Godley, Lieut., 157; Capt., 158–160; Bt. Major, 193
Godwin, Maj.-Gen., 16, 17, 18, 22, 23, 26, 27
Goodall, Sergt. A., 14
Gordon, Lieut., 156
Gordon, Capt. A. D., 140
Gordon, Major A. W., 158, 162, 170, 183, 187, 188, 192, 193; Bt.-Lieut.-Col., 199
Gosling, Lieut. G. F., 14, 17, 18, 30, 65; Adjt., 71, 85; Capt., 140, 141
Graeme, Lieut. L. A. M., 30, 71, 96; Capt., 140, 144
Grant, Lieut. W., 1
Grant, Lieut. C., 14, 30, 31, 37; Capt., 37, 40, 47, 59, 68, 74, 76, 77, 79, 90, 91, 109, 112, 118, 130, 131
Grant, Gen. Sir Patrick, C.-in-C., 45, 64, 70
Granville, Lieut. F. J., 140, 141
Green, Ensign St. J., 141
Greene, L./Cpl., 160

Grimshaw, Capt. C. T. W., 192, 202, 209, 211, 213
Groom, 2/Lieut. W. T., 29, 40, 43, 46, 51, 57, 59, 70, 76, 78, 88, 89, 90; death of, 91, 130
Grove, 2/Lieut., 209, 211, 213

Halahan, 2/Lieut. J. C., 162, 173
Hamilton, Ensign A., 141
Hamilton, Lieut. F., 5, 13, 14
Hamilton, Lieut. G. J., 14, 17
Hamilton, Lieut. J., 14, 17
Harcourt, 2/Lieut. G. J., 13, 14, 17, 30; Lieut., 40; Capt., 140, 148; Major, 152; Col., 154
Hargood, Lieut., 40, 76, 81, 100, 105, 108; death of, 116, 130
Hartigan, Sergt.-Major T., 162, 194
Harriott, Ensign H., 1
Harris, Lieut. J., 14; Major, 47, 71, 93
Havelock, Brig.-Gen., 36, 45 et seq.; death of, 102
Hawes, Lieut. J. C., 1; Capt., 14, 17, 31
Hawker, Lieut., 181
Hawkes, 2/Lieut., 186, 187, 188
Hayes, Pte., 86
Heathcote, Lieut. H. F., 152
Henry, 2/Lieut., 184
Heys-Thomson, 2/Lieut., 187
Hicks, 2/Lieut. H. T., 153; Major, 158, 162, 165, 169, 171–173; Lieut.-Col., 193
Higgins, Sergt., 87
Higginson, 2/Lieut., 158; Capt., 206
Hill, Lieut. W., 1; Major, 14, 17, 24, 25, 29, 31
Hill, 2/Lieut., 158
Hoey, 2/Lieut. C. B. R., 189, 193, 199, 202, 209; Lieut., 211
Holloway, L./Cpl. F., 194
Holloway, Clr.-Sergt. L., 194; Lieut. and Qmr., 202, 206, 211
Holmes, Major, 156
"Honours" for Second Burma War, 31
Hooper, Capt. B., 1
Hope-Grant, Gen., operations of, 116 et seq.
Hopper, Ensign F. H., 1
Hornsby, Lieut. H. F., 71; Capt., 140, 148; Major, 152
Hosey, Cpl., 100

Q

[*Vol. II.*

INDEX

Hosford, Sergt.-Major, 220
Howden, Lieut. J. H., 1; Major, 5
Hudlestone, 2/Lieut. G., 157, 158, 162, 180
Hughes, Capt., 156
Humfrey, Lieut., 148
Hurd, Pte. J., 111
Hutchinson, Lieut., 152
Huxham, Lieut., 85

INDIA, Regt. leaves for England, 147
India, Regt. ordered to, 210
Itala, defence of, 196–198

JACQUES, Cpl., 78
Jeffreys, 2/Lieut. R. G. B., 163, 184, 192, 193, 199; Capt. 202, 206, 211, 213
Jellalabad Fort, 109 et seq.
Jepson, Major H. J., 140, 141; Lieut.-Col., 151, 152
Johnson, 2/Lieut. A. M., 189, 193, 199, 202, 209, 211
Jones, Lieut., 181
Jones-Parry, 2/Lieut. S. H., 14, 19 et seq.; 93, 94, 97, 99, 108, 140
Joseph, Asst.-Surgeon, 30
Jourdan, Lieut., 12
Joyce, L./Cpl., 160

KEENAN, Sergt., 170
Kelly, Lieut.-Col. H. M., 1
Kelly, Pte., 17, 20
Kelly, Clr.-Sergt. J., 59; Q.M.S., 120
Kerr, Lieut. J., 1
Kerr, Ensign C. R., 148; Lieut., 152; Major, 156
Kinsman, Capt. H. J., 202
Kirkwood, Asst.-Surgeon, 148
Kitchener, Lord, assumes command in South Africa, 185
Knox, 2/Lieut. E. V., 184, 188–190, 199, 202, 209, 211
Kyd, Major, 3

LAMBERT, Commodore, 15
Lamprey, 2/Lieut., 173, 181
Lanigan-O'Keeffe, Lieut., 213

Lawrence, Sir Henry, 57
Leahy, Pte., 96
Lefroy, Lieut. B. P., 162, 184, 193–198
Le Mesurier, Capt. N., 193, 199
Lennox, Capt. C. E., 140, 141
Lidster, Sergt., 86
Lindsay, Capt. W. B., 152
Linking of 102nd and 103rd Regts., 151
Liptrot, Pte., 20
Little, Q.M.S., J., 194; Lieut. and Qmr., 199
Lloyd, Lieut., R.A.M.C., 162
Localization Scheme for Army, 151
Lonsdale, Capt. M., 199, 202
Loveband, Lieut., A., 156; Capt., 193, 202
Lowndes, Capt. and Bt. Major, 209, 211
Lucknow, first relief of, 76; second, 100; evacuation of, 102; final capture of, 114, 115, 121; Regt. back again at, 144

MACBEAN, Capt. J. A. S., 193, 194
MacDonnell, Capt., 187, 188, 192
MacDonnell, L./Cpl. P., 194
Maclear, Lieut. & Adjt. P., 162; Capt. and Bt. Major, 193, 208–211
Maclean, Lieut., 209
Macleod, Lieut., 162, 170, 194
Madras, ordered back to, 121; reception at, 125–129, 213 et seq.
Magee, Clr.-Sergt. V. J., 170
Mahoney, Sergt., wins V.C., 73, 105 221
Mainwaring, Capt., 158, 192
Malacca, operations in, 4
Malta, 199
Manning, Lieut. W. J., 1
Mansel, Capt., 156
Mansfield, Gen. Sir William, 144
Marshall, Ensign S., 1
Mathews, Ensign J. S., 1, 6
Maude, Capt., Royal Artillery, 70; Major, 73, 74, 108
Maule, Ensign J., 141
McCarthy, Pte., 46, 87, 160
McCaskill, Lieut., 148; Capt., 152
McClory, Pte., 17, 20
McCormack, Pte., 194; L./Sergt., 200
McGee, Pte., 46
McGill, Pte., 88
McGrath, Sergt., 47
McKenzie, Lieut., 12

INDEX

Medal for Second Burma War, 32; for South Africa, 198
"Mentions" for South Africa, 193, 194
Menzies, 2/Lieut. R., 14, 17, 29
Mills, 2/Lieut. G. R., 153; Lieut.-Col., 160, 162, 178–180, 184, 186, 188, 189, 192, 193
Molesworth, 2/Lieut. E. A., 158, 162, 173; Capt., 199, 202, 206, 211, 213
Molony, 2/Lieut. A. W., 202; Lieut., 211, 213
Mood, 2/Lieut., 206, 209; Lieut., 211, 213
Moore, Pte., 20
Moore, 2/Lieut., 162, 189, 194
Moore, Qr.Mr., 141, 148
Moran, Cpl., 194
Morrison, Major, 156
Mounted Infantry Company formed, 158
Murphy, Sergt. H., 194
Mutiny, commencement of the, 37 et seq.
Myron, Cpl. P., 194

Napier, Col., 83, 88, 90, 107, 110; Gen., 144; Lord, 153
Neill, Capt. J., 14, 21, 25, 31; Lieut.-Col., 37 et seq., 40; letter from Havelock, 62; Brig.-Gen., 76; death of, 80, 81, 123, 130; inauguration of Neill Memorial Fund, 129, 130, 220
Neill, Lieut. C. B. S., 140
Newby, Ensign W., 6
Nicolay, Capt., 14, 17, 20; death of, 28, 31
Nutting, Ensign C., 1; Capt., 5

Oates, Lieut., 152; Capt., 156
O'Brien, Pte., 160
O'Connor, Paymaster J., 152
O'Hara, 2/Lieut. H. D., 213, 216
Oliver, Lieut. C. L., 140
Olpherts, Capt., Royal Artillery, 42, 65, 73, 74; Major, 83
O'Neill, Lieut. W. H. S., 156; Major, 158, 163, 179, 193
Order, Valedictory, from C.-in-C., 145
Organization, etc., changes in, 154

Outram, Gen. Sir J., 36; his General Order, 69, 74; at Alam Bagh, 103 et seq.; gives over command, 115

Palmer, Lieut., 152
Pandoo Nuddi, action at, 51, 52
Parker, Pte., 88
Parry, Lieut. R. C., 99, 140, 148
Patey, Lieut., 187
Peard, Pte., 88
Pearse, Capt., 158
Pegu, operations at, 17 et seq.
Pentland, Lord, 218
Percy, Lieut., 181
Persia, Regt. ordered to, 36
Philby, Lieut., 213
Pilson, Lieut. A. F., 158; Bt. Major, 159, 160, 193
"Plassey," pet tiger, 150
Preston, Pte., 46
Preston, Ensign G. V., 141
Preston, 2/Lieut., 206, 209, 211
"*Primus inter Pares*," suggested as motto, 9
Proctor, Sergt. E., 194

Quinlan, Pte., 87

Raikes, Lieut. T., 14, 29; Capt., 66, 76, 86, 88, 102, 114, 131; Bt. Major, 119; Lieut.-Col., 140, 143, 148, 151
Reception at Calcutta, 123, 124; at Madras, 125–129, 213 et seq.
Rees, Capt., 13, 14
Reeves, Capt. F., 152
Regiments, British, 5th Dragoon Guards, 184, 186; 7th Hussars, 113, 117, 119, 120; 8th Hussars, 162; 19th Hussars, 181; 5th Foot, 72, 75, 76, 83, 93, 103, 109, 112; 10th Foot, 42; 19th Foot, 141; 31st Foot, 152; 32nd Foot, 83, 87; 38th Foot, 113; 51st Foot, 17, 141; 53rd Foot, 113; 57th Foot, 153; 64th Foot, 47, 67, 71, 76, 83; 75th Foot, 94, 103, 109, 141; 78th Foot, 47, 59, 63, 65, 67, 71–74, 83, 87, 89,

93, 103, 109, 113; 81st Foot, 141; 84th Foot, 47, 58, 63, 67, 71, 72, 83, 103, 109, 112; 90th Foot, 72, 74, 83, 93, 103, 109, 113; 91st Foot, 141; 93rd Foot, 94–98; 102nd Foot, 141; Border, 164; Camerons, 199; Connaught Rangers, 161, 163; Dorset, 178; East Surrey, 184; Inniskilling, 161; Leicester, 162; Liverpool, 183; Middlesex, 173, 178, 181; Northampton, 211; Rifle Brigade, 117; Royal Irish Rifles, 164; York and Lancaster, 186
Regiments, Indian, 4th Light Cavalry, 12; 12th Light Cavalry, 103; 13th Irregular Cavalry, 42; 1st Bengal Infantry, 85; 6th Bengal Infantry, 43; 37th Bengal Infantry, 42; 48th Bengal Infantry, 85; 5th Madras Infantry, 16, 18; 7th Madras Infantry, 12; 10th Madras Infantry, 12; 13th Madras Infantry, 141; 19th Madras Infantry, 28; 27th Madras Infantry, 103; 32nd Madras Infantry, 12; 40th Madras Infantry, 141; 41st Madras Infantry 12; 79th Madras Infantry, 16; 1st Punjab Infantry, 117; 5th Punjab Infantry, 117–119; 110th Mahrattas, 211; 123rd Outram's Rifles, 211
Renaud, Capt., 14, 21–23, 25, 27, 31; Major, 36, 40, 45, 47–49, 52; death of, 130
Reeves, Capt. F., 152.
Riccard, Lieut. C. B. J., 158; Capt., 163, 175, 184, 187, 188, 193, 202, 206, 209, 211
Richardson, Lieut., 40, 48, 59, 60, 130
Riddell, Lieut.-Col., 158
Roberts, Field-Marshal Lord, assumes command in South Africa, 175; hands over command, 185; letter from, 207
Robertson, Asst.-Surgeon, 40, 76
Roddy, 2/Lieut., 157
Rogers, Lieut. E. J. V., 141, 148
Romer, Lieut., 158
Roy, Capt. J., 5
Royce-Tomkin, Lieut., 158
Rutherfoord, Lieut. A. H., 156; Major 187, 189, 193, 199, 202, 204
Ryan, Pte., 84, 89, 106, 221

SAMWELL, Capt. and Paymaster F., 141
Saunders, Pte., 20

Scott, Capt., 156
Scott-Elliot, Lieut. C., 14, 17, 18, 24, 29, 31
Sennett, Major, 187, 188
Seppings, 2/Lieut. J. W. H., 158; Lieut., 162, 179, 180, 194
Seton, 2/Lieut. J. L., 14; Lieut., 40, 53, 59, 71, 113; Capt., 140, 144, 147
Shadforth, 2/Lieut., 153; Major, 158, 175, 182, 183, 187, 188, 193, 200
Shah Nujjef, fighting at, 96, 97, 98
Shairp, Lieut. S. W. S., 5
Shamrock, to be worn on St. Patrick's Day, 172
Shannahan, Cpl., 86
Sheppard, Lieut., 156
Shine, Lieut., 213
Ships, R.N., *Euphrates*, 154; *Himalaya*, 147, 155, 156; *Malabar*, 147; *Pearl*, 125; *Serapis*, 147; *Sphynx*, 14; *Tamar*, 153
Simpson, Lieut. E., 1; Capt., 5
Sladen, 2/Lieut. E. B., 14, 29, 120
Smith, Capt., 158
Smith, Pte., 16
Smith, Pte. J., wins V.C., 96, 106, 159, 221
Smithwick, 2/Lieut. S. G., 180, 187, 193, 199, 202; Capt., 209, 211
Smyth, Surgeon R. B., 141, 148
South Africa, Regt. ordered to, 161
Sowden, Pte., 88
"*Spectamur Agendo*," motto granted, 10
Spurgin, Lieut. J. B., 14, 17, 28, 29, 40, 43, 46, 48; Capt., 57, 76, 80, 87, 89, 112, 131; Major, 140, 141; Col., 151, 152; Lieut.-Gen., appointed Col., 157, 161; death of, 201
Steel, Brig.-Gen. S. W., 16, 22, 26, 29
Stenson, Qr.Mr., 153
Stephens, Capt., 29
Stephenson, Capt. J. L., 14, 17, 18; Major, 44, 48, 50, 58, 60, 63, 65, 68, 74, 76, 77, 79, 85, 86, ; death of, 88, 90, 103, 105, 130
Stevens, Lieut. N. J. C., 140, 141, 148
Stevenson, Col., 36, 37
Stinton, Lieut. T. C., 1
Stirling, 2/Lieut. W. F., 163, 184, 194; Lieut., 202
Strickland, Capt., 158
Supple, Lieut., 192
Swift, Capt R. M. F., 162, 173, 182, 183, 186, 187, 191, 193, 206; Major, 209, 211

INDEX

TABUTEAU, Lieut. T. R., 141 ; Col., 216
Taylor, Lieut. H. D., 14 ; Capt., 94, 97, 98, 99, 101, 131, 143
Taylor, Lieut. A. A. C., 192, 193
Taynton, Ensign M. R., 1
Thomson, Paymaster, 148, 153
Title, changes of, 139, 154
Todd, Capt., 175, 182
Tonghoo, 29, 30
Transfer to Crown, 132 et seq.
Transports, *Aligator*, 4; *Bavarian*, 162–4; *Brahmaputra*, 57, 58; *Dunera*, 202; *Graham*, 14; *Imogen*, 4; *John Wells*, 39; *Jumna*, 70; *Mahanuddy*, 21; *Mirzapore*, 45; *Moozuffer*, 14; *Nerbudda*, 21; *Oriental*, 36, 37; *Poona*, 156; *Sydney*, 125; *Tantallon Castle*, 158; *Tasmania*, 36, 37; *Zenobia*, 39, 40
Transvaal, war in, 153 et seq.
Traynor, Cpl., 87
Tredennick, 2/Lieut., 185
Tremenhere, Lieut., 148
Tulloch, Capt. C., 14, 17, 31
Turner, Ensign T. B., 141, 152
Tyrrell, Asst.-Surgeon W. J., 141, 148

UNAO, actions at, 59

VENOUR, Lieut. W. J., 158 ; Capt., 193, 202
Vereeniging, peace of, 189, 190
Vetch, Capt. W. F., 152 ; Lieut.-Col., 156 ; Maj.-Gen., to be Col. of Regt., 201 ; death of, 211
Victoria, death of Queen, 185
Victoria Cross, awards of, 105, 106, 221
Vincent, Pte., 20
Virgo, Band-Sergt. A., 194

Vivian, Lieut.-Col. Sir R. J. Hussey, 12, 37 ; Maj.-Gen., 140
Volksrust 181, et seq.

WAHAB, Brig. J., 9
Wallace, Pte. C. N., 194
Waller, Lieut., 12
Waller, Ensign J. H., 141
War, Burma, thanks to Army for services, 2
War, breaks out in South Africa, 160
Ward, Lieut. A., 13, 14, 17 ; Capt., 30
Ward, Qr.Mr. J., 158, 162, 193
Warthen, Pte., 109
Watson, 2/Lieut. H. A. F., 158 ; Lieut., 162, 172, 193
Waugh, Lieut.-Col., 1
Weir, Lieut. R. D., 1
Weir, Pte., 20
Welbank, Ensign R. T., 1
Weldon, Lieut. K. C., 157, 192
West, Capt. J., 14, 17, 18
Westerman, Ensign, 120, 130
Wethered, Lieut. H., 162
White, Ensign J. C. V., 141
Whyte, Lieut. W. H., 188, 199, 202
Williams, 2/Lieut. J. M., 14
Wilson, 2/Lieut., 206, 209, 211
Wing, 2/Lieut. J., 14, 29, 31
Winnington, Lieut. J. F. S., 162
Wodehouse, Lieut. A. H., 187, 202, 211
Woodcock, Lieut. J., 14, 17, 30
Woods, Lieut. J. A., 40, 43, 71, 76, 93, 94, 96, 99, 101, 117, 119, 123, 140, 141 ; Capt., 147
Wynne, Lieut. S. J., 152

YOUNG, Lieut. C., 5
Young, Pte., 88
Youral, Cpl., 80

www.ingramcontent.com/pod-product-compliance
Lightning Source LLC
Chambersburg PA
CBHW080544230426
43663CB00015B/2700